Praise for *Sulekha Select*

"What emerges in all these writings is that elusive but all pervading character of 'Indian-ness' which goes beyond ethnicity, religion, language, behavior, lifestyle – an ability not necessarily to transcend, but certainly to contain the many diversities that characterize the people whose origins are in South Asia, particularly India."

> – **Shyam Benegal**, director of *Ankur, Nishant, Manthan* and *Zubeidaa*

"This impressive new publication may well serve as a springboard for a new generation of writers from South Asia."

> – **Amitav Ghosh**, author of *The Glass Palace, The Circle of Reason* and *The Calcutta Chromosome*

"*Sulekha Select*, an attempt at capturing the diverse experiences of the Indian diaspora is a delight."

> – **Malavika Sanghvi**, editor, *The Times of India* and *The Sunday Review*

"Vibrates with life and creativity like the website that gave birth to it."

> – **Allen Quicke**, editor, *Asia Times Online*

"...This eclectic collection of writings...reflects the unpolished, off-the-cuff style of the e-writer. There are heartfelt musings, embarrassing confessions, hilarious escapades, painful autobiographies and plenty of parodies of that condition peculiar to the global Indian community known as *desiness*. *Sulekha Select* will make you laugh hysterically and cause tears of painful empathy to course down your cheeks."

> – **Mira Kamdar**, author of *M̶ ̶ ̶ ̶ ̶*

"This wonderful collection shows the power of the Internet to find fresh voices and fresh ideas. I recommend it, and Sulekha.com, to anyone who is tired of the tedious, imitative writing elsewhere."

- **Sreenath Sreenivasan**, professor of journalism at Columbia University and co-founder, *South Asian Journalists Association* (www.saja.org)

"*Sulekha Select* is extremely interesting, stimulating and enriching. What I found refreshing is the remarkably diverse, candid and unvarnished writings by people who write for just one reason: they love to do so. *Sulekha Select* offered me the rare opportunity to go into the minds of Indians around the world and get to know their feelings and opinions. I wouldn't be surprised if one of these stories gets made into a movie."

- **Santosh Sivan**, cinematographer and director of *Terrorist*

"A wide variety of topics and formats have been used here, making the collection vibrant."

- **Bharati Kirchner**, author of *Shiva Dancing* and *Sharmila's Book*

"If the Internet is about connecting people, there can hardly be a better proof of it than Sulekha. What sets the site apart, and which, I believe, is the principal reason for its success, is the eclectic mix of writings available on the site…. The best of these writings has now found its way in *Sulekha Select*."

- **Rajesh Kalra**, CEO, NaradOnline.com

"A must-read. Witty, thought-provoking, inspirational and at times nostalgic…. The width of experiences, differences in profiles of the writers, and the range of topics…provide a vibrant and highly involved reading experience."

- **Geet Sethi**, VP, Satyam Infoway and six-time World Billiards Champion

"Witty, vibrant and engaging…"
– **Pravin Gandhi**, Co-Founder, Infinity Technology Investments

Praise for Sulekha

"Thank us for telling you about Sulekha.com. (Sulekha is) one of the finest Indian websites."
  – *The Times of India*

"Tremendously popular...a hit!"
  – *India Abroad*

"(Sulekha is) one of the biggest creative and vibrant online community of Indians."
  – *Rediff.com*

"Winner of the 1998 Golden Pebble award for the most original site."
  – *Austin American Statesman*

"(Sulekha) is an extremely multifaceted site and one of the biggest and most vibrant communities of Indians that's bubbling over with creativity, opinions, wit and wisdom."
  – *Femina*

"I thought the romance with the net was over. And then I found...Sulekha.com. Sulekha represents what's exciting about the net itself...(Sulekha is) a whole cauldron teeming with creativity, wit and fun. And I think the operative word is *Indian*. Pluralism has probably never been so witty, sharp, and genuinely pluralistic."
  – *Free Press Journal*

"Encourages new writers, new opinions and thoughts...fills a unique need in the community for it allows people to express their creativity and communicate with others – that is, be a part of a community."
  – *Little India*

SULEKHA SELECT

The Indian Experience in a Connected World

Smart Information Worldwide

Austin   Chennai

Published by Smart Information Worldwide, Inc.
4926 Spicewood Springs Rd., Suite 101,
Austin, TX 78759, United States
201 Royapettah High Road, Chennai 600004, India

ISBN 0-9708157-0-0

Editorial Team: *Ruchika Joshi, Sangeeta Kshettry, Satya Prabhakar
and Venkatesh G. Rao*

Sulekha Review Editors: *Bharadwaj, Ruth Bushi, Kris
Chandrashekhar, O. Jaantrik, Abhijit Ghosh, Suraiya Ishaque, Amy
Laly, Julie Rajan, Sailendra Singh, Reeta Sinha, Jenny Wren*

Production Team: *Sangeeta Kshettry, Nishat Laika, R. Parameswaran,
Anup Pandey, Satya Prabhakar, Venkatesh G. Rao and Srini Vasan.*

Cover design by PrintGlobe.com
Cover art by Prof. V. G. Chavan, from the Sulekha Art Gallery

Part of the proceeds from the sale of *Sulekha Select* go to: Child Relief
and You (CRY), Asha for Education, NetIP, Raksha, Association for
India Development (AID) and Saheli.

Inquiries and additional copies:	**Smart Information Worldwide Inc.**
	Email: editor@sulekha.net
	Phone: (512) 231 9226 (US)
	Fax: (512) 231 0123 (US)
	URL: http://www.sulekha.com/select

Foreword

Sulekha Select achieves the impossible. It integrates what I always thought could never be integrated. The complete Indian experience. It is so varied, so magical, so differently hued that I always believed India would forever remain an assemblage of multiple experiences held together by a tenuous thread of nationhood or *Hindutva*, or however you may choose to describe it. I always believed that the Bengali experience, the Tamil experience, the Maharashtrian experience, the Kashmiri experience, all added up to create the sum total of what we often describe as the Indian experience. An experience that cannot stand on its own otherwise. But *Sulekha Select* has proved me entirely wrong. I now discover that it is possible in a wired world to actually have a cohesive and complete experience that can be actually described as Indian. Totally Indian. I guess this is what modern technology and global connectivity has brought about: an integration that we never thought was possible through politics. It has brought about a mindset that is complete and yet extremely dynamic, ready to confront any challenge, any experience.

These 42 pieces create a geography and a landscape that makes me extremely proud to be an Indian. An Indian whose country is spread out across the world, whose sense of nationhood spans so many different cultures, whose pride exults in being part of a world that is constantly changing, constantly evolving, and yet whose tradition, whose roots, remain with him wherever he goes, wherever he decides to settle down. Sulekha Select says one simple thing: India is where you are; India is wherever you go.

Pritish Nandy
Mumbai,
March 15, 2001

Pritish Nandy *is a columnist, TV host, Member of Parliament and chairman of a multimedia firm. He was Publishing Director of* The Times of India *for nearly a decade and was awarded the Padma Shree for poetry in 1977.*

Preface

Step by step as you go,
The Way shall open unto you.

– Zen saying

This book you are holding is a milestone of sorts in the short history of a tiny Web magazine that evolved, in little over two years, into the biggest online community for Indians worldwide: Sulekha.com. A bustling, effervescent, and occasionally anarchic sub-continental club-house, constructed and kept current by its members and visitors. On its way to becoming the definitive online Indian community, Sulekha has become the home-on-the-Web to tens of thousands of Indians, from Calcutta to California, from Sydney to St. Kitts. In this edgy world of passionate discourse that is Sulekha, an amazing, dynamic portrait of the world of modern Indians emerges. A portrait, we feel, that no individual observer can ever hope to capture.

Selected by the Sulekha community from nearly 1200 featured writings by Sulekha members, this collection of 42 easy pieces is a distillation of the essence of the revolution that Sulekha represents.

So who are the writers featured in this book? A marketing manager in Chicago, and an IAS officer from Orissa. An engineer-turned-filmmaker from Hyderabad and a movie script-writer from Bollywood. A CEO of an IT company in Singapore and another who runs an ad agency in Mumbai. A 16-year-old African-Indian who just started her freshman year in the US and a fresh graduate in Britain. A Ph.D. student at an American university and an Anglo-Indian in Australia. An entrepreneur in Calcutta and a banker in the Silicon Valley. A software engineer at Infosys and a hardware designer at Maxtor. A fisherman-sailor turned freelance travel-writer from Kerala and a Bangladeshi writer with a finger on the pulse of Dhaka. And many, many more.

So, what do these people have in common? It is that ungraspable, fascinating feeling of being *'Indian'* in a fragmented, yet connected, world. A world in which the economy pulls us apart but the Net brings us together. A world in which we have little disposable time to socialize, but our longing for belonging and our need for a stable cultural context runs deep. More than *expression*, Sulekha is about *connection;* more than pageviews (though we are not, truth be told, averse to them), Sulekha is about creating magic from the collective power of a myriad brilliant and, on occasion, bizarre minds. If the Net is about connecting people, then *Sulekha Select* is a striking testimony to the power of those connections.

Sulekha.com and *Sulekha Select* are not about writing or about showcasing extraordinary talent (though you will find that in abundant measure) *per se*. The driving purpose behind this book is neither to showcase literary excellence nor to capture the clichéd 'voices of South Asia'. It is, rather, to get at that complete picture of being 'Indian' in this new world, where merry continent-hoppers, idle humorists, incessantly-analytical philosophers and angsty soul-searchers together define an entire culture.

You will notice that *Sulekha Select* is eclectic in its choice of content. This is by design. There is humor and satire, prose and poetry, analysis and commentary. There are even a few pieces that we find somewhat incomprehensible; but we have been assured by some cultivated minds that it's good stuff. We think you will enjoy them all and zap us an email demanding to know when the next *avatar* of *Sulekha Select* will be out!

You will find both British and American spelling in *Sulekha Select*; this is because the writers in it are of all ages, and come from all over the planet. You are welcome to post your own comments in response to any of the articles in *Sulekha Select* on Sulekha.com.

We at Sulekha thank the following for helping make Sulekha happen:

- *soc.culture.indian*, a reflective and rambunctious Internet Usenet group that has been in existence for more than 15 years, and which helped us fashion Sulekha,

- *Dakghar,* a mailing list of IIM Calcutta alumni and their spouses, that propelled us to create Sulekha,

- Sulekha's early writers, columnists, editors, contest directors, hosts, Coffeehouse warriors and numerous other active participants, who made Sulekha what it is,

- Our investors, who believe in the concept of Sulekha; they make it all possible,

- Our reviewers, who were gracious enough to manufacture some time to read the book and send us their comments.

We welcome you to come visit us online. We are home all the time and there is no need to call ahead. The address: *sulekha.com*

More importantly, consider contributing to Sulekha in any of its numerous sections (details on the next page). We will showcase your contributions and connect you to thousands and thousands of Indians from around the world who visit Sulekha. And perhaps feature you in the next *avatar* of *Sulekha Select.*

Team Sulekha
March 14, 2001

p.s. Let us know what you think of *Sulekha Select* by sending us an email at editor@sulekha.com; you will make us happy and improve future editions.

CONNECT!

Sulekha welcomes you to join its virtual metropolis of thousands of active members, to contribute to, and participate in these forums.

❖ **Articles and Columns**: Hundreds of articles on a variety of topics. Read, enjoy, comment and join the global club of Sulekha writers.

❖ **NewsHopper**: A constantly-updated listing of insightful news stories from world media on all things Indian, contributed by members. Plus a hot, interactive discussion forum on the news stories.

❖ **Coffeehouse**: A happening place with thousands of conversations and discussions in many forums. Open 24/7.

❖ **Contests**: Play the Cryptic Tuesday, Peril, Geetvala and more. You can even set contests.

❖ **Art and Photo Gallery**: Hundreds of delightful pieces of artwork and photographs. Browse our gallery, send them as ecards or, better yet, contribute your art and photos.

❖ **Movie and Book Reviews**: Before you buy a book or go to see a movie, find out what others thought of it. Plus post your reviews so others can make informed decisions.

❖ **Events**: Check out what's happening in your city; post your comments on what you have seen, and publicize an event you are organizing.

More information: www.sulekha.com/contribute.html

Contents

Marriages are Made in Heaven

Ramesh Mahadevan

Ajay Palvayanteeswaran just could not believe his ears. (Okay, okay. I confess. This is the fourth Ajay Palvayanteeswaran story that begins with the same line. But just this one time, let me get on with the story). Ajay wondered if it was for real. The voice at the other end of the telephone: was it a human voice or was it a computer chip? Computer chips don't have ABCD daughters waiting in line to get married.

Ajay went through an instant replay of what had just happened. First the phone rang and when he answered it, a thoroughbred,

"Ask him for a BMW as dowry. If he doesn't come down, then make sure you ask for at least a Subaru. If nothing, at least let him get you an engine tune-up and oil change."

thick, South-Indian accent responded. At first, Ajay thought it was the usual call to extract five bucks from him for the Tamil Association or some nuisance call about a forthcoming music concert.

"Good evening, Mr. Palvayanteeswaran. My name is Srinivasan Iyer," the voice introduced itself. "Let me be direct with you. I got your name from the Jyotishi Vijai Maharaj of Tantra Corporation. You see, I have a daughter and I am

Mahadevan Ramesh grew up in Chennai, India. After a rather uneventful childhood, he migrated northwards to Kanpur for his undergraduate studies and then made a beeline to the US to pick up a doctorate degree in physics. Currently, he works for Maxtor Corporation, designing and productizing their latest high-capacity hard disk drives for personal computers. Ramesh believes that life is one heck of a hilarious odyssey, (even corporate life) and his writing is a direct product of this naiveté. Ramesh's other interests include jogging, stock market investing, cooking and classical music.

looking for a good alliance from well-placed Iyer boys. You seem to be a nice boy high up in the Iyerarchy."

Good! Somebody had finally realized Ajay's true worth in dollars and was taking the initiative to ring up and discuss a possible marriage.

"We call her Molly, short for Malini Ammal," the man went on. "Very nice girl – she has the best of our culture and this culture – the kind of girl who could make stuffed asparagus *parathas* with a dash of fresh thyme. A child of sound moral values. By the way, can I have a copy of your horoscope? You can fax it to me."

'Why not?' Ajay thought. After all, he always carried his horoscope and never left home without it. In fact, when he cashed his checks, he frequently showed his horoscope as an ID.

"What are you doing this Friday night? Why don't you come to our place for a dinner? You can also meet my daughter," the prospective father-in-law pressed on aggressively. "By the way, you are still employed, aren't you?"

Ajay didn't even hesitate, and accepted the invitation immediately. "If the marriage deal doesn't work out, at least I can get a good dinner," Ajay rationalized. Ajay had only known seventeen women in all his life. If you discounted his various aunts and cousins, the

...he always carried his horoscope and never left home without it. In fact, when he cashed his checks, he frequently showed his horoscope as an ID.

number dropped to just one or two, which too were faces from way back, from his kindergarten days. Now he was going to have his own wife, that too an American-born one! It was now time to bring out all the repressed passionate thoughts.

Ajay already started to daydream and drool. 'The first romantic thing I must do with my woman,' Ajay dreamed on, 'is to take her to India and go straight to my old IIT hostel and show her my ex-hostel room.' He would take Malini to Piscataway, New Jersey for their honeymoon. And when he showered her with lusty kisses, his toothbrush-like mustache might come in the way and brush her teeth, but he could always sacrifice a little and shave it off. Then one day, they would be blessed with a healthy baby boy. He would have an elaborate 'naming ceremony,' followed the next day by an equally elaborate 'nicknaming ceremony.' He would call the child Munna, after his favorite mess worker in his old hostel. His parents would come from India and linger on for months to look after the baby. Then one day, in a ceremony resembling the change of palace guards at the Buckingham palace, his parents would leave and Malini's would arrive from New Jersey, maintaining the continuity of grandparents for the lucky brat.

For days afterward, Ajay experienced a new joy, a new lightness, something akin to floating on cloud nine. He tried to visualize how Malini Ammal might look. Perhaps he would have to teach her Hindi and Tamil. That would be a lot of fun, especially the foul words. He found himself pointlessly humming an ancient Talat Mehmood song in total ecstasy all the time. He had half a mind to call his dad in Madras and simply tell him 'Boooooo!' But then, he was still scared of his dad and didn't want his dad to screw up things from across the ocean. However, he did call his wingmates and ex-classmates. They all had advice to offer him.

"You should be firm when negotiating with these dudes," cautioned Srini from Hostel Ganga, Ajay's bum pal, from the other side of the phone. "This Iyer dude sounds very tough. Ask him for a BMW as dowry. If he doesn't come down, then make sure you ask for at least a Subaru. If nothing, at least let him get you an engine tune-up and oil change. Don't sell yourself short."

On the appointed day, Ajay borrowed the whitest *kurta* from his roommate, emptied a bottle of perfume on himself, and checked five times to see if his fly was zipped up. He asked his roommate Bala to accompany him for moral support,

"But, *machi*, don't dress like a prospective bridegroom and ruin my chances," he begged. Bala's friend, Srini, who was visiting him from some godforsaken place, and a couple of anonymous friends who landed up hoping to initiate a booze session, were also asked to accompany Ajay. After getting lost a million times in the suburban jungles, they finally located Iyer's house from the *sabji* smell. Ajay and his buddies wandered in.

❖

"Hello, I am Ajay. This is Srini, Bala, Srini and Bala."

"Ajay, *Namaste*. I am Srinivasan, Srini for short. My full name is Iyer. This is my wife," Mr. Iyer introduced a big woman wearing a kilometer of *sari* to Ajay.

"Hello," Ajay said shyly. "Nice meeting you Auntiji. Er, umm, I didn't catch your name."

"Good, good, your horoscope is a killer one. Guru is in the fourth house and Saturn is in the garage."

Mr. Iyer interrupted. "That doesn't matter. You see, like many other *desis*, I don't ever care to mention her name in introductions. Now we no longer remember her name. Everybody only knows her as Wife #32454."

"Oh, what a nice number," Ajay said.

"What would you like to drink?"

"Whatever you have on tap. I will have a pitcher."

"Ajay, Malini is getting dressed. When she is done you can go inside and have a one-on-one chat with her. Stay at least four feet away from each other. Good, good, your horoscope is a killer one. Guru is in the fourth house and Saturn is in the garage. We can start our interview now itself, if you wish. Do you have any questions about Malini that I can answer?"

"Yes, what is her cholesterol number?"

Time stood still while Malini Ammal got ready for Ajay. In the meantime, Mrs. Iyer went from the kitchen to Malini's room *hazaar* times. Finally, Malini was ready and Ajay was slowly escorted inside. Ajay felt like a sacrificial lamb being led to the slaughter. As the two potential mates began their 'interview', a tense lull fell on the living room. Anxious, everyone fell silent and pensive.

Iyer began to remember his own early days. He had started out as a Chief Administrative Officer for the Maharaja of Travancore, till one day the Maharaja woke up and realized that Maharajas and kingdoms had been abolished several decades ago, and summarily fired Iyer. This sent Iyer searching for greener pastures and greener cards. Eventually he landed up in the US, and sold his soul for a few hundred dollars and a coupon for three dollars off a large pizza, and now firmly believes that he is helping India from the outside. He remembered somebody's theory about *desis* in this country, and how *desis* are like drops of water. If they land up this side of the continental divide they end up in New Jersey, and if they are at the other side, they end up in the Silicon Valley eventually. Now he is as New Jersey as the Turnpike. After years of hard work, he has moved up in the hi-tech corporate world and now designs the on-off switches for personal computers.

The rarified atmosphere, with whiffs of onion *pakoras* getting deep-fried, numbed Iyer's senses and made him think deeply. 'Just exactly who is cheating whom?' he wondered. 'Am I cheating the poor boy by forcing him to marry my dud daughter? Is he cheating me by marrying her purely for a green card? Is my daughter cheating him by marrying him just because he is a qualified professional, otherwise she might end up as an exotic dancer? Are the four thugs, friends of Ajay, cheating me by coming here and freeloading a dinner? Am I cheating these four boys, because even if the Ajay Palvayanteeswaran deal falls through, I can always go after one of the other guys and try to get him hitched to my dud daughter? Is my wife cheating on me?'

Iyer was like a thinking machine, as he rambled on to the next line of thinking. 'Hmmm! The modern man has evolved so much,' he felt. 'In prehistoric times, man made crude implements out of stone, polished them all day and spent entire days hunting animals with the implements. He then made fire and cooked his kill. The modern man, on the other hand, simply reaches out and calls in a pizza. Look at how much the institution of marriage has changed over the centuries!' His father and mother, Archibald and Abigail, were married when *Malini is a product of East and West. She is five percent* Mundaka Upanishad, *seven percent* Rush Limbaugh, two *percent* Kamasutra... they were just three years old. In fact, they went to the same kindergarten and sang lewd versions of *Ba-Ba-black sheep* together. When he got married, about eighty-two relatives on his side and his wife's side negotiated the deal. Now, the boy and the girl were doing all the dealing!

The four 'friends of Ajay' had just finished eating the fifth plate of *pakoras*.

Malini is a product of East and West. She is five percent *Mundaka Upanishad*, seven percent Rush Limbaugh, two percent *Kamasutra*, and eight percent Ann Landers. The rest of her life is based entirely Taco Bell commercials. When she was young, she learnt *Bharatnatyam*, till one day when she was executing the Krishna *abhinaya*, the floor opened underneath her dancing feet, and she fell onto the pool table at the basement and had to walk around dragging the pool table for several days. Each summer, she would go to India and learn music under the tutelage of the famous Lady King of Classical Music, Begum Kabuthar of the *Piya-ka-Gharaana*, until one day when the Begum was on her deathbed, she made Malini promise she would never sing again. Malini struggled with her high school courses and finally, thanks to a football scholarship, she even went to college and enrolled in a popular major, 'The Care and Feeding of the Horse'. After three days, she dropped out and now works as a mannequin in *India Sari House*.

Ajay tiptoed into the room, checking one last time if his fly was zipped up. Malini Ammal didn't look un-pretty. She was like a cross between an old Madhuri Dixit and a young Mother Teresa. Ajay had this incredible urge to just blurt out that it was all a big mistake and run for his life, stopping at a bathroom *en route*. His knees felt weak. Instead he said a sheepish "hi" to Molly.

"Hi," replied Malini.

"Hi," insisted Ajay.

"Hi," responded Malini.

"Yes, isn't the weather nice today?" said Ajay, and broke the ice.

Soon, the young couple relaxed and rambled on pointlessly from one topic to another, like Ramesh Mahadevan's Internet bulletin-board writings. Just when Ajay thought that things were going well, Malini dropped a bombshell.

> *"Bob is my boyfriend. He is a very jealous kind of person and knows karate and has a collection of guns," Malini explained*

"Ajay, I would have gladly married you except for Bob."

"Who is Bob?" he asked.

"Bob is my boyfriend. He is a very jealous kind of person and knows karate and has a collection of guns," Malini explained, "It was with him that I had my first hug, my first kiss and my first everything."

Ajay was petrified, "You mean, first everything?"

"Yes, everything."

"*Everything?*" his voice was quivering.

"Yes, *everything*," replied Malini. "You see, I wasn't interested in this Indian-style marriage deal. It was all Dad's idea."

"Yes, even I wasn't very keen on this thing. It is all your dad's idea," said Ajay, fearing for his life.

"Ajay, it is nothing personal. If Bob and I break up and you are still interested, we will contact you."

"That's great. Will you then explain all this to your dad? Now, if you will excuse me, I have to rush to my apartment," Ajay said, resigning himself to several more months, perhaps years, of celibacy.

"You can do better than that Ajay," replied the *femme*. "Why don't you at least have dinner and complete this evening? My mother is a good cook."

Exeunt omnes

So Who Speaks Hindi?

Abbas Tyrewala

(In which a frustrated scriptwriter attempts to explore and expose the myth of Hindi as a spoken language, in a pathetic display of the defensive instinct towards his stilted film scripts.)

As a scriptwriter, there is nothing I dread more than the moments of pained silence after the reading of a script.

I know this pause. I've heard it before and I saw it creeping up on me once again even as I read *Scene #43B. Counter-Intelligence HQ. Int. Day.*

There is an uncomfortable sequence of coughs and a reflexive lighting up of cigarettes. Slowly, visible reactions are diffused in the haze. Everyone feels a little more secure (quitting cigarettes is such a trauma in this trade). Each one waits for the other to remark that it didn't 'work' and **This is also the reason there are so many idiots in this trade. Not enough of them are told, early on, that they're idiots.** therefore become the perpetrator and symbol of rejection to somebody who might, one day, become quite famous.

This is the response-muting, reaction-numbing, sensibility-obstructing, integrity-negating fear in the film industry today. This is also the reason there are so many idiots in this trade. Not enough of them are told, early on, that they're idiots. What if this is a mistake and the guy is not an idiot? Then some day he's going to be a force to reckon with and he'll never forget my volunteering adjectives for his person. Then these idiots

---

Abbas Tyrewala, 26, was born and raised in Bombay, India. He has worked as a copywriter with Ogilvy & Mather and as a Creative Consultant with a couple of TV companies. He currently pens scripts and lyrics for Bollywood. He enjoys reading, writing and pretty much anything involving ideas. Abbas lives a quiet, non-filmi life in Bombay with his parents.

hang around long enough for a lot of other idiots to figure that if they've been around this long, maybe they aren't idiots.

And so slowly, we become an industry of idiots wherein a man who has the misfortune of recognizing idiocy and not wanting to associate with it has a problem. This is a pretty fascinating tangent I'm hitting, but the negative connotations of the noun defeat the promise of the adjective and so I'll come back to my point.

Which is the suspended comment, "It didn't work."

Of course it didn't. I sensed that. Maybe someone cares to elaborate – idiots! Instead I say (after an adequately long pause which suggests okay, fine, I guess you feel that way and it's alright that you feel that way), "Hmm. Why?" More pauses, long drags, coughs and I feel desperately like smoking. (Promise of relief, promise of everything instantly reverting to "OK" mode.) I hold out and wait for awkward coughs to run their course. Someone suggests, finally, that the dialogue doesn't work. The floodgates are open. The offender is marked. Subsequent opinions are vaccinated, immune to vengeance.

"It sounds too stilted."

"It doesn't sound like people talking."

"Sounds false."

And the classic: "The indicative dialogue in English sounded so good. Why couldn't you capture that?"

I know. I saw this coming. I felt it as I wrote but once again, I allowed myself the luxury of a familiar lie – that no one would notice.

They always notice. No one talks like that.

So why don't my characters sound like they are talking? Why don't they sound like people we know? The simplistic answer is that such people don't exist, that people don't talk like that. But the premises and conclusion of the implicit syllogism are not quite clear.

I write these characters,
they sound like no one,
therefore I don't write the way people talk.

Or…

I write these characters,
they sound like no one,
therefore no one talks the way I write.

This latter is interesting Not that I don't write the language that people talk, but that no one talks the language I write. While the two may seem mutually redundant, they are not. I write fairly decent, clean, universal Hindi.

So is the problem with me or with Hindi?

Who speaks Hindi? Where does this language come from?

I will not claim to have researched this subject and discovered any startling answers. But from discussions and snippets and the odd conversation, I am increasingly of the opinion that Hindi in its pure form is not spoken anywhere in significant quanta and frequency. Hindi is a language of twentieth century scholastic expression that enjoyed a promotional thrust in the post-independence era – a synthetic language has *never been adopted by a people.* At least not for any significant length of time.

As a result, it has no traces of the idiom, the colour, the richness that stems from a familiar misuse and abuse of **Sure, it has a motley bunch of idioms, lovingly called** muhavaras **and drilled by the pathetic handful into students in school.**

words and phrases. It lacks the poignant clusters of words, which in their literal relation to each other mean absolutely nothing, or perhaps something quite in contrast to their understood implications, which may be profound or incisive or just plain silly. These elements are rendered almost impossible by the very *scientific* nature of the language – it is so fixed and harsh in its pronunciation that there is no question of play, pun and misinterpretation. A certain syllable is that syllable only: unflinching in its dull fixedness, invulnerable to the seductions of creative interpretation.

Sure, it has a motley bunch of idioms, lovingly called *muhavaras* and drilled by the pathetic handful into students in school. The usage of these *muhavaras* is so unfamiliar and academic that kids are actually compelled to first *write their meaning* and then to construct sentences using such endearing phrases as "*lohe ke channe chabaana.*" (chew on grams of iron – execute a tough task) and "*sirr mudaate olé padé* (encounter hail immediately after shaving one's head – a double whammy of

> **The Urdu-enriched 'Hindustani,' the colourful vulgarity of 'Bhojpuri' and various other dialects that have a gratifyingly tangential relationship with Hindi.**

sorts). Idiomatic elements in a language are traditionally a contrast to the scholastic form. Together, they elevate language to communication and expression. Here, we find a fervent attempt to *academically enforce* this necessary aberration to give the language a pretense of plebian usage.

Hindi in its various *adapted* avatars and related versions is rich in idiomatic content and the homegrown turn of phrase. The Urdu-enriched 'Hindustani', the colourful vulgarity of 'Bhojpuri' and various other dialects that have a gratifyingly tangential relationship with Hindi. A little Urdu here, some Farsi there, and a hint of English adulteration – especially prevalent in Bombay – and the language is rocking.

So who speaks Hindi? Where have people accepted this language as their own, bringing to it therefore the beauty of their lives and experiences, adapting it to create a sense when it had not the words to express that sense, using words to hide and silences to express and bringing to it the ring that only love and usage can bring? (I can just hear indignant voices shouting "Allahabad." Well... yeah, okay. One point for you, but I'm still ahead.)

Which is the oldest epic written in this language? What are the literary achievements in Hindi that inspire and evoke? A couple of names come to mind right away. Munshi Premchand, and of course, Harvanshrai Bachchan and his rich metaphors in *Madhushala*. Before I go further into this discussion, can we just remember that Premchand seldom used wordplay? His entire approach was one of elevating simple emotions to epic proportions. In fact, the prosaic nature of the language actually helped in keeping it simple, which is what critics commemorate in Premchand's style. And the poetry of Madhushala stems not from any dance of words but from the dance of thought, from the deceptively profound idea underlying the *simple* ode to a drinking house. As we say in Bombay, *"Idea ka paisa hai."*

That's the mantra. Keep is simple, and the language can handle it. From what I remember of the Hindi literature I studied through school and college, it consisted of simple stories told directly – where the emotions and images took the narrative forward – or the great Hindi tradition of *vyangya* (satire). Satire was somehow the predominant theme in Hindi literature. Political and bureaucratic satire. Sarcastic looks at relationships and families. Ironic statements on the times. Remember Sharad Joshi?

Satire is what this language most readily lends itself to. Not to beauty, not to abstractions, not to wordplay and unconventional creative expressions. Because at the turn of the century, when Hindi first started to find a voice, the mood was one of Nationalism and rebellion – emotions that could not be expressed openly. So the dominant stylistic form became one of hinting, and implying...but keeping the language obvious, so that even a child could grasp the 'encryptions'. And in the aftermath of independence, when I believe this synthetic language really came into its own, the mood was one of cynicism and failed dreams. The people reacted with bitterness, the intellectuals with sarcasm. And Hindi became a tool for the scholastic class to cleverly express their disgust – with the reflexive tendency to suggest and imply and veil – but only in the emotional content. *Not* in the language. Hindi is poorly adapted to any other higher form of expression.

Which Hindi film sounds like anyone talking? I understand that Hindi films necessarily speak to an entire nation. Therefore it has to transcend idioms and usage that may alienate different the regions and communities of such a vast country. But isn't talking to no one too high a price to pay for talking to everyone? Will flavour and colour and authenticity always be sacrificed at the altar of universality?

In Hrishikesh Mukherjee's *Chupke Chupke,* a professor of botany drives a senior man up the wall by taking his affinity for *shudh* Hindi to an extreme, underlining that when used in its purest form, Hindi becomes a caricature of itself. (Of course, at one point, the golden-hearted protagonist expresses the concern that he might be mocking something as beautiful as 'language'. The other responds saying that language is inherently so sublime that you cannot mock it. Having thus covered their backsides, they gallop right ahead, mocking the language with deceptive viciousness.)

So will the odd word borrowed from English and Urdu continue to rescue spoken Hindi and infuse it with vitality? Or will this language actually be embraced by a people and come into its own as a language of the people?

And will my characters ever sound like people talking? I don't know.

Perhaps dialogue in Hindi cinema will necessarily become focussed and localised with the new trend of regionally segmented markets. The 'universal' film is fast becoming a myth along with its degenerate cousin, the 'formula' film. Maybe filmmakers will have to take cognizance of the fact that their characters have to come from *somewhere*, and speak like *someone*. They will have to anticipate the markets where their films have a greater likelihood of succeeding and make their characters localised, relevant and consequently real. Their characters will share local or regional concerns, pasts and dreams.

Which Hindi film sounds like anyone talking?

Where does that leave me...he of no colour save the gray squalours of Bombay? Hey, maybe I'll just write films in English. Maybe I'll talk the way people in Bombay talk, without worrying too much about the language. Maybe I'll just do story lines and scene breakdowns and let a man with a past do the dialogue. I don't know.

Why did I write this? Again, I don't know. Frustration-induced intellectual masturbation, as far as I can tell. Have I offended anyone? Perhaps. If so, to him I say, *"bhaasha apne aap mein itni mahaan hoti hai ki uss ka mazaak udaaya hi nahin jaa sakta."* (Language is inherently so great that you cannot mock it.)

Interesting to note here that *'mazaak'* is an Urdu word that helps this harshly angular sentence come around and curve into place. Hmmm.

Sulekha Reader Comments

DA: I was a copywriter too, 'but please don't tell my mother, she thinks I play the piano in a whorehouse'. My epiphany came when I heard some of my copy translated into Telugu. The Telugu translation sounded like a civics lesson from a government Telugu textbook. The only thing the translated copy lacked was Ramu and Sita. It sounded like no Telugu I've ever heard. Then again, it did sound like a civics lesson from a government...(The same copy was also translated into Urdu and it sounded like poetry. But this I think was largely due to my minimal understanding of formal Urdu. To be honest I liked the sound of the translation. For a brief minute I considered going out and buying a *sherwani*, getting drunk and writing melancholy odes to my courtesan with the heart of gold if only that pimp brother of hers would leave us in... *Magar, mai shayar tho nahi...*) From then on I was intrigued by 'tone' in Indian languages.

This lack of varied tones in Indian languages when compared to English is depressing for those Indians who are more fluent in English. Eventually 'we' are confronted with the fact that we can twist English to match our needs but fail miserably when it comes to our mother tongues. This fact is all the more strange when we realize that English is a relatively new to us. A lot of it has, I think, to do with the fact English has been worked over by hundreds of thousands of writers in the last two hundred years. Not just by authors of fiction but by academics, scientists, comedians, screenwriters, journalists, musicians and many others and yes copywriters too. Each one us owe our 'individual' language to the hundreds of writers that we might have read. No amount of sheer brilliance by a few writers will gives us the language that the modern mind craves for to make sense of its environment. You can't have Joyce without a hundred years of Dickens and you can't have Dickens without a couple hundred years of Shakespeare. And most of the highly educated Indians who normally might have added the required layer upon layer to their respective languages take the easy road that English is. I think it would take thousands of us, many decades of treading on a path to make an Indian language resemble the six-lane expressway that English is.

Amitabha Bagchi: Please Mr. Tyrewala, let me submit to you that the language known as Hindi which New Delhi has been trying to construct is a weak attempt to flatten a rich array of dialects. You agree with me on that, I think. Do not buy the government propaganda on what is Hindi. Do not buy the classicist argument that says that anything with a Persian sounding word in it is not Hindi. That is just insecurity talking. Please do not say that beauty cannot be expressed in this language. You want beauty in classical Hindi, read Dharamveer Bharati's *Andha Yug* or Mohan Rakesh's *Aashad Ka Ek Din*. You want beauty in Urdu-flavoured Hindi read Krishna Sobti's *Dil-o-Danish*. You want beauty in local dialected, influenced Hindi, stay with Krishna Sobti and read *Mitro Marjani*.

Apurva Mishra: Delightful little essay. Your remarks on Hindi were bang-on and very funny. Yet, however stilted the use of *shuddh* Hindi in the country is, the use of *shuddh* English is infinitely worse. I'd say the stiffest *muhavara* you pick out of a Hindi grammar-book is still much more real to the Indian populace than the Wren-and-Martin stuff they used to force on us in my little 'convent' school. And you who complain about stiffness in Hindi movie dialogue – have you ever heard a 13-year-old small-town schoolboy attempting to recite *Lochinvar*? Hindi at least has the advantage of now and then falling back on regional or vernacular flavor for earthiness or relevance. English (in India) has none. English *babuspeak* has been ridiculed so much it's not even funny. But to my mind the utter lack of connection of Indians and English is demonstrated in its most pathetic form in the stiff, unnatural usage that passes for English slang among city college kids in India.

On a Wing and a Prayer

Mahesh Krishnaswamy

Now I've heard everything. *The San Francisco Chronicle* reported some weeks ago that a Hindu priest in Silicon Valley called Umashankar Dixit is in great demand to perform Lakshmi *poojas* when e-commerce startups are launched by Indians, as an increasing number are. Mr. Dixit says modestly that he is considered a 'lucky hand' because his God is Ganesha, the remover of obstacles. He – Mr. Dixit that is, *not* Ganesha – has been compensated in cash and stock options by several startups, and says he has already done very well from the IPOs of successful companies like Exodus Communications. A few Indian and American publications have since come up with their own breathless takes on Mr. Dixit, reporting among other things that he spends an hour every morning, presumably just after *sandhyavandanaam*, on the Internet, monitoring the financial markets.

Or he may favour a simple kumkum pottu—in effect, despite all the gadzillions Sun Microsystems spends on advertising, it may actually be Mr. Dixit who is the dot in dotcom...

It's not clear from the articles whether Mr. Dixit is an Iyer, in which case he would normally wear three bands of *vibhooti* on his forehead – ideal, one would think, for launching

---

Most of Mahesh Krishnaswamy's work over the past twenty-five years consists of plaintive letters to the editor of The Hindu, the Madrasi's patron saint of lost causes. He had a B.Tech. thrust upon him in 1975 by IIT Madras and later shrewdly invested in an M.B.A from IIM Calcutta in 1977. Neither institution seriously interfered with his education. Mahesh lives in Singapore, which he says is no laughing matter. He describes his writing as being of merely comic, rather than cosmic, proportions. His wife Radha and he are bringing up two daughters while wrestling with a small software company and a large mortgage.

companies that specialise in broadband networks. On the other hand, he may be an Iyengar who wears a U-shaped *naamam* on his forehead, more suitable for launching ASIC design companies. Or else, he may have decided to assist as wide a spectrum of startups as possible, and may favour a simple *kumkum pottu* – in effect, despite all the gazillions Sun Microsystems spends on advertising, it may actually be Mr. Dixit who is the dot in dotcom.

It is likely, although both the papers are unaccountably reticent on this point, that Mr. Dixit's *poojas* are integral to the business plans of his clients and the willingness of canny VCs to part with vast amounts of negotiable tender. I have it on good authority that the average e-commerce startup in the Valley usually has its business plan scribbled on a napkin and requires you to sign a 20-page non-disclosure agreement before it will show the napkin to you. Mr. Dixit's clients have probably jotted down a business plan that typically goes something like this:

1. Come up with brilliant idea for a B2B category-killer but don't tell anybody
2. Get copies of founders' horoscopes for name selection
3. Consult Dixit on launch date and *muhurtam*
4. Finalise funding of $6 million
5. Locate suitable garage
6. Order pizza
7. Don't use this napkin to blow your nose

"So who's Dixit?" asks the VC. "Oh, he specialises in ultra-long-distance wireless communications," says the entrepreneur. "Wow," says the VC as he fumbles for his chequebook, "so that's where you're going, huh?" "That's where the whole world will eventually have to go," says the entrepreneur, "but we're giving you an opportunity to get in on the ground floor!" And so it goes.

The *Chronicle* describes a typical Lakshmi *pooja* performed by Mr. Dixit in lyrical detail. The CEO of the company has set up a small, colourful shrine in a tiny conference room for the ceremony. 'There is a basket with 108 US coins, symbolizing the 108 different names and forms of Hindu gods; a platter with coconuts, limes and other offerings; and small silver bowls of turmeric, the yellow-orange seasoning signifying wealth, and *kumkum*, the red powder that Indians use to dot their foreheads. The ceremony, which involves a lot of chanting and tossing of flower petals, lasts about 45 minutes.' As an honorarium, Mr. Dixit receives 51 dollars and 5,000 stock options. One assumes that for good measure, he also tosses

As an honorarium, Mr. Dixit receives 51 dollars and 5,000 stock options.

some *akshathai* on the heads of the VCs, not to mention the *Chronicle*'s correspondent. And so it goes.

The startup buys two Porsches and sets up shop in a garage to begin work on its brilliant idea. Very soon, it is first-round funding *swaaha (an incantation used while pouring butter into the ritual bonfire)* as Mr. Dixit might say, and more money is needed although no product is in sight. That's when the entrepreneurs hide the Porsches and go out and hire a couple of IIT graduates. If all the column inches of pure baloney that have been written about IIT graduates in the past one year were placed end to end, they would reach the moon. "Can I see the scar on your thumb you got from the workshop?"[1] whispers the VC reverently. "Aw, gee," says the bashful IIT graduate, "you should see the one I got when they did my frontal lobotomy!" Immediately, even more money rolls in, and our intrepid entrepreneurs organise a *homam* that is, naturally, performed by Mr. Dixit. "We're increasing our burn rate," the founders reassure the investors. And so it goes.

---

[1] Ed: A reference to a story in the American press about the success of IIT graduates in the Silicon Valley, in which mention is made of the rigors of the engineering workshop training at these institutions.

Soon, everyone wants to meet Mr. Dixit who duly arrives in his modest Honda Accord. In the Valley, nobody thinks his silk *veshti* and *angavastram* are particularly odd. "Willya look at those cool threads!" the investors remark, eyeing his *poonal*. "So how's it going?" they want to know. "It's all His *leela,*" says the devout Mr. Dixit, looking skywards. "We're a pure e-commerce play" translate the entrepreneurs. By this time, breathless articles in publications like the *Chronicle* have caused normally cautious people to buy sleeping bags and camp out on the grass outside the company to get a piece of the action. The entrepreneurs use part of the windfall to buy homes in Sausalito. The *grihapravesam* is performed, naturally, by Mr. Dixit. And so it goes.

The *Chronicle* doesn't say specifically what Mr. Dixit thinks of the whole dizzy dotcom world, although Rediff.com reports that he thinks the economy and the markets will recover very soon, praise be to Vigneshwara. The *Chronicle* is far too busy asking Dr. Mark Juergensmeyer, Professor of Sociology, who studies Indian religion at the University of California at Santa Barbara what he thinks of the idea of Mr. Dixit receiving stock options. Mr. Dixit will no doubt be reassured to know that Prof. Juergensmeyer thinks that stock options for priests aren't incompatible with Indian culture. "Some Hindu priests," the good professor says, "receive more than others, just as they do in other religions." *Ayyaiyyo*, for these kinds of penetrating insights they gave Juggu a Ph.D.?

What Ganesha thinks is another matter for speculation. The prudent Mr. Dixit says he's already using a part of his high-tech portfolio to construct a *Durga Siddhivinayaka* temple in Bangalore, so it may well be okay with Him too. I guess day-trading beats removing obstacles hands down, especially if He already knows which way NASDAQ is going and how the Microsoft saga will end. *Sarva Vighna Upashaantaye (May All Obstacles be Removed)...*

Inheritance

Ruth Bushi

This is how she remembers her birth:

Their wooden homestead was slightly apart from the cluster that comprised the village. The other houses sprang from the dust, and were mantled by a powdery compound wall: to keep the road out, to keep the village in. Her father's dwelling was embedded in a verdant field, other watery fields undulating from that given point in every direction as far as he might care to walk.

Raising eyes to the heavens, even the clouds would not deign to move that morning; airless they hung, flat and white, pasted onto a cerulean sky. Completing the overhead arc back to the dust clouds rising above the village that framed the squat little house: her father stood on the veranda, his white cotton *lungi* dropping to his ankles, shirted in crisp cotton. He smoked. Behind him the swollen house loomed.

Inside the house, the mother lay in the marital bed, her face beaded with sweat, her belly above her tumescent and veined translucent.

Inside the house the mother lay in the marital bed, her face beaded with sweat, her belly above her tumescent and veined translucent. An ancient woman basted her brow with drops

---

Ruth Bushi was born in Rajahmundry in Andhra Pradesh, South India. She grew up in England, and currently lives in the Lake District. Ruth has worked in publishing and new media, and aims to write professionally in the future. She attained a Master's in English from the University of Durham in 1999. Her writing interests are dark and diverse, and not limited to the South Asian experience, although that was her first inspiration. She dedicates this story to her family, and to the memory of her late father, Joseph.

wrenched from a soaking rag. A child hid among the folds of her stained *sari* and fearfully watched the twisted face. Another girl, too young to be afraid, was charged with minding the baby; together they mewled on the earth-dirt floor, and rolled between the wooden legs of the cot.

Inside the foetid cabin the wretched woman opened her mouth and roared out the dank breath from her womb: she sprawled her knees, and strained to spew out the monstrous seed. Outside, the villagers crept around the house as the walls rose, and rose, and burst forth with her screaming; in the intermittent silence they strained for a joyous wailing.

The women had come with rainbow-stolen scarves draped over muddy skirts and blouses. Some of the men wandered close to her father and milled on the veranda, but at he last hung back.

The racking sobs ceased. So too did the rolling whispering of the crowd. They waited with one breath. Far away in the fields, where nothing mattered, the long reedy grass danced from side to side, but outside the homestead even the wind stilled and let the sweat stream un-cooled on her father's brow.

The ancient woman shuffled to the door, swaddling clutched to her chest, her milky eyes running over as she searched for the patriarch. He strode towards her, his eyes fiercely searching hers, but she would not be examined. She thrust the bundle at him and began the wail of blessings: his head fell forward in humble triumph to receive them.

Around him the prayers of the dowager were caught up and expanded by the ululating cry of the villagers. A drum began to beat, a single, solid pulse, then was joined by the fiercer rumbling of a second. To the reverberating throb the women added the jangle of ankle bells. Their clapping grew to a sideways swaying, a silken rainbow stretched out over their heads, the edges of the frayed squares caught and lightly tossed in the wind. Under their feet the grass was trampled in frenzied circles, the dust was freed by their cracked heels and rose about their hems.

Some had bought coloured powders, pure enough to outshine the rainbow silks, and now the rising zephyr carried it high above their heads to rain down upon their raised faces. They called to voice shrieking song, and in the midst of all, planted as firmly as Atlas with the child raised high above his head, her father's triumphant wail resounded above all.

As the throb of the drums grew faster, so too did their feet fly over the flattened field. Her father lowered the silent bundle that all might gaze on the immaculate face. The wailing grew to a climax; the wind mocked harder, and seeped *The singing stopped. The dancing stopped. The dust fell, but still the swaddling rags fluttered gaily in the breeze.* between the bloody rags, prying them from under his fingers. As the howling became bacchanalian, the swaddling fluttered once, twice, and then billowed out freely. He turned his face to gaze down upon the folds, his eyes frozen, his lips pulled back in revulsion.

The singing stopped. The dancing stopped. The dust fell, but still the swaddling rags fluttered gaily in the breeze. The headscarves dropped, wrapped tightly around averted faces as the colourful forms bled away.

"What is the meaning of this!" Clutching at the newborn he turned to roar at the wise old woman, but she too had shuffled away, her milky eyes shining happily. Inside the gaping black doorway only her sisters stayed to face the rage of her father. Only one dark pair of eyes met his with fearful understanding, and then turned away in shame.

Black, White and Various Shades of Brown

Man from Matunga

I came across a project report written by an executive of a US-based multinational company, which is considered to be a leader in the beauty care business. He had been sent to India, some months ago, to carry out a market survey for a new fairness cream. This particular fairness cream had done very badly in the US despite a very positive pilot study, and the company was stuck with a large inventory, which it had thought of dumping in a suitable third-world country. The MNC had no previous base in India. This is the report that he sent.

Summary: India is a phenomenal market for fairness creams and our product should do well beyond all imagination. Despite the logistical problems of setting up a company in India (Annexure A), I believe that not only should we market the cream in India, but we should also set up our own base in India – not as part of a joint venture with a local company, as we had thought of doing earlier. Not only that, I believe that we should even be prepared to shift our production facilities to India if necessary, at short notice.

Observations: Indians are obsessed with skin color. A careful study of the classified matrimonial columns in the local and national newspapers shows that the majority of the ads follow a set pattern. 'A fair, good-looking, Gujarati/Sindhi/Punjabi/Tamil lady wanted for an educated, well-settled man...' If the girl is advertising for a groom, the ad goes something like, 'A fair girl with good temperament looking for....', or if

---

Man From Matunga is the pseudonym of a Mumbaikar who in his mid-30s has finally decided to go back to his first love, which is writing. Using a website, www.manfrommatunga.com as a springboard, MFM, as he likes to abbreviate himself, writes essays, articles, rants and reviews, and dreams of writing a novel sometime in the near future. He is a doctor by profession and recently became the father of twins; both these nearly full-time occupations have added depth to his writings, but taken away the time that he needs to devote to his writing.

the girl is not fair, euphemistically, 'A girl with a wheatish complexion...'. Never in the last few months, have I come across an ad from either side mentioning a dark-skinned lady. This is because all things being equal (and sometimes even if not equal), a fair woman has a much better chance of bagging a good husband. (For an explanation of the concept of matrimonial ads and arranged marriages and their importance in the Indian scenario, please see Annexure B).

As soon as a child is born and its sex is known, the next thing looked at is the skin color. A dark skin in a boy is still acceptable, but in a girl is considered a liability. (Please see Annexure C for a more detailed local explanation.)

Indians have a poor tolerance towards races darker than them. In places like Kenya, where there is a large Indian population, a very derogatory attitude exists towards the native African population. The Indians there refer to them as *kaalia* or *karo*, meaning black. (Annexure D for articles regarding this). A similar attitude exists towards Africans who come to study in India. They are looked upon with suspicion and in the event of even the slightest trouble involving them or their places of residence, they are arrested and considered guilty unless proved innocent. (Annexure E for reports in the press including protest letters by the Nigerian embassy). A couple of years ago, an African couple was denied entry into a South Mumbai pub, because the owner thought the couple would cause trouble. (Annexure F for a *Mid Day* report on this). As an Indian friend tells me, 'Our attitude towards the blacks is worse than the attitude that the whites had towards us – the apartheid spectrum seems to have shifted to the right of the color range.'

Just to illustrate this point further. I am sure you are aware of the controversy that Indian and Pakistani cab drivers in New York got into, when they refused a ride to Mr. Danny Glover, the actor, on the grounds that they were scared of blacks and would prefer not to go to areas with a predominant African-American population. (Annexure G for the New York Times coverage of this incident).

There is a sizeable community of Indians in the US. Though marriages and interactions between the white population and Indians are known, it is very rare for Indians to have emotional or sexual relations with African-American individuals. (Annexure H for a report by an Indian-American on this topic).

There are two popular brands selling fairness products in the local Indian market – they account for most of the market share. Of these two, one is actually a bleach, (we can stress this point in our ad campaign and run the company out of business) and the other is a cream similar to ours. (Annexure I contains copies of press advertisements of these products as well as statistics regarding their sales and market share).

In the Southern parts of India, where the people are much darker than in the northern parts, being fair is considered a godsend. In their movies, fair actresses and heroines are much better appreciated than dark actresses, even though the majority of the population is dark. (Annexure J for pictures of fair Southern movie actresses).

Marketing Strategies: There are two target populations. The first is women in the age group of 17-25 whose need to be fair is directly proportionate to their urge to get married. At this stage, they are extremely vulnerable to suggestions from any source, including ads, about products that would help make them fair. The second target population is men – they should be made to see the virtues of our cream using subliminal messages in our ads. They would then support the use of our product and sometimes maybe even suggest its use to their daughters and wives.

The two competing products mentioned above blatantly extol the virtues of being fair in their television ads. There is no opposition from the public or the advertising council regarding these racist ads, which would never have been allowed in our politically correct country. With our superior advertising and marketing concepts, we can push this divide even further – we can show how being dark is shameful and that nothing works like being fair, creating a situation where anyone even remotely affected by color, will have no choice but to use our products.

To this end, we can use some fair actresses to advertise our product. This concept is very prevalent in the soap industry and though the actresses are expensive by Indian standards, the amount of money involved is not much by our standards (approximately $100,000 or so for endorsement).

If we could get Michael Jackson to endorse the product in India, that would work wonders. We can show him during his *Thriller* days and compare that MJ to the new one, to show how even the darkest of dark people can become fair with the right attitude and skin-care products.

There is a tendency to believe anything that has even the slightest scientific background to it. Shampoo and face-care companies run countless television ads showing pretty scientists in research and development departments strutting around extolling the virtue of their products that ostensibly have been developed after extensive experimentation. Since we have an R&D department, we could do the same by showing a dark, academic-looking Indian asking a fair, Indian woman scientist, working in our R&D department, leading questions about our fairness cream and looking terribly impressed by the results shown, so much so, that even she starts using our cream and notices a change, within a month.

Conclusion: To reiterate, India is a country, prime for the picking. We should see phenomenal sales and profits for our product in the country.

There is an interesting epilogue to this. The executive's superiors in the MNC approached his observations with the proverbial pinch of salt and thought he had gone overboard in his enthusiasm. The project was nixed and the extra stock of the fairness cream was dumped in a landfill. The frustrated executive quit the company and formed a start-up with venture capital finance from some Silicon Valley Indian entrepreneurs who were the only ones who believed in the potential of his project that would include the manufacture and sale of a new, unique fairness cream in India. For those interested, the grapevine has it that the project is nearing completion and a product launch is just around the corner...

Sulekha Reader Comments

Mallika: This article cracked me up! It is true that Indians are obsessed with skin color. I live in the US and every time I interact in an Indian social group, stereotypes are always made against me! Cos, you see I am 'extremely fair' for a South Indian according to 'North Indians' and that simply can't be! And of course, I get stereotyped by South Indians as well. They take one look at me at parties and jump to the conclusion that I must be a North Indian cos of my skin color. Americans think I am Middle Eastern cos I don't fit the profile of an Indian. One of them actually told me that I don't look 'that brown'! After all these stereotypes, I feel like filling the race section in a form as "fair and confused"!

Kannan:

1. Does the average skin-color conscious Indian consider dark to be 'shameful'? I don't think so. Any attempt to establish this,

in my opinion, would backfire badly. I have not found 'dark' to be 'shameful' to those for whom 'fair' skin is 'desirable.' An idle question: is it 'racist' to prefer blondes to brunettes or redheads?

2.   Preference for a certain color does not automatically translate to 'racism'. The bias against a certain color (like the examples of bias against African students or African Americans) is.

3.   Glorifying dark skin as a thing of beauty in response to the preference for fair skin is a reactionary expression of "I am not like that." Preferring dark skin is no different from preferring fair skin. Neither is glorifying dark skin. By itself, I don't hold either preference to be racist. Some people may just find blonde hair aesthetically appealing. If blondes are assigned a characteristic that is not related to being blonde (such as being 'dumb', as in the notion of 'dumb blondes') that is a problem. Similarly, you might say, preferring dark is not necessarily being fair. Just as the opposite of 'being in love' with someone is not 'hating' that someone. The opposite of being in love is indifference.

Aesthetic preference rules a lot of our choices consciously and unconsciously. Our guard has to be up in the matter of causing no injustice because of our aesthetic preferences.

Happiness, Just a Battle Away

Nagesh Kukunoor

Half the battles you fight are in your head.

I told myself this repeatedly. I had other *mantras*, of course. One I stole, you know from where – *Just do it!* Anything to remind me that there was a higher purpose; that I was meant to do something else. Yet, the days went on and the excuses mounted. Excuses to not break away. Excuses to put off pursuing the dream until the next paycheck. I blamed everyone – my parents (the best anyone could dream of having) for the way they brought me up, my siblings for their lack of support, my friends for their lack of ambition. Anything to shift the blame from myself.

> *Plus, filmmaking is not exactly revered in educated Indian society, occupying one secure notch above, say, prostitution.*

There wasn't one defining moment when it happened. Just a bunch of little things that eventually led to that explosion. Coming from a stable middle class Telugu family, I took one of the obvious routes – becoming an engineer. My brother, coincidentally, chose the other. Yup, becoming a doctor. Ironically, my parents encouraged us to do whatever the heck we wanted, not coercing us onto time-tested routes. But conforming is a way of life in most of India, and mavericks are not really looked up to. Plus, filmmaking is not exactly revered in educated Indian

---

A chemical engineer by profession, Nagesh Kukunoor gave up his career as an environmental consultant to make Hyderabad Blues, *a film that won critical acclaim at numerous film festivals and commercial box office success around the world. Nagesh has created a new genre in Indian cinema — that of the low budget film that breaks the traditional barrier between commercial and art cinema. His next venture is* Bollywood Calling, *starring Om Puri.*

society, occupying one secure notch above, say, prostitution. So we became the ideal family: a doctor, an engineer and my sister a double master's in communication.

How dare I rock this boat! What will people say? *"Log kya kahenge?"* More excuses, more fears. But no decisions. I did have something working in my favor. I was unhappy. I mean *unhappy*. Not just a general feeling of dissatisfaction, but *'I-hate-my-existence'* unhappy. I think it is necessary for a lot of us to reach this stage in order to take the next step. Sure, right now it would be easy to pass off what happened in the past few years – when I broke away from my mundane existence and 'boldly went where few men have gone before' – as courage. But the truth is that I was miserable doing what I was doing and, being human, I did what came naturally – selfishly sought my own happiness. I was not embarking on some journey to change the world and help humanity. It was merely a personal search for happiness. If we only stopped to think of what makes us truly happy, we would all choose the paths that would lead us there. Paths, when you think about it, are not difficult at all. I admire the people who've given up their lives in the service of mankind. That's noble. On the other hand, maybe that's what makes them happy and their pursuit is as selfish as mine.

I actually sat down and subjected myself to a little introspection. Wow, what a scary thing! Most of us nine-to-fivers have no idea what that means, and we look down upon the 'artsy-fartsy' people who do. Yeah, it's natural to be scared of the unknown, scared of what you might find. When I spoke to myself (didn't have to fork out any cash to a shrink), my Everest (it seemed like that then) was clearly defined: make a movie! I hung out with that goal for several weeks, never really doing anything with it but just happy that I had reached that stage. One fine day no different from any other – one of those days when you feel you can kick anyone's ass – I decided to start taking courses and workshops, anything that would help me get there. I knew random enthusiasm would not be enough. I needed a databank that would give me the requisite confidence. I was Mr. Double Life, engineer by day, actor-writer-whatever by night. I found that I had bucket loads of energy at the end of the day to do what made me happy. It was cool. I did this for several years.

Then it felt right. Again, no great or incredible day, just one of those I-can-take-on-the-world days. I walked in and did the most difficult thing I have ever done. Said no to the paycheck. Was just about ready to puke out of fear. But once the deed was done, a numbness settled in that was perversely enjoyable. I had always felt that I did my best work with my back to the wall, and this was the one time I had to prove to myself that that was true. On I went my merry way, losing the apartment and the car (this hurt since I drove a Dodge Stealth in those days), giving away my stuff and beginning a nomadic life (three years later, I'm still floating). And off I went to India. Bollywood, Tollywood, here I come.

The dream run came to a screeching halt. They didn't want me as much as I wanted them. They didn't want some NRI (sometimes it is used as a *gaali*) trying to teach them stuff they already knew. I think at this stage I was truly devastated. I had failed...well not quite. Then it hit me. If failing was what I was petrified of, then I would simply be prepared for absolute failure to begin with. Starting with this worst-case scenario, I could only do better. I was going to make the worst film ever made. If it turned out to be good, that would be a bonus. This cheered me up. I realised that not finding out if I could do it was a lot scarier than finding out that I wasn't good at it. That is a little perverse philosophy, but here's one piece of unsolicited advice: it works. In this depressingly cheerful state I wrote *Hyderabad Blues* (seven days in long hand), budgeted it, did some math and figured out that I needed some more *moolah,* and that my savings were not going to be enough. I came back to the US and took up a job again and started hoarding like a madman to build up that bank balance. Giving up a cushy high-paying job

In this depressingly cheerful state I wrote Hyderabad Blues (seven days in long hand)...

the second time around was as difficult as the first time. I have no clue how, but I guess I was possessed enough to do it. And then began my true journey. My road to happiness.

And I still say, half the battles you fight are in your head. Just get used to winning them.

Sulekha Reader Comments

Suchitra: I liked your article and would like to offer another perspective. Before that, let me just say that I am very critical of movies and 'Hyderabad Blues' is amongst the few movies that I loved, especially because of its simplicity.

Well, the Indian pressures of stereotyping are enormous. I always wanted to write, and despite everyone's advice, set out to do my B.A. in literature and journalism. Being a science student, and a good one at that, 'arts' was a total disillusionment in both content and format. I ran back desperately, conformed and I am an engineer today! And I love my work!

I still write, however, but am glad I did not make it my profession. You could say that I found my dream in a manner opposite to yours.

Madana's Call

Shanti Aiyer

The sun rode vain in the mid-noon sky,
leafy shadows danced on the hilltop green,
he sat under a canopy of swishing palms
and poured a thousand dreams into his bamboo flute.
Far away, languid goats gently grazed
content, serene, drugged with the mid-day sun.
All valley heard his fluted dreams
waft softly down the pine-sweet breeze.

She came, floating down the winding path,
red mud-pot bouncing cheekily on her bronzed hip,
eyes throwing sharp-sweet darts of laughter
as dangerous as the arrows of Madana.
The sun bounced off the blues and golds
woven by crafty hands into the rustle of her robes,
as she snaked down the curving hill-top green
to the river chortling against mossy rocks.

He gazed at her, goats and flute forgotten,
winding her way through the murmuring pines,
mud-pot on hip, mischief in her eyes
and a hundred unknown aches tore his virgin heart.
He waited, noon after noon, under the silent palms
for the sinuous grace that never came.
Bird-song ceased in the twilight purple
distant lamps pin-pricked the weary village.

Shanti Aiyer received an MBA from the Southwest Missouri State University, and currently works in Chicago. She enjoys writing and has contributed some essays on classical music to Sruti, *an Indian monthly dedicated to the classical performing arts.*

That night all valley heard his fluting call
wafting down-hill from the scented pines.
They heard a pain, an ache, a want, a plea,
they fathomed not, nor did he.

The Witness

Syed

He slung his brown cloth bag on his shoulder and set off for home. The group of young men and women that had collected in the Gandhi square had already dispersed, and now only a few latecomers, some of them with long vermilion streaks on their foreheads, were poring over the newspaper. Subbiah, his master at the shop, had told him that the 'essesee rejultz' (SSC results) had come out that evening, and these people were checking to see if they had passed or failed. He did not really know what it was all about, but realized that it was a big deal, from the expressions on the faces of all those young people.

> The song from the new Chirru movie was playing over the loudspeaker on top of the soda shop at the street corner. He really loved the song...

The song from the new Chirru movie was playing over the loudspeaker on top of the soda shop at the street corner. He really loved the song, with its delicious references to red apples with red flowers on them. Whenever he heard the song he would imagine a heap of shining red apples piled on a cart, decorated with bright red flowers.

"*Pandu pandu pandu, yerra pandu, apple daani peruuuuuuu; yerra puvvulundu, bujji pandu....*" he sang along with the loud speakers.

Syed was born in Proddatur, Andhra Pradesh; legend has it that a bright light descended from the skies at the time of his birth. He did his schooling in Hyderabad. After finishing B.E., he left for the US where he completed his M.S., after which he took up work as a design engineer in a Silicon Valley company. He is single, but is getting a tad bit bored of such a life. He writes his stories while at work, when his boss is not looking. He also claims to write Urdu shayari, but refuses to show it to anyone.

His gait now had a spring in its execution. By the time he reached the dirt road that wound between the paddy and sugarcane fields to his village, Mullakanmpa, he was in very high spirits, and had already forgotten about Subbiah's abuses and beatings that evening for spilling the lentils.

"Haiii! Haiiyya!"

A bullock cart turned onto the dirt road behind him. He turned around and saw the two dirty white bulls approaching him with their characteristic, swaying walk. He ran toward them and got into the cart without saying a word to the indifferent cart man.

"Em tatha, yaddiki?" ("What grandpa, where to?") he asked the cart man.

"Kottachinnayapalem," he replied.

"Aite nen yeru kaada digtale."("Then I will get off at the creek.")

"Theyya!" the cart man whipped one of the bulls for no apparent reason, and the bulls started walking faster.

"Pandu pandu pandu, yerra pandu...." he started singing lustily again in the stillness of the fields, to the accompaniment of the *latt-patt-ghatt-khatt* of the cart's wooden wheels.

"Em kurrakai chana hushargundave!" ("What boy, you are in high spirits today!")

"Manam yeppudu inte!" ("We are this way all the time!") he announced; by now he was feeling on top of the world.

"Tha..tha..tha.." the old man prodded the bulls on with his feet, with a smirk.

The boy jumped off the cart at the creek, and without saying a word to the old man, walked off toward his village. He could hear the cart man for some distance as he prodded his animals on. Up ahead there was a man approaching, swinging a long stick in one hand, with two animals ahead of him.

"Hoi hoi!... cluck cluck...paph paph pah," the straggling farmer approached, driving his bulls home.

"Yem bi? Bheki vachhinave nedu?" ("What boy? You have come early today?") the farmer asked. He knew the boy well, as he went to Subbiah's shop for his *beedis* in the evenings.

"Aan! Ayya pendliki ponaadu!" ("Yes! Master has gone to attend a wedding!") he replied without stopping.

"Ramayya pendli kaaa?" ("Did he go to Ramayya's wedding?")

"Aaann." ("Yes.")

A little further down a frog hopped into his path, and he immediately picked up a stone to squash the creature right there. As he raised his hand to strike, he remembered his friend Basha telling him never to kill a frog, that he would beget dumb children if he did. The hand came down slowly, reluctantly, and the lucky frog leapt away without realizing its brush with death. Basha had also told him that one gets the reward of giving half a piece of bread in charity for killing a chameleon, so he searched the nearby bushes for one instead. He found a big one resting on a stem, and with a perfect shot smashed its skull against the stem it was holding onto. He felt happy about it; he had done a good deed for the day.

As there were no more chameleons around, he walked on, singing his *'pandu pandu pandu'*. He looked up and saw the huge railway bridge ahead. This always made his feel grand. His father had told him that his *thatha's thatha* (grandpa's grandpa) had 'constructed' it. He felt that in a way he was the owner of the bridge.

He could hear the distant *'kook'* of the train (though it sounded more like a *'boo-ooonk'* everyone called it the *'koook'*, probably because the diesel engine's predecessor, the steam engine, had announced itself with a *'kooooooook'* for over a hundred years on that same track).

He instantly knew what was going on, and started running towards the man, his bag and his shirttails flapping against the wind

But what was that man doing up there on the tracks? He could only see the silhouette, but the man was walking towards the bridge...now he was sitting on one of the tracks a short distance from the bridge, and now he was lying down on the tracks!

He instantly knew what was going on, and started running towards the man, his bag and his shirttails flapping against the wind. The patch of land between the railway track and the path was not under cultivation, and was strewn thick with the wild thorny bush that grows everywhere where there is any untended land. The train was still some distance away, and he knew that he could easily reach the track in time. The bright circle of the engine's headlight, and the long cone it formed in the dusk ahead of it were plainly visible on the other side of the bridge, but the '*koook*' was still quite faint.

The gravel and tiny pieces of stone hardly bothered his bare feet, which seemed to know their own way through them. Even in the twilight, they invariably landed in the safest spot for each stride he took. Suddenly he stepped on a dry thorn and let out a little cry, hobbling a few paces before sitting down on the ground with his right leg in his lap. The thorn had pierced his heel and was sticking out, but fortunately had not gone too deep. He pulled it out without feeling much pain. Then he squeezed the flesh on his heel around the tiny red spot, and a tiny bead of red formed on it. He wiped it off with his thumb, and squeezed again. Another droplet of blood oozed out, but it was tinier this time. He rubbed it off again, and squeezed. Nothing. He picked some earth, and rubbed it on the wound, and squeezed again. Nothing. He got up, and looked for the train. It was about to enter the bridge now. The huge brick-red iron frame of the bridge glowed brightly in the engine's light.

Boooonnnnk...the engine screamed impatiently.

He looked at the bump on the tracks above him. There was very little time now. He started running again with renewed vigor, without waiting to pick up his bag.

The railway track, maybe on account of the bridge, ran several feet above the ground level. The embankment on which it ran was just a continuous mound of earth covered with fist-sized stones, and more of the wild thorn bushes and trees.

He reached the base of the incline just as the engine entered the bridge with a resounding '*BOOOOONK*'.

By now, the silhouette of the man on the tracks was beginning to yield more details in its yellowish red light. As he started struggling up the incline, he realized that it was hardly a man up there. It was one of the youths from the village, whom he had seen many times at the shop, though he did not really know him.

By now the rhythm of the train's wheels jumping across the gap between sections of tracks, *'Tthakk Dhuk Tthaa Da...TThakk DHukk TThaa DA..THAkk DHUk TTHa DA...,'* was rising in a crescendo, amplified by the bridge's ironwork and drowning all other sounds except its own loud honk.

'BOOOOOONk!' the train engine screamed urgently from the bridge, followed again by the *'TTHAkk DHUK TTHAa DA'*... the light on its forehead, bright and flickering through gaps in the iron framework, provided a terrific visual effect to match the sound.

Two big thorn bushes formed an arch at this spot, and he decided to take that route as it appeared to have been used by people before. As he crawled through panting heavily, and reached the top of the incline, the youth turned towards him. There was a long red vermilion line on his forehead and he lay right across the tracks. The boy stood there a few feet from the tracks, and looked on, breathing heavily. As he met the young man's melancholy eyes, he started singing to himself in a low voice, "*Pandu pandu pandu...*," glad that he had made it.

The train's engine burst out of the bridge with an ear-shattering

"BOOOOOOOOOOOOOOOOOOOOOOOOONNNNNK!!!"

This would be the first time he would actually see someone die. He had only heard of it before.

Dance, Mathematics, Happiness, *Vedanta*

Arun Kumar

Letter from Austin, March 1999

When I lived in Bangalore I ran across one Professor Venkatesh, a physicist, who had retired from the Indian Institute of Science and had set himself up as a teacher of *Vedanta*. One of my fellow engineers, and a good friend, Ravi Amur, was his disciple. Ravi's wife had completed her doctorate in theoretical physics at the IISc. That was his connection.

...the girls disdained you in favor of wealthier, better-looking, and more presentable hotdogs. So, what's a young fellow to do with a loose evening?

I went along with Ravi a few times to Professor V's house, just because he was such an interesting person to talk to; and because the girls disdained you in favor of wealthier, better-looking, and more presentable hotdogs. So what's a young fellow to do with a loose evening?

Some people radiate peace and good will, and Professor Venkatesh was one of those. Also you could discuss anything at all with him – be it religion or the design of the processor

---

Arun Kumar was born in Jodhpur, Rajasthan. He designs embedded systems for image and video compression in Raleigh, North Carolina, where he lives with his lovely wife, Abha Varma, and their two delightful chit-pits. He likes to write articles for kahany.com, and letters to his friends and enemies in a mailing list called Dakghar. He was awarded a B. Tech. by IIT Kanpur in 1975; an M.B.A. by IIM Calcutta in 1977; and an M.S. and a D.Sc. from Washington University, St. Louis, in 1986 and 1990 respectively.

you were building. He was a man of quick wit and deep learning.

I also asked him about *Vedanta*. I asked, if I wanted to be his student, would he accept me? He said he'd be happy to. I asked what I'd have to do. He said that the first thing to do would be to learn Sanskrit. That was like having a bucket of cold water poured over me. "Professor Venkatesh, it is quite a job to learn Sanskrit. I'd be forever learning Sanskrit. I'd never get to *Vedanta*," I said.

I had spent a lot of good youthful time in school declining Sanskrit verbs *ad nauseum*, but read almost nothing in the language that made more sense than poop. School education in India is more than wrong. It is an exercise in imbecility. But that is another subject. About the only nice thing in Sanskrit that I remember from those days is a fragment of a *Saraswati Vandana*:

> *Ya kund-endu-tushaar-haar-dhavala,*
> *Ya shweta-vastravrita*
> *Ya veena-varadanda-manditkara,*
> *Ya shweta-padmasana.*

Having gotten used to long words in German and Dutch often fielded by Ingrid and Leonard, Sanskrit seems almost manageable now. Also since I have decided to read the *Mahabharata* and *Vetal Panchvinshati* in the original, I guess I will have to learn Sanskrit one of these days.

Professor Venkatesh said, "To every discipline there is a language that is proper to it."

"If you wish to learn physics without learning mathematics, is that a good way to learn physics?" he asked.

"And how would you describe the sound of a bamboo flute played at sunset in Hindi or in English?" he asked. "That's impossible. The proper language to describe that feeling is the language of the flute itself. Nothing else will do."

"Likewise," he said, "the language of *Vedanta* is Sanskrit."

I said, "Professor Venkatesh that is all very well but what happens if you teach me first Sanskrit and then *Vedanta*, and you know that I'm not a very bright fellow. What if I just cannot learn? What if I just don't get it?"

"That happens to me all the time with everything," I said.

He said, "We have been teaching *Vedanta* for thousands of years. We can teach *Vedanta* even to a donkey."

I have always found *Vedanta* very attractive. *Vedanta* says that Man has three needs: Perfect Knowledge, Perfect Happiness, and Perfect Being.

Perfect Knowledge is something I could really use. Perfect Happiness sounds okay too – if it is anything like the feeling after some perfect sex. Perfect Being seems a little abstract to me. No death? No illness like the flu I am stricken with today? No headache? What the devil is Perfect Being?

Vedanta goes on to say that *you can have it all!* That is a claim, I hope you'll agree, of rather breathtaking audacity.

In fact *Vedanta* claims we already have perfect knowledge. And Perfect Happiness. And Perfect Being. And that all that is lacking is the realization that we have it all. This claim has always worried me. It appears to suggest that the method of *Vedanta* may consist either in part, or entirely, of a process of

> *Perfect Knowledge is something I could really use. Perfect Happiness sounds okay too—if it is anything like the feeling after some perfect sex.*

convenient redefinition, whereby you redefine everything so that at the conclusion is inescapable that you have it all – but you still feel like the same sad old dog in your underwear. You still have holes in your socks. And no money. And your head still hurts from the mere thought of thinking about the true meaning and purpose of the Heine-Borel theorem.

It is my private and personal theory that there are two kinds of learning. There is the Learning Of The Head that comes when you have worked hard with much expenditure of ink, electricity, and gray matter, and the problem begins to make sense, and the answer too, maybe, and you begin to think that maybe the world is all right.

And then there is the Learning Of The Heart, coming later perhaps, perhaps never, where you feel the problem and the answer in your belly and your bones, and there is no thought at all. Just pure feeling. You know that such and such theorem is correct, and that you could always make up a proof, or five. That is a much more fulfilling kind of learning. It has become a part of you, and it shall never ever again be taken away.

The head kind of learning is volatile. It tends to evaporate. It leaves you still with an empty hunger in your stomach.

When I was twelve I went to one Pandit Khastgir at my school in New Delhi and asked to learn music. He put up with me for about a week and then he told me as gently as he was able (which wasn't much): "Look here," he said, "You are wasting your time. And you are wasting my time."

"Why don't you go in for radio engineering or something?" he said, "That is also a good hobby."

I was telling this story one evening in St. Louis to Professor Ranade, a musician visiting from Bombay University, who had just that evening performed before a large gathering. I told him about what Professor Venkatesh had to say about being able to teach Vedanta to a donkey. "Why can't you people do something like that?" I asked Professor Ranade, "I'd really love to be able to sing half like Bhimsen Joshi."

Without batting an eyelid he said, "Oh music is music! It is not *Vedanta* that we could teach it to just anyone." And he laughed a nice shaking laugh, and we all laughed too. Maybe if I had had some *Vedanta* under my belt, I could have sung him something then and there to show him that even a donkey could sing. That should certainly be a part of the promise of Perfect Being, don't you think? But the musicians have this bee in their bonnet about something they call *swar gyan* (knowledge of notes). Either you have it or you don't.

I remember once sitting and chatting with Professor Venkatesh in his veranda, when a lizard dropped almost directly on me from the ceiling above, and I all but took off in fright.

Professor Venkatesh laughed. "You who would become one with the *Brahman*," he said, "you will have to learn to put up with lizards."

I find religion distasteful. About 10% of it I like because it has to do with music, poetry, literature, architecture and dance. But the remaining 90% of it is so thick with mumbo-jumbo and miscellaneous unadulterated garbage, that I find it very difficult to believe that any half-sensible person would have any truck with it. And the existence of politico-religious schmucks like the BJP and Bajrang Dal *wallahs* rather proves the point. I was open about my distaste for religion with Professor Venkatesh. I said I hoped that no sort of prior belief in anything would be assumed of me.

He was very reassuring on that point. He said that no belief was needed of me that I did not already have. He said that if a point of view were found convenient or necessary, I would be led to it in a way that it would erupt spontaneously from within me. He said that the methods of *Vedanta* vary with the personality of the disciple. There are *bhakti*-oriented people who have to be handled differently from the sort of people who will defile every idol with doubt and thought. Whose primary relationship with any sort of authority is one of opposition and disbelief. I found it very satisfying to learn that the teaching of Vedanta took all that into account. So why does Indian education today treat every child as an equal donkey?

Vivek Basrur sent me an article about teaching mathematics by way of dance. I think there is little in the world as enchanting as a *Kathak* or a *Bharatanatyam* performance. *Kathak* and *Bharatanatyam* I am very partial to. *Odissi* also I do like, but less. I have seen Sanjukta Panigrahi and her son dance the *Odissi*. In *Kathakali* I very much like the *abhinaya* in parts, but I am sorry to say that I find it a bit of a drag to sit through an entire performance of *Kathakali*. As a vehicle for mathematics, however, my feeling is that dance is not quite the right language. Dance is very good as a celebration of the animal form. Even of the plant form perhaps. I remember Bui telling me once during a storm when she was two or three: "Look Baba, even the leaves are dancing!"

But for mathematics nothing serves quite as well as a few scrawls on a piece of paper. Dance is not its language.

Forced Choices

Rupa Gawle

In this day and age we ABCDs (American Bred/Born Confident *Desis*) pride ourselves on our choices and the home runs we hit with the curveballs life throws us. We take pride in our flashy jobs, cars, MBAs, condos, stock portfolios, social lives and high-flying lifestyles. Yet, many of us can't boast about making the choice of a life partner on our own. This incredibly important task is still left to Mommy and Daddy.

I don't get it. Lately it seems that many people are going back to either India or their 'home-states' to marry someone their mom and dad have picked for them. While I must admit it's usually guys who go for that option, I know a few female friends who have opted to go the 'arranged marriage' route. I can't say I understand or relate to it, but it scares the bejesus out of me. It scares me to think that one can commit oneself, overnight, to another person emotionally, mentally and physically without knowing much about that person.

It scares me to think that one can commit oneself, overnight, to another person emotionally, mentally and physically without knowing much about that person...

I just don't understand how these seasoned players of life, who are so cutthroat when it comes to their personal lives and professions, cannot make such a major life decision on their own. Is this the ultimate cry for the need to break the umbilical

Rupa Gawle was born in Bombay and moved to the US when she was 13. She has a B.A. in Business from City Univ. of NY and is certified in Textile Management from North Carolina State College of Textiles. She enjoys living in NY, her pets, traveling the globe, Impressionist art, home and antique restoration, writing about being a single, independent Indian-American woman, and dislikes being mistaken for a feminist. She is a 10-year veteran of the New York fashion industry.

cord? After several friends started dropping like flies I decided to probe this a bit. It piqued my curiosity.

One friend, who I'll call Raj, is a successful ophthalmologist in his first year of private practice. He just bought his own house, lives alone, drives a loud Range Rover, and has dated the *crème de la crème* of women. He's decent-looking, smart, educated, successful and I'm unaware of any shortcomings he may have. After a recent visit to the West Coast he came back engaged to someone he had met for two days. I was floored. Was she gorgeous? Had he slept with her? What, *what*? I couldn't figure it out. I knew him and it didn't add up at all. She was a very nice girl from what he said, though her beauty didn't blow him away, but he thought it was 'time'. I didn't buy it because it sounded like hogwash.

I found out, after much prodding, that his parents had put an awful lot of pressure on him. He'd been feeling it for months, and while I knew he was meeting people his parents were setting him up with, I had no clue that he was under such intense duress. He felt cornered. The numerous reasons used were: *'We made you a doctor...now that you are settled, it's time you bring a wife and make us happy.' 'We are getting old, why are you putting us through so much stress and not allowing us the benefits of having a daughter-in-law?' 'We want to see grandchildren before we die and our days are numbered'.* I was a little tickled. He actually fell for this emotional blackmail? I saw through it, so why couldn't he? He said he did; yet he felt guilty. He said he felt inadequate as a son, and felt the need to make them happy. The whole concept of marrying someone to make a third party happy doesn't sit too well with me. What about the repercussions?

I have another friend; we'll call him Jay, who is freshly divorced. He married a girl to make his parents happy. Over the 7 months he was married, they both learnt that they were incompatible. They were both pressured into it and while neither had a gun to his/her head, they married each other with the 'end of the road' concept in mind. Neither of them was happy and both realized that it had been a mistake to get married. The marriage turned sour and they ended up divorced. His parents were devastated. He resented them, didn't even want to talk to them or deal with them.

That annoyed me no end. "Why are you blaming your parents for the choices you made?" I asked him. He was angry with me for not understanding. "Try living in my shoes over the past couple of years and know what it's like." He was apparently put through vehement coercion everyday, and all sorts of emotional blackmail, with Mom crying and Dad threatening a heart attack. So while he wasn't dating anyone, and had no prospect of his own in the background, he just gave in to his parent's wishes and got married to whomever they picked.

Another friend (we'll call her Neela) couldn't convince her parents to let her marry the man of her choice, and after her mother had a stroke and her father tried to blame her for it, she agreed to marry someone they selected. The guy was nice and came from a nice family. She moved to Chicago after getting married and for a while we lost touch. One day, some four months later, I decided to give her a buzz to see how she was doing.

He was apparently put through vehement coercion everyday, and all sorts of emotional blackmail, with Mom crying and Dad threatening a heart attack

I reached a very agitated mother-in-law who wanted to know if all the girls from New York were 'like that'! I was puzzled and politely excused myself off the phone. I made a bunch of phone calls and finally tracked her down, living at her aunt's in New York. I was so confused. Why wasn't she at her parents? I met her over coffee where she explained to me in tears what a difficult time she had with her in-laws and her husband, and how she felt stifled and couldn't work around it. She had come back home and her parents had refused to take her in, instructing her to go back home to her husband and make it work because it wasn't like he was 'hitting her or abusing her'. I didn't understand. Was getting hit the only reason for a woman to walk away from a man? Why do parents behave this way? I felt so sad for her. She was even more sad...not on the break-up of her marriage but on the lack of support from her parents, who told her that she was being flaky and not working hard enough on her marriage.

I know of at least four divorces over the past year that came about as a result of these forced marriages. I don't need a statistical analysis from the government or a study by some university to sit up and take notice of so many marriages breaking up among young Indian-Americans. Marriages that were 'forced' in the name of 'obligation'. That word sounds harsh. I find it hard to believe that these professional and hardcore adult New Yorkers blame their problems on their parents. How can something like a 'bad marriage' be blamed on parents? I find it shameful. I make all my decisions. Sometimes they are good decisions and sometimes they are bad ones. I couldn't blame my parents for it. Yeah sure, they can be difficult but I make the ultimate decisions of my life. Whatever choices I make I can only blame or congratulate myself. Isn't it rather cowardly to blame your parents for the seven *pheres you* take? Why then are so many resentful children blaming their parents for their failed marriages lately? I'm not saying marriages that people enter into on their own don't break up, but so many 'arrangements' are falling apart that it makes me sad. Is the sad statistic of '50% of marriages end in divorce' now applicable to Indian marriages as well? Did we ever think such an old and sacred institution that boasted of so many successful unions would get so tainted?

For a lot of guys I've questioned, who've had failed marriages or who opted for marrying someone their parents chose, it came down to this: "my parents have to live with this person day in and day out...if I don't marry someone that they like, the rest of *their* lives would be very miserable, not to mention the unfairness to the woman I'd marry." It's a mind game. There is almost an 'upper hand' power position when it comes to parents and wife. If the parents pick the wife then they will always have the upper hand, and if the wife and husband pick each other, without the parents consent, the wife will somehow have the upper hand, and hence power. What happened to good old-fashioned love? Yeah, I know it's not an Indian concept but for God's sake, we aren't exactly still in India! Why do these people who date and mate with everyone suddenly grow a conscience and go marry some unsuspecting person? Isn't that pretentious and deceptive?

Our parents who raise us with good values and lessons in culture and love, drive us to soccer practice, send us to the best colleges, and encourage us to take up the best professions are the same parents who can't let us decide on our own who our life partner should be? What happened to trust? What happened to wanting our happiness? What happened to treating their children like adults?

I dream of getting married some day. Hopefully to a man I'd be in love with. It makes me sad when I hear such stories. No one should be forced into anything, especially something as sacred as marriage.

Sulekha Reader Comments

Rose: One day I decided I wanted a cat. I didn't know where to look. I asked my friends, I looked up the newspaper. All I knew was that I didn't want to pay for it. I found my cat through a listing. I didn't date it. I didn't spend time talking to it to see if we were compatible. I just brought it home. I love my cat. My cat loves me too. Wish things were so simple.

Doesn't Matter: Don't necessarily disagree with the theme of the article, but I wonder if this whole 'love match' thing among the Indian crowd in the West isn't a bit contrived. To begin with, you are 'arranging' your marriage after a fashion because you are specifying the ethnicity (and probably religion too) of your prospective mate. When you are less than 1% of the population, it is not as though there is a great deal of spontaneity in this matter for all the talk of dating/mating etc. The closest I came to this magic was with a small town American girl, but didn't go through with it because I didn't feel it was in the cards, given the differences in backgrounds. I am curious if the guys you have cited as examples had similar experiences and then went the 'arranged marriage' route. Given the slim possibility of falling in love with someone of the same background (and it is not as though you have an infinite amount of time), they may have just taken the practical way out.

The Moon

Ashini J. Desai

I see this woman of the night
shed more each time –
First, while draped in black velvet,
she winks a pearly smile.
She has a secret she's longing to impart.
Carefully she tugs away the darkness
and slowly reveals her glowing bosom.

Embarrassed for her, I look away.
But she lures eyes to gaze
upon her voluptuous curve –
Hands reach out to touch a fantasy
of smooth marble marred only by the evening
shadows.
She feigns bashfulness
behind a fan of feathered clouds.

Lonely sighs grope for solace and
their breaths graze across her cheek.
Lovers, so entranced, forget each other.
She was their First.
Come closer, she whispers,

---

*Born in India and raised in the US, Ashini Desai's creative efforts
explore cultural issues and diverse personas. Her online
publications include poetry, essays, reviews for various sites, and a
column for new writers on Sulekha. She has published work in a
1997 anthology Shakti Ki Awaaz. She has an English degree and is
currently pursuing a Masters in Information Science. Living in
Pennsylvania, she and her husband recently became parents of a
baby girl.*

their hearts swell, fed by her luscious promises.
She tosses back her hair, glimmering with stars.
How coy of her! She knows the limits.
Forsaken, they ebb and flow away.

Each night she bares more, dropping her silken veils.
In her fullness, she is divine;
her crimson bloom is unrivaled.
She can fuse the hues of the blue night
and melt into the drippings of the setting sun.

Isn't this too much? Does she know what she's doing?
Hungry for attention, she shouts in the darkness.
She resonates loud, brassy, jazzy tones –
she pulses to a tempo of her own
sings an aria to her soul
she shares all she has.

Oh she knows what she's doing.
Sublime and surreal,
she shines.

Dolphin's Day

Tabby Balasubramanian

For many years now, I have been reading, with open-mouthed incredulity, about dolphins. Though I have yet to encounter a dolphin in real life, I marvel as I watch, on the *National Geographic* channel, their toothy Buddha-like grins and acrobatic movements. As bemused grown-ups and captivated children pet them and talk to them, there they are, these large gentle creatures, responding with such natural facial expressions that their intelligence and sensibility is almost palpable. Some say that interacting with dolphins is an awesome, almost spiritual experience.

Too often, it seems that we human beans have perversely, even arrogantly, appointed ourselves overlords of the planet and its resources. Everything that we find about us is seen to be good or noble, only to the degree that we find some use for it in extending our suzerainty over an already anthropocentric world. We seem to find nothing disturbing about ransacking the earth exclusively for our own advantage, reserving areas of wilderness for the other beasts, and that too, with extreme reluctance. It is as if we have found

> *I marvel as I watch, on the* National Geographic *channel, their toothy Buddha-like grins...*

T.A. Balasubramanian, known fondly as Tabby, is the creative half of Maxigen, an advertising service based in Mumbai that he founded in partnership with his spouse, Gita, in 1993. Born in Mumbai, India, in 1953, he romped through an early education in Secunderabad, Andhra Pradesh. He is a Chemical Engineering graduate from IIT Madras, and a post-graduate of IIM, Calcutta. Before Maxigen, he was a zealous software professional for 14 years. He is passionate about creating inspiring books, short stories and playful poetry. Like his 12-year-old son, Kartik, he loves fun, grace, harmony, learning, love, mastery, playfulness, vitality and wisdom.

no use for the wilderness, when every other species thrives in it.

Dolphins seem to demonstrate a rare attribute that we beans have not yet learned with any consistency. They show an incredible capacity to cooperate with other earth creatures. Even as long ago as 62 AD, it was Plutarch, the Greek moralist and biographer, who observed that "to the dolphin alone, beyond all other, nature has granted what the best philosophers seek: friendship for no advantage".

What's more, the dolphin seems to have been blessed with a refined sense of humour. These pranksters have been known to silently sneak up behind unsuspecting pelicans, snatching their tail feathers. Other exploits include grabbing unsuspecting fish by the tail, pulling them backward a few feet, or teasing slow turtles by rolling them over and over.

If an ambassador were to be identified to talk on behalf of all creatures, the dolphin would be a perfect choice. It appears that these chatty swimmers do conduct conversations in whistles, clicks, chirps and a range of dolphinese sounds. So it was not particularly difficult to let a dolphin speak to Dr. Moose. The latter is a fictional biologist, but he is derived, in part, from a teacher of biology I knew in my high school days. His real name was Dr. Rao, but the image he conjures up for me is that of a bull moose. A hard-nosed, pudgy, gruff, unsmiling character, he spent hours educating us about the insides of frogs. Thankfully, we never got round to doing live dissections, and learned all we needed to know about anatomy from charts and diagrams. But he had a gentle side, too, which we found out, much to our amazement, when he sang a song at a cultural function.

Dolphin's Day

"Human beans," the dolphin said
  "Are partly green and partly red."
"How can you be so obtuse?"
  Said the snooty Dr. Moose.

"Darwin put you in your place
Far behind the human race.
Keep in mind your fishy stature
And your petty, lowly nature!"
"Green is when you care for trees
Red is when you shoot the geese!"
Said the dolphin, grinning wide
Bobbing nose from side to side.
"Dolphins cannot be our teachers
Humans are not simple creatures!"
Said the angry Dr. Moose,
Snorting like a ruffled goose.
"Green for painting daffodils
Red for making oil spills,"
On the smiling dolphin went,
"Life is not an accident
Every act of noble reason
Has a countervailing treason."
"Some you win, and some you lose,"
Said the cranky Dr. Moose.
"Green for every tiger spared,
Red for every turtle snared,"
Sang the dolphin, with a grin
Flipping on a teasing fin,
"Creatures all can still be free
If only beans would let us be!"
"Spare me," said the frosty Moose
From your existential blues!"
"Green is every singing bird,
Red is every vanished herd,"
Beamed the fish with gentle guile,
Treading water with a smile.
"If only beans could tolerate
The diversity of our fate!"
"You've said enough, I'll blow a fuse"
Said the horrid Dr. Moose.

"Green for every panda's life,
  Red for every carving knife,"
Doggedly, the dolphin prattled,
  Leaving Dr. Moose quite rattled.
"I'm just being hard and bitter,
  I can see that you're no quitter!
Human beans have no excuse,"
  Said the thoughtful Dr. Moose.
"Oh, that's music to my ear,"
  Said the dolphin, with a tear.
"Life is precious to us all,
  Though we walk, or swim, or crawl."
"Beans are smart, we all agree
  But every species must be free
To live and grow and pick and choose,"
  "It's time we quit this confrontation
No more coloured accusation,"
  Crooned the dolphin, with a swirl,
  Dancing like a giddy girl.
"Right, my friend, let's call a truce,"
  Said the humbled Dr. Moose,
Jumping in the dolphin's pool,
  Wet and dripping, like a fool!

Sulekha Reader Comments

Ravi M: Nice article, Tabby. The rhyme at the end was superb. The whole piece reminded me of something Douglas Adams said at a lecture that I attended. Apparently, they were trying to 'train' this dolphin by giving it a fish to eat every time it jumped out of the water and made a sound. In the beginning, the dolphin was doing pretty well, and getting the fish every time it jumped out of the water. Later, its actions became more erratic. Sometimes, it would make no sound; sometimes it would make a really loud sound etc. - all apparently random. The researchers figured that the dolphin was dumb. Later, somebody looked at an oscilloscope (or whatever it is that they used to measure its sound) and found out that there were some startling regularities in the way the dolphin responded. Turned out that the dolphin was actually doing all the 'experimenting' by calibrating the human hearing range! It would vary amplitude and frequency until it figured out in what range humans could hear! Fairly amazing, I thought.

A friend tells me that dolphins, along with man, hold another distinction. I don't know how far this is true, but this exemplary mammal is the only one (apart from us) to indulge in gang rape. A disturbing thought. They must be much more like humans than we ever suspected.

Thanks for a thought-provoking article.

Rita:

Hello there
Thank you Tabby
Your piece made me blabby
Reminded me of the good old days
Of bird and beast and simple ways.

When life was full of simple fundas
Even 'hellos' had no hidden agendas
Liked your piece very much you see
Hope man and beast live in eternal harmony.

Come to think of it hope man and man work towards living in peace and a strife-free world too.

The *Desi* Professor and the Italian Mafia

Mukund Narasimhan

"I want my advisor polished off," Anand Gopalakrishnan told Tony in a desperate tone.

"Boy! That's serious business," replied Tony, the *Marco's Pizza* guy.

Anand revealed his intentions to Tony because he knew he would get some help. No *desi* graduate student had resorted to such desperate measures, but Anand had made up his mind. Even after nine revisions to the thesis, Prof. Natarajan (Nutty) was not willing to let him graduate with a Ph.D. It wasn't that his research was not up to the mark, but it was just that Nutty constantly needed some hapless guy on whom he could vent all his frustrations.

The Mafia would do a clean job and nobody would suspect anything. Anand liked the idea.

"Yeah I am serious. I need your help," Anand said. Tony offered his help.

"I have a buddy of mine, Joey, in New York who can help you. He has contacts with the Big Boys, if you know what I mean."

Anand knew exactly what Tony meant. He had often boasted of his contacts with the Italian Mafia. The Mafia would do a clean job and nobody would suspect anything. Anand liked the idea. That Saturday he rented a car and drove to New

Mukund Narasimhan was born in Bangalore but has had the chance to live in Bhubaneshwar, Chennai, Mumbai and New Delhi. He completed his Master's degree from the Pennsylvania State University, State College, and had the privilege of receiving his degree certificate from the hands of President Clinton. Nowadays he and his wife, Prema, live in a peaceful town called Findlay in the Northwest part of Ohio. He makes a living as an engineer, and writing fictional pieces is his main interest. Mukund also enjoys traveling.

Jersey and stayed at a cheap motel. The next morning he took the subway to Queens, where Joey was waiting for him. Joey took him to Eddie, the Bull. And the Bull took him to the Boss.

When Anand entered the run-down building – the *Headquarters* – in Queens, he was shaking like a leaf. Inside the room The Bull did the talking while the Boss observed.

"Will you have something to drink?"

"Yes, Pepsi with no ice, please."

The Bull looked at the Boss, and the Boss shrugged his shoulders.

"What do you think this is, some kinda Pizza Hut? Don't you drink any heavy stuff?"

"Do you have Mountain Dew?"

The Bull gave Anand a blank look.

"It has more caffeine in it," explained Anand.

The Bull offered him the drink and continued to talk.

"So who's this guy you want to finish off?"

"Professor Natarajan."

"Professor who?"

"Natarajan."

"Who?"

"Natarajan, we call him Nutty."

"So why do you want this nutty professor out?"

"He won't let me defend."

"What's that? Defend?"

"Well, he won't let me defend my PhD thesis in front of the committee."

The Bull looked at the Boss, and the Boss shrugged his shoulders.

"Look here, you fruit! You gotta tell us why we have to kill this professor so that we can understand."

"Well, I have been working for this professor for seven years now. He is the worst guy you can work for. I do all the work for him and he goes and presents it in all these conferences and makes himself look good. I don't get anything for it. To graduate I have to write a report – a thesis – on my research work and defend it in front of a committee. He is in the committee, too. But he won't let me defend my thesis, so I am not able to graduate."

"So how will it help if we kill this guy?"

"If Nutty is packed off then Dr. Stevens will become my chief advisor – my supervisor – and it will be a piece of cake after that."

"So you are telling us that if we stick a couple of BB's through his skull, the way will be cleared for you."

"That's correct."

"You seriously want to do this?"

Something snapped inside Anand. Blood rushed to his head and all the pent up anger burst out like water from a broken dam.

"Have you ever worked for a *desi* professor? Do you know what it is to be abused day after day? Have you any idea what it feels to work continuously for four years without a chance to go home and see your family? No other graduate student has had to go through what I am going through here. You think I would come all this way to talk to you if I was not serious?"

Have you ever worked for a desi professor? Do you know what it is to be abused day after day?

"Hey! I was just asking," said The Bull defensively.

"Yeah, I am serious as hell."

"So what's in it for us?"

Anand opened his bag and pulled out three of his latest bank statements.

"You can have all of this, save a thousand bucks," he declared, with the confidence of a CEO closing a billion-dollar business deal.

The Bull looked at the statements and turned towards the Boss with an incredulous look on his face; the Boss shrugged his shoulders.

"Are you out of your mind," yelled The Bull. "Do you think we would be willing to kill a guy for less than five grand?"

The Bull grabbed Anand by his shirt and started to drag him out of the room when the Boss stopped him.

"Cool it Eddie. I think this will be a good one for Frankie."

He was referring to Frank Maldini, a new member of the gang. Eddie sent for him and Frankie entered the room.

"Give the details about the professor to him," commanded the Boss.

Anand pulled out the brochure of the Materials Science and Engineering department and quickly turned to the page that had Professor Natarajan's picture with his research interests.

"This is the person you need to put to sleep."

"I can hardly see the guy in here, do you have another picture?"

"No. We will not need that. I know this guy very well, and I have got it all up here," said Anand, gently tapping his temple with his right index finger.

"Nutty is going to a conference next week in Dayton, Ohio. That will be the best time to dust him off."

Anand knew exactly what Nutty did on those trips to Dayton. He had been there with Nutty a few times and watched him make the presentations. Nutty followed the same routine every time. Anand laid it all out in great detail, for Frankie to go after the kill, and they discussed the plan at length. That night Anand drove back to his college and the following Sunday Frankie took a flight to Dayton.

The next day, as advised by Anand, Frankie drove to the Indian restaurant near the Dayton Mall around 11:30 a.m. He wanted to get there early and wait for his prey. The restaurant had barely opened, so he went to the bar to have a couple of drinks. Frankie looked around the restaurant. He liked his seat. From his secluded position he could see both the entrance and the buffet table. Frankie felt confident about spotting his quarry. He pulled out *The New York Times* and pretended to read, but he was actually closely watching the entrance. People came in groups and Anand had told Frankie that Nutty never came to the restaurant with anyone else. So he continued to wait. A few minutes later a middle-aged man walked in through the doors all by himself. Frankie felt his muscles tighten a bit. He pulled out the brochure to take a second look at the picture. He discerned a similarity between the picture and the person standing at the door: dark, penetrating eyes behind thick glasses, a nervous look and unkempt hair. No wonder Anand dreads this guy, Frankie thought to himself.

"Please come in this way, professor," the waitress greeted him. Frankie now observed him like a hawk. The professor didn't even have the patience to sit down and order a drink; he walked to the buffet table even before the waitress could offer him some water. He walked past the salad bar as though it did not exist, and picked a plate and filled it up with rice. Then he called the waitress to make sure that everything he wanted to eat had no meat in it. And, once having confirmed that the dish was a 'pure vegetarian' item, he dug into it generously. Frankie saw the professor eat ravenously, as though he had never seen Indian food before. With each trip to the buffet, he became more sluggish, walking a bit more slowly and taking longer to decide on the item that he wanted to eat next. Frankie counted four such trips to the buffet, and what he saw on the fourth trip confirmed it for him. He watched the professor fill up his plate with rice, then walk to the salad bar and pour *raita* (salad in yogurt sauce) all over it. Frankie had not believed it when Anand had told him about this, but now he saw it with his own eyes.

He paid his bill and quickly went back to his car, started the engine and waited for the professor. About fifteen minutes later the professor walked out unsteadily. Frankie aimed the gun at the professor's head and kept a finger on the trigger. The professor got into his car and before starting the engine, lowered the windows to cool the car. Frankie pulled the trigger and the professor fell on the wheel with a dull thud. Frankie had used a silenced gun and nobody heard a thing.

Before boarding the plane back to New York, Frankie called Anand's apartment to inform him of the good news. When the phone rang, Rajesh, Anand's roommate, answered it.

"Hello, this is Frankie, is Anand in there?"

"No he is in the lab, can I take a message?"

"Yeah, can you tell him that Frankie called? Tell him that eleven Bengal tigers died at the Orissa zoo." As agreed, he gave the coded message.

"Actually it is twelve," replied Rajesh.

"What?"

"Actually one died a day later, making it twelve. It's so tragic, isn't it?"

"No, just tell him that *eleven* Bengal tigers died at the Orissa zoo," Frankie insisted.

"I checked it up with *The Indian* and *The Hindu*, I'm pretty sure it is twelve."

"Listen you imbecile. If you don't want me to come there and blow your head to pieces, just tell Anand that *eleven* Bengal tigers died at the Orissa zoo," said Frankie in a threatening tone.

"OK. OK. I will leave a note for Anand with *your* message," said Rajesh, and hung up.

That evening Anand read the note and smiled to himself. He retired to bed a happy man.

The next morning he checked *Rediff.com* to confirm the news. "An Indian Professor shot dead near the Dayton Mall" read the headlines. Anand clicked on the item to read the whole story. His jaw dropped when he read the article. Frankie had bungled it. He had bumped off the wrong guy – a professor from the local Wright State University by the name of Sundaresan. There was no mention of Natarajan in the article. Anand panicked. He called Frankie at the *Headquarters*.

"Frankie, what the hell did you do?"

"What do you mean?"

"Did you read the news?"

"No, why?"

"You have got the wrong guy! You shot a professor from a local college in Dayton. It was not Nutty."

"But I observed the guy closely. I could swear he looked like the guy in the picture that you gave me. He ate at the restaurant exactly like the way you described it to me. He gorged like there was no tomorrow and he poured *raita* all over the rice and ate it, too."

"But did you confirm his identity by listening to his talk at the conference?"

"Hey, I didn't take this job to listen to some professor talk about his research. I'm paid to seal people's lips, not to hear them talk."

Anand hung up. He went back home and collapsed into his bed. He stared blankly at the ceiling and into an uncertain future.

In Dayton, after hearing about his advisor's murder, Ajit rejoiced silently. The program chairman requested Prof. Russell to become Ajit's chief advisor. After seven years of hardship, and nine revisions to his thesis, Ajit finally saw some light at the end of the tunnel. That fall he graduated and held a party at the Indian restaurant next to the Mall. When all his buddies gathered at the bar that evening, Ajit raised his glass of champagne and said, "Friends, this one is for that blessed soul who cleared the way for the successful completion of my PhD"

Everyone in the bar knew what he meant, but none of them had ever heard of Frank Maldini.

Sulekha Reader Comments

Roopesh: I knew a guy whose advisor virtually imprisoned him in his lab and made him work long hours. He wanted this student to give him a legal undertaking that he would do a Ph.D. with him and would not run away. The way my friend got out of it was to give him a legal undertaking that he planned to do his Ph.D. with the Prof. The catch is that you can plan to go to the moon, but whether you make it or not is another thing. Some lawyer made 500 bucks for legal advice!

Mirrors

Jawahara Saidullah

I lived in a world of mirrors. Staring at my own reflections, trying to craft my individual realities through them. I looked, at first, with great hope, toward the mirrors facing me. What revelations did their hard, polished surfaces hold about me? In response to my quest for an identity, they glinted in the moonlight, reinforcing their presence, and blinded me during the day, until I had to shield my eyes and look away.

Into the life of any minority comes the awareness of being the 'other'. And with that awareness follows the realization of the difficulty of bridging the gap between 'you' and 'them'. This can be a slow dawning or an epiphanous flash. For me it was the latter.

And so I made the discovery of the 'other' in me one languid August afternoon.

Brought up on a diet of nationalistic fervor, and an abiding belief in India, the wondrous, wonderful idea, I was protected at home, and within the high walls of St. Mary's Convent for twelve years. Our eight-hour school days left little time for more than the most superficial of conversations. Until, I went to the strike-ridden Allahabad University, where the professors' hit-and-miss attendance, strikes and lockouts gave us plenty of time to converse. And so

Jawahara K. Saidullah grew up in the fierce summers and dramatic monsoons of Allahabad. Transplanted to the US in the late 80's, she proceeded to move from the south to the west to the northeast and back to the west. Perhaps one day she will find a permanent home. Till then she contents herself with her day job as Content Manager while writing as a weekly columnist for Mid-Day newspaper in Bombay. She currently lives on the US west coast with her husband.

I made the discovery of the 'other' in me one languid August afternoon.

A group of girls sat around the platform encircling the girth of an old Banyan tree, at the Allahabad University, eating *pakoras* from the canteen.

"Hey, you want to know what this *jyotishi* told my *mama jee*? He said that by the year 2000 all Muslims would be eradicated." Claps and approval erupted as I sat there, retreating into myself. And I see my first reflection, consciously. An identity that had played hide and seek with my life till now, but one I had largely ignored. An insect to be eradicated. Different. 'Other'.

More importantly, invisible. Because, as they said, they did not think of me as a Muslim. That satisfied me, for a while. I was accepted, acceptable. I grasped at any straw, just trying not to be the 'other'. I refused to learn Urdu and scoffed at the delicate fervor of Urdu poetry, alienated myself from all Islamic rituals and festivals, anything that in India could identify me as a Muslim. Foolish, child-like, useless grasping, because nothing really ever changed.

Scattered comments fell around me like the sting of the early monsoon, as the years continued to roll past. "Oh, Muslims are so dirty, so cruel, so uncultured, did you know they boiled live cows in huge cauldrons of water? Why they sound barely human don't they? Why didn't all of you just leave in 1947?" As the years progressed, the language used became sophisticated, shaded with subtlety, and camouflaged in ambiguity. The Internet universalized it a few years ago, but the message came through loud and clear.

The mirrors of the other side chanted my name, as well, and made me look into them. "Your name is not Muslim enough, how come you don't know Urdu? Why are none of your friends Muslim? You're just too wild. What were this girl's parents thinking?" And I wondered where was I, as a person, a woman, a...a Muslim? Nobody else wondered about that, because labels are easier to classify, file away forever. Indeed, what space was left for me to slide neatly into, as I had seen so many others do? The slots were too narrow, because I could never fit.

My eyes burned, staring into the heat and glare of a dozen mirrored suns, everyday. They glowed until it felt like the trapped rays of heat reached into my soul, and plucked out my hopes and dreams, tainting my being with doubt and self-hatred and lack of trust. So hard, inflexible, those mirrors, so cruel in their unrelenting reflections. And the number of mirrors increased, until they totally surrounded me.

Coming to America transformed me into another type of 'other', as it did all those who journey to this country. And here, as a group, once more united, all of us Indians, battled for our realities together, for a while. Until of course, the Marathi *Mandals*, Telugu associations and Islamic associations arose to claim their own, and herded them away. One large 'other' splintered into many.

I married a one-time Hindu, who's now a Zen Buddhist. For once, both groups of mirrors agreed. "Oh, did you hear s/he is not converting? They would not dare do this in India. There we could teach them a lesson. They are not married in the eyes of God. Their poor parents. These children of today. How can this work? What about their children when they have some? What religion will they follow? It won't last more than a year. These things never do. They are not practical. All this new-fangled nonsense."

I clap my hands over my eyes, like a child blocking out a scary movie. Until I realize, like that child, that my unguarded ears let in the scary sounds of the monster awakening. The mirrors called my name repeatedly, softly, like the rustling of a cobra's scales on dry leaves. No place to run.

Of course, this alienation was not something to be discussed with others. Who, other than someone else, achingly in love with their homeland, yet forever forced to prove their allegiance, could truly empathize and understand? Certainly not those who fly green crescent flags from their Indian homes. And, not those who create convenient, monolithic whipping boys of an entire, extremely diverse group.

So, I searched relentlessly and alone, for a cool, soft reflection in rippling water, for respite from this lone desert. And then, just a few days ago, an Indian catholic friend, who had never understood before, now says she does. She – my friend with whom I have lived with for years – says she feels the 'otherness' now. And others do too. Those who still believe in the India of before, and those who hold fast to unfashionable principles like secularism.

"They would not dare do this in India. There we could teach them a lesson. They are not married in the eyes of God..."

There is a certain sweet sadness in the revelation, however, and an inevitability. Sectarianism based on religion or ethnicity is a raging fire that refuses to be put out, and continues to devour everything in its path. Once one group is vanquished, move to another, ravaging people, lives, freedoms, individualities. Witness the birth of the Shiv Sena in the 1960's as an anti- South-Indian group, to its current evolution as just simply an anti-minority force. Witness the clout of a man who holds no elected office, but who can force state leaders to resign, and who essentially runs the government. The fire moves on to new victims, the more, the better. That is what keeps the fire alive, makes it robust. Hatred keeps the embers alive, sometimes dormant, but always just glowing beneath the surface.

I challenge anyone who talks of the RSS and the BJP or even the ISS, as being hapless victims of malignment, because I have witnessed what they have done to my country, to my people, on all sides of the religious divide. I do acknowledge their right to exist, as I do the rights of the KKK in this country. Indeed their thoughts, ideas and ideology coalesce with frightening ease, with those of their kin across the seas. To the 'others', it means that we must live with a fear we really

ought not to, in a secular democracy. If, until and whenever,
we refuse to be scattered and stand firm.

> *Standing in the middle, I see the melded glints of their*
> *many surfaces. And I see myself reflected in each one,*
> *with cruel clarity. Always my face a little askew, just*
> *off, blurred. Never belonging to either group. And a*
> *new wonder: do I really want to belong to either side?*
> *The second epiphany of my life. The sledgehammer of*
> *my realness feels wonderfully hefty in my hands. I*
> *swing high. With a great tinkling of glass, the mirrors*
> *vaporize at my assault. And I see my face, centered,*
> *crisp and alive, in the gentle river of my own true*
> *identity.*

Mine

Tamara Lila Giwa

I'm looking back
for a history I can relate to,
and I see a past I cannot recognize.
For it is not mine.

I'm searching
for something to hold onto,
But I come back empty-handed.
For this culture is not mine.

So I look ahead
and wait patiently for the day to come
when I can proudly claim
what is justly mine.

Tamara Giwa was born in Harare, Zimbabwe, but has lived in several countries around the world, including Austria, Switzerland, and Kenya. She has a keen interest in French and English poetry and literature and spends much of her time reading and writing. Being half Indian, she is also interested in the issues of identity and multiculturalism. Currently, she is a freshman at Duke University (North Carolina), where she intends to study chemistry.

Chandra

Jenny Wren

Not a statement in science, not an observation, not a thought exists in itself. Each was ground out of the harsh effort of some man, and unless you know the man and the world in which he worked, the assumptions he accepted as truths, the concepts he considered untenable, you cannot fully understand the statement or observation or thought. – Isaac Asimov

I borrow these words from Isaac Asimov, because I could not possibly express it better myself.

I have been travelling a lot this past month of October. On one of such trip to Montreal, my inborn radar system directed me to a second-hand bookshop called *Ex Libris* on *Rue Maisonneuve*, a couple of blocks west of the *Musée des Beaux-Arts*. If you are a second-hand book collector, particularly those out-of-print ones, and in Montreal, I recommend this shop – courteous owner, organized shelving – as just the thing! Here I found the subject of my piece – a biography of Subramanyan Chandrasekhar (*Chandra: A Biography of S. Chandrasekhar*, K. C. Wali, U. of Chicago Press, 1992), a delicious collection of interwoven anecdotes that take you into

Jenny Wren was born in Gujrat, India. She grew up in different parts of India and the UK, and received her bachelor's degree in manufacturing engineering from the University of Hertfordshire, England, UK. Having lived and worked in various nooks and crannies of Europe and the US since 1991, she is currently in Kalamazoo, MI, as a marketeer for an engineering multinational. Her writing interests fluctuate between the sundry genres of creative prose. Lives by Benjamin Franklin's words: "If you would not be forgotten, as soon as you're dead and rotten; either write things worthy reading, or do things worth the writing."

the mind and life of an Indian scientist. K. C. Wali, his biographer and a former student, did his undergraduate and master's degrees in physics and mathematics in India and graduate work at the University of Wisconsin, Madison, specializing in elementary particle physics. After two years at Johns Hopkins University as a Research Associate, he joined the High Energy Theory Group at Argonne National Laboratory in 1962. Since 1969, he has been at Syracuse University as Professor of Physics. Wali's deep and abiding interest in both his subject and the science really shine through in this narrative. As Dyson, another physicist, said, "Wali has given us a magnificent portrait of Chandra, full of life and color, with a deep understanding of the three cultures – Indian, British, and American – in which Chandra was successively immersed. If the book is only read by physicists, then Wali's devoted labors were in vain."

Chandra was an astrophysicist and a Nobel Laureate. But, these two facts alone are not what drew me to him. In 1983, the news that he and William A. Fowler had won the Nobel Prize in physics for work on white dwarf stars registered vaguely in my pre-teen consciousness. Our physics teacher told us that he was related to the famous C. V. Raman, and, then she went on to glorify the virtues of C. V. R., without elaborating on Chandra's. Years later, when I was devouring everything written by and about Virginia Woolf, I discovered Chandra again. He had, in his 3-minute Nobel Prize acceptance speech, quoted from her book *The Waves*. He concluded with this sentence of his own while describing black holes in the astronomical universe, explaining the simplicity in the underlying physics and the beauty of their mathematical description within the framework of Einstein's theory:

> "*If the book is only read by physicists, then Wali's devoted labors were in vain.*"

The simple is the seal of the true
And beauty is the splendor of truth.

His love for and attention to language came searing through later in *Truth and Beauty: Aesthetics and Motivations in Science* on the relationship between art and science.

After these sporadic introductions to an elusive and very private man, reading this biography was my first attempt at understanding him. I can still barely comprehend the discipline, rigor, patience and fortitude that Chandra must have possessed to make his stellar discovery in 1930 and not gain the full, deserved recognition for it till 1983. To have achieved this at age 19, only to then find himself in a huge controversy with Eddington (the leading figure in astronomy then; also considered largely responsible for Einstein's acceptance in the scientific world), who dismissed Chandra's work as incorrect and useless. To have all astronomers, without exception, view him as a Don Quixote trying to kill Eddington and those subscribing to his works. To have a mother who aspired for her son to return from England with the glory of Ramanujan, and outshine his famous uncle C. V. R. To have an uncle who was so dismissive of him and his pursuits in "the backwaters of science", that Chandra achieved his scholarships, publications and future accolades without the slightest intervention from that man. Finally, to have his own father quote Sir Walter Scott at him in a severely reprimanding response to Chandra's decision to obtain US citizenship thus:

> *Breathes there the man with soul so dead,*
> *Who never to himself hath said*
> *This is my own, my native land!*
> *Whose heart hath ne'er within him burn'd*
> *As home his footsteps he hath turn'd.*

As is often the case, the people closest to us have both a negative and a positive influence on our lives. And Wali is a very fair and thorough biographer. He reveals how Eddington's feud with Chandra influenced the latter's entire attitude to science. Chandra decided that the most important thing in science was to continue to be productive and active, to not worry about the controversies, and that if he was right, people would know in time. This was also one of his chief reasons for not returning to India after his Trinity Fellowship at Cambridge. At that time, there were bitter rivalries within the group of leading scientists in India. Raman and Krishnan, Raman and Saha, S. N. Bose and Saha, both Saha and Bose against Raman. In fact, Krishnan, with whom Chandra had shared a warm friendship for years, advised him in a letter around 1936 not to return to India for at least two years due to the oppressive scientific atmosphere. Chandra maintained that he would still have considered returning if a decent position, other than the directorship of an observatory, had been available to him. In later years, even Chandra's father acknowledged that India had used him ill, and that her enlightened citizens or those in power had given him no thought, nor cared for his work or his personality. When he was eventually offered a position by Bhabha at the Tata Institute, almost a decade after he had left India, he was unsure about being able to fit in again.

Chandra's parents were rather remarkable in their own way, which explains some of Chandra's early predisposition to science and literature. Sitalakshmi, his mother, was not, as per the norm for most women of her time, well educated. Yet, she studied English after her marriage and translated Ibsen's *A Doll's House* into Tamil.

When he was eventually offered a position by Bhabha at the Tata Institute, almost a decade after he had left India, he was unsure about being able to fit in again.

Chandra's father, C. S. Aiyyer was quite the writer too, and well versed in Carnatic music. Learned in the Arts and the Sciences, he passed on his rich legacy – in turn, received from his own father – to Chandra and his other children. There are several heartwarming and absorbing episodes in the book about Chandra's parents, their own upbringing and their subsequent nurturing of their offspring.

Chandra met his wife, Lalitha, while enrolled in a Physics Honors course in South India. She was 17, also an aspiring physicist at the time, and the only 'lady student' in the class. Her own heritage is quite unusual for a woman of her era. Her aunt was the famous Sister Subbalakshmi, a child widow who was instrumental in setting up a number of women's educational institutions in the 20's in India, by championing the cause long before Mahatma Gandhi started to do so. Chandra's father had been allowed to choose his bride and so was Chandra. There is a touching story of how he wooed her. Lalitha wanted to pursue her physics research too, after graduation. But, India had not made such progress yet, especially for an unmarried woman. I do wonder at what might have been, if theirs had been a collaboration of great minds at work as well, like that of the Curies. It is perhaps India's loss that we never did find out, and that such a history-altering event never occurred.

The work of a theoretical astrophysicist in those days was not an easy job (I don't suppose it is that much easier now), as Wali explains:

> *There are no controlled, reproducible experiments in astronomy. The laboratory is out in space. There is only one universe we know that came into existence some ten billions of years ago. Its beginnings and early moments, its present large and small-scale structures – the formation of galaxies, the evolution of stars, the fundamental constitution of matter – have to be inferred by theories based on our microcosmic understanding of terrestrial phenomena. The laws of physical science thus learned must then be extrapolated, sometimes to vast scales of space and time and to extreme conditions of matter very different from those encountered on earth. To interpret and deduce what is observable from such extrapolations requires a mastery not only of diverse mathematical techniques but also of several branches*

of the physical sciences, several orders of magnitude more complex than what is required, say, in one special area of physics.

Chandra's research mode, as Kip Thorne explained, was one of sitting by himself with zero interaction for days struggling with equations, trying to make the math fit the patterns, and then explaining it in mathematical terms rather than physical terms. In this kind of mathematical astrophysics, Chandra's contributions have yet to be surpassed. The amount of work he published was phenomenal. Little wonder, when you consider the kind of travel reading he had on his passage from India to England: Eddington's *The Internal Constitution of the Stars*, Compton's *X-Rays and Electrons*, and Sommerfeld's *Atomic Structure and Spectral Lines*. And this was all the material he needed to do his calculations and make his discovery while still on board; a young and solitary man, earnest in his passion. As this scientist grew in age and experience, his quiet elegance, simple style and graceful imparting of knowledge to his Ph.D. students (some of who went on to win the Nobel Prizes before he did) gained him an untarnished and world-class reputation. He did not care about the establishment, but only about the pursuit of knowledge and learning and productivity. His long and loyal tenure with the University of Chicago, despite more alluring offers from other esteemed institutions, is irrefutable testimony to these traits.

I once heard Harold Bloom say, on C-Span *Booknotes*, that in the lives that we lead today, it is not possible for us to get to know many amazing and wonderfully inspiring people intimately; and the only way we can do this is through books. Bloom is an avid bibliophile himself. For me, reading biographies in particular is also a deeper form of critical inquiry. How did X's life and work illuminate our cultural and intellectual history? What were the social, familial and cultural structures and traditions that nurtured his or her genius and outlook? How did X influence the way we think about ourselves and interpret our society? And finally, what can we learn from X's life and work that will be of use to us? This biography answers these questions rather generously – from the early influences that prevailed on Chandra to the paramount influences that he, in turn, brought to bear through his life and work.

Also, reading this life history brought to mind some of the great scientists such as Galileo, Kepler and Newton, and their amazing discoveries during the European Renaissance of the mid-15th to the 17th centuries. And, when one considers their intellectual masterpieces – *Dialogues Concerning Two New Sciences, Astronomia Nova* and *Principia Mathematica* respectively – one perceives that, somehow, their scientific goals went far beyond making those course-altering discoveries, per se.

It is believed, and I love this idea, that India also experienced a Renaissance of sorts in the heady years leading up to her Independence. Here's how Chandra put it:

> *In the modern era before 1910, there were no Indian scientists of international reputation or standing. Between 1920 and 1925, we had suddenly 5 or 6 internationally well-known men. I myself have associated this remarkable phenomenon with the need for self-expression, which became a dominant motive among the young during the national movement to assert oneself. India was a subject country, but in the sciences, in the arts, particularly in science, we could show the West in their own realm that we are equal to them.*

This was also the era, as most of you will know, when India saw 2 of her 5 Nobel Laureates make their mark.

Of course, all human beings, no matter how great their genius, have certain flaws and imperfections. But, time has a way of absorbing these minor imperfections, as Peter Kapitsa of the Royal Society of Engineers said once, leaving only a great man with an astounding brain and great human qualities.

So, I find myself unable to end without sharing another personal facet of this gentleman, the latest addition to my pantheon.

The same year that Chandra was awarded the Nobel, my youngest sibling and only brother, Pranav, was born. I was almost 11 years old. And, I watched in muted wonder, the growth of this prodigious child for the next eight and a half years. It has been over nine years since I left India, and I have seen the boy briefly twice. At nearly 18 now, he is a young adult and at the brink of some important life decisions. I am overwhelmed for him, and so brimful of platitudes. But, there is a distance between us that is more than just geography and age, which renders me quite speechless. Then, in this biography, I chanced upon this: Chandra's younger brother, Balakrishnan, wanted to be a writer, while their father wanted him to be a doctor. At such a time, Chandra wrote Balakrishnan a 15-page letter. I wouldn't even know where to begin writing to Pranav, even though he isn't facing the exact same dilemma as Balakrishnan. But, I would like to quote this from Chandra's letter for him, as indeed I wish someone had advised me years ago:

Of course, all human beings, no matter how great their genius, have certain flaws and imperfections. But, time has a way of absorbing these minor imperfections.

> *I wish I could divulge to you the sorrows of my heart, and tell you how I feel at times that my heart will break by the oppression of my ignorance. You are mistaken and so are others, if they think that I have proved anything at all. My progress I only know too well is positively shameful. What is essential, however, is to have the ideal of gaining knowledge and to work steadfastly towards the ideal. One should not care to worry about what happens. One must lay sound foundations, one must have enough enthusiasm, one must have a passion, one must be filled with the joy of*

study. That is enough. Age does not matter. It is never
too late to begin...do not damage your inner feelings
and aspirations...If your aspirations are deep-seated,
do not on any account damage them or molest them.

Sulekha Reader Comments

Mahboob: I have the book *Black Holes and Relativistic Stars* edited by
Robert M. Wald, and published by The University of Chicago Press. This
book is a collection of articles presented at a 1996 University of Chicago
symposium dedicated to the memory of Chandrasekhar. It contains
written versions of the talks given at the symposium banquet by
Kameshwar Wali and Lalitha Chandrasekhar. Very touching and
mellifluous articles these.

Lalitha recollects her first day at her husband's home when she sang a
Papanasam Sivam song about the cycles of birth and death. She draws a
parallel between them and Chandra's cycles of scientific endeavor:

"Each field of study, or cycle as we shall call it, took anywhere from
ten to fifteen years, for the selection of the subject for investigation,
study of the available scientific literature on the subject for
investigation, his own research that followed, the scientific papers he
wrote on the subject, and finally, the way he gathered all the material
that lay in front of him into a coherent whole that was his book on the
subject. After a cycle ended and he was searching for a new field to
enter, there was an interim. He referred to it as his fallow period. It
was depressing to be in a fallow period. My song gave him comfort and
soothed him."

She corrects two notions about Chandra's life:

He did not leave England to come to America because of his controversy
with Eddington. He left because Eddington and Fowler told him that his
chances of finding a position in England, after the end of his fellowship
at Trinity College, were nil. If he had secured a position, he would have
stayed on in England even after he was offered positions at Yikes and
Harvard.

I reproduce this one verbatim: "Chandra used to tell me often, 'You
know it is because of Eddington that I became the sort of scientist
changing my field periodically from one to another. I had to change my
field after the controversy, and I continued doing that after each field
was explored'. Kamesh Wali in his biography of Chandra suggests that

an analysis of Chandra's scientific life reveals this influence of Eddington. If Kamesh felt that Chandra was unaware of this influence he is mistaken, since Chandra told me of this many years before Kamesh even started his biography!"

And Jenny, I hope you are not getting carried away by the flattery lavished by readers!

The Roma and the Persistence of Memory

Subhash Kak

Historians tell us that we represent the fourth wave of major migration from post-Harappan India to the West. The first happened about 2000 BC as a result of the dislocations caused in north India by earthquakes that altered the direction of major rivers and caused the drying up of the Sarasvati valleys. It is soon after this time that the Indic element begins to appear all over West Asia and Europe. Some Druze and Kurds claim that they are descendents of Indians from this period, but this belief could be a modern myth.

Herodotus in his Histories *speaks of the contingents of Indian soldiers in the Persian armies that battled the Greeks 1,500 years later. Indian colonies were situated in Babylon, Alexandria, Memphis, and Rome.*

Herodotus in his *Histories* speaks of the contingents of Indian soldiers in the Persian armies that battled the Greeks 1,500 years later. Indian colonies were situated in Babylon, Alexandria, Memphis, and Rome. But this, as the previous migration, is remembered only by historians. This second wave extended over centuries. For example, Firdausi, the author of *Shahnamah*, tells us that during his reign, the Persian king Behram Gaur (fifth century AD) asked his father-in-law in India to send him 10,000 musicians. What influence this massive migration had on the music of Eurasia, we will never be able to estimate.

Subhash Kak was born in Srinagar. He attended school in various towns in Jammu, Kashmir, and Ladakh. His college education was in Srinagar and IIT Delhi. He lives currently in Baton Rouge where he is a professor at Louisiana State University. He has authored several books including The Astronomical Code of the Rigveda, The Secrets of Ishbar, Ek Taal, Ek Darpan, *and* The Wishing Tree.

The third wave is remembered with greater clarity. This was the Roma, or Gypsies, who left India a thousand years ago as a result of the Arab and Turkish wars. According to the *Chachnama*, a contemporary account of Muhammad al-Qasim's campaigns in Sindh in 712-3, several thousand Jat warriors were captured as prisoners of war and deported to Iraq and elsewhere as slaves. A few hundred thousand women were likewise enslaved. The process of enslavement was accelerated during the campaigns of Mahmud of Ghazni. Abu Nasr Muhammad Utbi, the secretary and chronicler of Mahmud, informs us that 500,000 men and women were captured in Waihind alone in 1001-2. During his seventeen invasions, Mahmud Ghaznavi is estimated to have enslaved more than a million people. According to Utbi, "they were taken to Ghazna, and merchants came from different cities to purchase them, so that the countries of Mawarau-un-Nahr, Iraq and Khurasan were filled with them." The famed linguist and historian, Ian Hancock, himself of Romani ancestry, has argued that it was to escape this ongoing enslavement in the battlegrounds of Middle India, that many soldiers, together with their families, migrated west. Some say they were mainly Rajputs, but perhaps they did not constitute a single group, rather representing a wide spectrum of Indian society. These migrating families became the ancestors to the Roma. So their experience is the experience of a part of India that was separated from it a thousand years ago.

Passing through various lands, the Roma started appearing in Europe in the Middle Ages. But very soon they discovered a horrible welcome: that of removal by expulsion, repression, assimilation and, later, extermination. Here are a few randomly chosen accounts in various European countries: The King of Denmark, in 1589, decreed that any leader of a Roma band found on Danish soil was to be sentenced to death. In the 17th century, any vessel bringing in Roma would be confiscated. From that time on, and until 1849, any Rom found in Denmark was subject to deportation. 'Gypsy' hunts were organized with rewards to those who captured a Rom. Sweden also enacted harsh laws to deter the Roma. They were not allowed to enter the country. Those who managed to do so were immediately expelled. Those who failed to leave were brutally attacked or hanged. This forced many Roma to go 'into hiding' and marginalized them from society, or forced them to assimilate.

France enacted a series of expulsion laws beginning in 1510. Throughout the sixteenth century any Roma caught in the country were flogged. In the following century, Romani women who were captured had their heads shaved and were sent to workhouses. The men were put into chains in galleys.

In 16th century England, Roma were ordered to leave or be imprisoned because the English believed them to be sorcerers, thieves and cheats. Signs were posted in the English countryside, telling the Roma that they must leave England. Those who remained were given forty days to leave. Failure to do so meant death. If they were lucky, they were deported to their colonies as cheap sources of labor. In most countries, the speaking of Romani was forbidden.

> *The fundamental hostility towards the Roma remained unchanged, reaching its most tragic limits in Hitler's Germany. The Roma were seen as 'asocial,' a source of crime and culturally inferior.*

Switzerland allowed 'Gypsy' hunts in the 16th century, as did Holland in the 18th century. In the former Moravia, it was allowed to cut off the left ear of all Romani women who were caught. In Bohemia, removal of the right ear was legal.

In the Romanian principalities of Moldavia and Wallachia the Roma were enslaved in the 15th century. Once freed, a number of restrictive measures were taken against them, including a 1740 law that stated that no Rom could perform metalworking outside his tent. This law was aimed at any attempt by the Roma to compete against native metalworkers.

The fundamental hostility towards the Roma remained unchanged, reaching its most tragic limits in Hitler's Germany before and during World War II. The Roma were seen as 'asocial,' a source of crime and culturally inferior. When Adolf

Hitler came to power in Germany in 1933, his Nazi administration inherited 'anti-Gypsy' laws that had been in force since the Middle Ages.

On 15 September 1935, the Nuremberg Law restricted Jews for the Protection of Blood and Honor, and Roma were added later in 1937. This law forbade intermarriage or sexual intercourse with the perceived foreign peoples. Criteria for classification as a Rom were twice as strict as those applied to Jews. If two of a person's eight great-grandparents were even part-Roma, that person "had too much Gypsy blood to be allowed to live."

In 1937, the Nazi-occupied countries began to force the Roma into concentration camps. Many of them were worked to death as slave laborers in the camp quarry or at outlying arms factories. At first, there were no gas chambers but thousands were shot, hanged, or tortured to death by the camp's guards. Other prisoners were sterilized to prevent them from having children of their own.

A few years later a program of liquidation began. Roma were beaten and clubbed to death, herded into the gas chambers, and forced to dig their own graves. The fate of the Roma paralleled the tragic fate of the Jews who were also imprisoned and exterminated. They were tortured, used for inhuman scientific experiments, and put to death in the infamous gas chambers.

It is estimated that over a million Roma were murdered from 1935 to the end of World War II. After the war, the Roma received little, if any, reparations from any government for their losses and suffering. Not a single Rom was called to testify at the Nuremberg Trials, or has been to any of the subsequent war crime tribunals. Until the 1970s, many Nazi-era laws remained on the books. In 1982, the German government was one of the first (and few) to belatedly recognize the atrocities committed against Romani people during World War II.

The Roma have survived in the most difficult situations and for this they deserve to be saluted by all. They have also given a lot to Europe – music, dance, arts and crafts, and shown an indomitable will to survive.

Here's what Ian Hancock told me about how the newly immigrant Indians in the West could build bridges with the Roma:

I think the 'theme' should be the tenacity of Indianness – the fact that, as diluted as we Roma are after 1000 years away from India, we have kept an incredible amount of Indianness in language, culture and (I think) behaviour and attitude. The other point is that Roma are in a time of crisis because of questions of identity and allegiance, which have perforce become political, and we [need] our Indian brothers and sisters to legitimize us. We are all Indians in the West, but separated by a millennium. It might raise the question of "how long do Indians remain Indian away from home" – I lived in British Columbia for many years (my parents still do) and there are many Panjabi families there several generations old. They're still Indian. I taught in Trinidad one year – Indians have been there since the 1800s – but you'd hardly know it. There's something about Indianness.

But what are the main Roma organizations in the US and Europe? Would they welcome interaction with more recently arrived Indians? This is what Ian had to say:

The two main ones are The Roma National Congress and the International Romani Union. We are in process of creating an Indo-Romani Alliance, Nidhi might have mentioned this to you. There is no policy regarding relationships with India, but those individuals who feel strongly nationalistic of course emphasize our Indian roots. There is, however, a vocal minority which insists that we don't bring attention to that, but instead try to be 'true Europeans'. My own argument to that is, in order to

be 'Europeans', the Europeans must want us to be –
and it's clear that they don't.

Nidhi Trehan, the Indian-born American scholar and activist mentioned above by Ian, has lived in Eastern Europe for almost past five years. She is researching power structures that inhibit Romani participation in the achievement of their own autonomy and emancipation. She is also trying to establish a Foundation for Indo-Romani exchange; *FIRE*. She hopes this will facilitate the process by which Indians, diaspora and *desi*, will get to know and understand Roma.

Sulekha Reader Comments

John Smith: Can the Roma be called the *Dalits* of Europe? It appears so. I am surprised then that European Christians criticise Hindus in India for the historical injustices against the Dalits when their own record against the Roma is even worse. At least the Indian *Dalits* were not physically eliminated, as was the case with the European *Dalits*. The experience of the Roma also tells us that Europe's human right record is quite abysmal. And it continues to be so. The Roma are still being hounded out of their settlements in most European countries and they haven't been given the same rights as other citizens.

Rohini Ramanathan: A book you may like to check out is, *Bury Me Standing: The Gypsies and Their Journey* by Isabel Fonseca. Interestingly, the cover page testimonial is from Salman Rushdie. Here is what he says: "A revelation - a hidden world, at once ignored and secretive, persecuted and unknown - is uncovered in these absorbing pages." Years ago, I had read an op-ed piece in *The New York Times* by Yul Brynner in which he traced his Gypsy roots to Punjab. I got a real kick out of this revelation as he's one of my all-time favorite actors, and I had seen him on stage in *King and I* just a few weeks before that.

VGR: Thanks for the concise and interesting account of the migration of the Roma people to Europe. I have heard from other places that there is a movement within the Gypsy community worldwide to building closer ties with their Indian roots. Whether it will be successful remains to be seen, of course. For those interested in the Roma and the gypsy culture in general, World Network (Germany) has compilations of Gypsy music.

Fathima and the Alchemists

John Swamy

Prologue:

Kuttalam was the legendary resort of Agastyar, the alchemist sage of Southern India. Its forests are rich in medicinal plants and have natural caves, which are now places of worship. Though Agastyar is part of the cave pantheon, *Shenbagadevi*, a goddess, rules over these hills. A temple dedicated to the goddess and an exquisite waterfall named after her attract many pilgrims from the plains. The tradition of the *Siddhars* (South Indian alchemists) moved out of these hills long ago, but the place still survives, pregnant with all its memories. This story is based on a real event that happened in these forests.

Karuppaiyya Thevar makes delicious coconut chutney using herbs.

Karuppaiyya Thevar makes delicious coconut chutney using herbs. He picks them early in the morning after bathing in the waterfall. "They are more sensitive than we are. If we aren't clean – both in mind and body, they lose their power even before we reach them. Some of them hide, you know, he

John Swamy was born in 1962 and raised in Kollam, Kerala. After school, he joined deep-sea fishing trawlers and worked in them off the east and west coast of India, for about three years. He then joined merchant ships where he worked for another 15 years. He left ships in 1997 and has been a freelance writer ever since. He has a deep affection and respect for forests, sacred groves, the ocean and the powerful gods connected to them. He's single and lives with his ageing parents in Kerala.

says with a toothless smile. That's why I pray after bathing and, while collecting them, I keep chanting *Devi*'s name."

Thevar slept in a small shrine near the waterfall during weekends. The deity inside was a shapeless black stone, draped in red pleated cloth. His bedroll was hidden behind the idol all day and taken out after sunset. During the 'season', pilgrims thronged this shrine. Thevar sat at the entrance selling dried herbs tied into small clumps. Before he dispensed them, he held them to his heart, murmured a prayer and handed them to the pilgrims with a pinch of sacred ash. They were sold at a rupee a clump. Herbs for erectile dysfunction cost three rupees and were sold out well before the end of the season. On weekends, Thevar drank a quarter bottle of rum and ate meat that he cooked himself. "She appeared to me in a dream and said, go down to the plains, eat meat and enjoy!" he used to sing when drunk.

Ramaswami has a pension and that makes him the most moneyed hermit around. He looks down upon Thevar and calls him a thief. Thevar believes it's the pension that makes him arrogant. He occupies the cave of Agastyar. It has two chambers, one for Avvai, the poet-goddess and the other for the sage. He is the caretaker-cum-high-priest of the cave and won't let anyone spend the night there. When Thevar collects herbs, he gives some to Ramaswami, who gives it to pilgrims who come to him for divining. During the lean season, when pilgrims are scarce, Ramaswami shares his meals with Thevar but makes him work for it. "He's nuts! Don't ever eat his chutneys...I had a bad stomach for two days after trying one of them!" warns Ramaswami. Between the two of them, they share this spirit-nourished patch of land on the edge of a thick tropical forest.

At the place where the river plunges into the plains, there are huge boulders of rock with shallow crevices. Fathima used these crevices for a living. When pilgrims returned from Shenbagadevi, they had this light-headed, relieved feeling about them that normally follows the end of an arduous pilgrimage. Fathima sat on a prominent boulder with her sari

hitched up to her knees, chewing betel leaves. She returned the
stares of pilgrims going back and managed to lure a couple of
them every day during the 'season'. The love-chamber, a snug
crevice, had a brightly-coloured *lungi* spread over dead leaves.
Fathima never took off all her clothes. She used to pull out her
breasts from under her blouse and carefully hitch up her sari
before lying down. Most of her clients were nervous with guilt
and always left immediately after the act. She had a hare-lip
and a large gap between her front teeth. It showed only when
she smiled. Adolescent boys from the plains used to hide and
watch her at work, during school holidays. She knew they were
there, but didn't bother.

All calamities that came upon the hermits and the hills
were credited to Fathima. The moral brigade was often led by
the affluent, Ramaswami while Thevar, who knew poverty
better, was more tolerant. "She's the curse of the hills," said
Ramaswami, "and the cause of all floods." Though none of
them had the courage to look her in the eyes, she remained the
butt of all curses. He spat in disgust whenever he passed her in
the forest. Telling the police was of no use, because many
constables were part of her clientele.

Unlike others of her profession, Fathima worked in
daylight. Nobody really knew where she spent the night.
People say she stays at a mental asylum down in the plains
with the cook and some even say she has leprosy. She always
waited for Karuppaiyya Thevar, the last person to leave the
hills on weekdays. When she saw the old man she knew it was
time to go home. They greeted each other. "*Amma*, how are
things?" he asked. The conversation lasted a few minutes and
she always waited for Thevar to reach a certain distance before
she followed him downhill.

Then, one evening during the dry season, Thevar didn't
turn up. It was *Amavasi* and there was a trickle of pilgrims to
the shrine. Most of them were regulars, and Fathima couldn't
work much that day. When she went to her 'chamber' to collect
her *lungi*, she found monkey droppings on it. This was the first
time in all her 15 years that the monkeys had done this. To

Fathima, this was a bad omen and a strange tremor in her stomach told her something was really wrong. The sun was already behind the hills and she knew it would soon be dark.

As she was folding her *lungi* and tucking it into her plastic carry-bag, she was confused. Fathima liked the old man and knew something was terribly wrong. If she went uphill there was no way she could return, as it would be too dark. Her heart wasn't letting her go downhill either. She started to climb down from the boulder

The men were drunk and, from their shaven heads, she knew they were the keepers of the Ganja *plantations higher up in the hills.*

when she tripped and fell. The fall was short, but it scared her. She got up from the ground, took a deep breath and walked uphill towards the caves.

It was dark by the time she reached the caves. She had been here before when a drunken rice merchant from the plains demanded she accompany him for a bath in the waterfall. As she approached the shrine, she could hear loud voices and saw a fire lit outside Ramaswami's cave. She stopped and walked back slowly around the caves unseen and reached a place from where she could see the fire without revealing herself. There were four people seated on the floor around the fire. In the firelight she could see they had shaved heads. There were many steel utensils, brass lamps and food provisions piled up on the ground next to them. Ramaswami was lying on the floor with his hands tied and he was groaning, *"Devi,* help me! *Devi...Devi...DEVI!"* Her heart was hammering at her breasts as she looked around desperately for Thevar. He was nowhere to be seen.

The men were drunk and, from their shaven heads, she knew they were the keepers of the *Ganja* plantations higher up in the hills. They were supplied food and provisions by their employers, but sometimes the supplies were delayed. Hunger drove them to small forest towns where they looted small shops for supplies. Cigarettes were hot on their list and in passing they grabbed everything they could. These men were violent and Fathima had heard stories about them. In the firelight she could see their eyebrows were shaved too. Then a fifth person appeared from the shadow holding Thevar by his long, grey hair. Thevar had his palms joined in prayer and was begging the man to let him go. When they reached the fire, the man shoved Thevar away from him and spoke to one of the seated men. The man rose and walked towards Thevar who was lying on the ground. Thevar grabbed his legs and began to plead. The man kicked him but Thevar held on till he shook himself loose, cursing loudly.

In the darkness, Fathima began to shake uncontrollably and her legs gave way. She sat on the ground leaning against the boulder and prayed. She prayed to all the gods she could remember and swore to shave her head and do anything if they could spare the hermit. Then suddenly, she heard Karuppaiyya Thevar scream loudly and something snapped inside her. Her shaking stopped and a great calm came upon her. She noticed there were fireflies around and smiled at them. The dark night had suddenly become alive. She rose from the ground, walked around the rocks and turned towards the fire. The men around the fire slowly got up and walked towards her.

Just before he passed out, Karuppaiyya Thevar could see one of the men pulling her to him and as the darkness covered him he heard her laugh. When he came to, it was morning and there were policemen all over. They were questioning Ramaswami. There was no sign of Fathima and the policeman laughed at him when he asked about her. "She's having a good time with them now, what's your problem, old man?" asked the policeman laughing. Thevar limped painfully to his shrine and reached behind the idol for his bedroll. It was still there. The temple and a small shop selling cigarettes had been looted and they even took away the sweets kept in bottles.

For four days Thevar limped painfully up to Fathima's boulder to see if she had come back. On the fifth day he saw her. She was folding a new *lungi* into a plastic carry-bag. She looked older but her eyes were shining. Thevar could only say "*Amma...*" as he looked into her eyes for the first time. He then joined his palms and, bowing his head, he whispered, "*Shenbagadevi!*" and walked slowly downhill. She stared at the old man's retreating figure for a long time till the sharp call of a jungle fowl brought her back to this world.

Epilogue:

Karuppaiyya Thevar was an orderly in the army when he shot a serviceman dead for attempting to rape his officer's wife. He served five years in the Andaman & Nicobar penitentiary before he was released with many others when India became independent. On returning home he found his wife living with another man and his only son, serving time for theft. He left home and reached Shenbagadevi Falls at Kuttalam where he spent the rest of his days as a hermit. About ten years ago, he disappeared and was never seen since.

Ramaswami was a peon in a govt. office at Madras and came to Kuttalam after he retired. He still occupies the same cave and continues to spit on the ground when he sees Fathima. He has good divining skills and makes excellent *sambar*.

The keepers took Fathima across the state border into Kerala and dumped her at the periphery of a wildlife sanctuary there. She caught a bus back to Kuttalam. She's old now and sells slices of fresh pineapple to pilgrims during the 'season', a few meters from her favourite boulder.

An Insurgent Day

Viswanath Gurram

Part One

The light that shines comes from thine eyes;
The day breaks not: it is my heart...

Daybreak.
John Donne, 1573 – 1631.

Their lives were very well organised.

Every morning Sachin Bhowmick would come downstairs, nattily dressed, kiss his wife on the cheek and then sit down to breakfast. They would listen to the morning news coming on the All India Radio, followed by Carnatic classical music.

The breakfast would be usually accompanied by strong Karachi coffee. Whatever she had fixed, he would say, with genuine pleasure, "This is wonderful, dear!" And because she knew him and his sincerity, she always enjoyed his compliments. Only once, in their seven years of marriage had he said, "This is wonderful, dear, but I think it needs a pinch of salt!" And having said that, he had looked up with such an expression of contrition that she had laughed. She went into the

Viswanath Gurram was born in India and is a resident of Canada. He is the grandson of the illustrious scholar, Gurram Subbaramayya. Viswanath is a graphic artist, web designer and translator and spends every moment away from work in reading, writing and freelancing as a journalist. He writes in English, French and German and also in Indian languages under the pseudonym of 'Gangadhar'. Viswanath's work has appeared in publications like The Indian Express and Upbeat and has received much attention and appreciation. His debut novel will be completed soon. The writer's web presence begins at gurram.terrashare.com, from where his online work can be accessed.

kitchen to fetch the salt, and realised that she had tears in her eyes. She knew, in that one moment of gazing upon his remorseful face, that their love was a survivor because it was singularly honest. Her heart felt safe in his hands.

He would then leave for work, taking with him the three-tier lunch carrier that she had prepared for him. After his departure, she would work in the garden, then take a bath, meditate for a while, have lunch, and then sit down to write; she was a regular contributor of short stories and poems to women's magazines, and she enjoyed giving her imagination free rein over the lovely ivory paper that Sachin bought for her. He had also gifted her, when she had first begun to write, a bottle of Camlin's *The Hunter Green* ink, with which she had immediately fallen in love. From then on, he made sure to bring her a new bottle every month.

He had also gifted her, when she had first begun to write, a bottle of Camlin's The Hunter Green ink, with which she had immediately fallen in love.

He would come home in the evening; they would have Jasmine tea, and then go for a stroll, or to see a play, or just stay at home. They were so comfortable and relaxed in each other's company that the days and years went by as happy floats in life's parade.

They sometimes had guests, and then it was only her sisters, who adored their youngest sibling. They were proud of her and treasured every line that she wrote. Their greatest sorrow was that she was childless.

Four years ago, the doctors had declared that Naveena would not be able to conceive; she had been much disturbed and had suggested adoption, but Sachin was not very keen on the idea. "It will never be the same, darling," he had protested. "They would grow up and wander off to find their own roots, and where will we be? Hanging on to squandered love..."

"It need not be like that," she had tried to reason with him. "I know of several people who were adopted and who grew up to be the best things that happened to the parents who took a chance with them! And then, dearest, love is never a waste..."

Her arguments led nowhere, and soon they decided to never raise the issue again. "He feels complete and whole just being with me and I feel the same myself," she had later told her sisters. "I am really reconciled to the idea of not having children. Your children are as good as mine!" And she was a very generous and devoted aunt to her young nieces and nephews.

Part Two

And Lo! The Hunter of the East has caught
The Sultan's Turret in a Noose of Light...

Rubaiyat of Omar Khayyam
Edward Fitzgerald, 1809-1883

This August morning was much like other mornings. They ate a sweet-sour monsoon fruit salad, along with hot cardamom coffee. After the news, the usual classical music floated in the room, while they discussed a few domestic matters. He then took his lunch-carrier and drove to King's Road, where he worked as an adjuster for a large insurance firm. She finished watering the plants, and her other morning occupations, lunched while listening to Austen's *Persuasion*, dramatised on the BBC, and then went into the sunlit parlour, where her lovely rosewood desk awaited her.

She was very excited about the play she had begun writing a week ago. It was turning out very well, and it being her maiden endeavour in this artform, she was anxious to conclude it and get feedback from Sachin and her sisters. She took out her manuscript from the desk drawer, and reached for the inkbottle to fill her fountain pen, a peerless creation made of silver and sheathed in interlacing sandalwood strips, with a tiny ruby on the top of the cap. The bottle was empty, and there wasn't a new one beside it. She remembered that she had spilled some ink a few days ago, and had forgotten to mention it to Sachin. "He'll be getting me a new bottle tomorrow anyway, it being the first of the month," she told herself with a sigh.

But an hour later, she was feeling so frustrated that she decided to go out and get the ink herself. "My muse cannot be put on hold," she informed her reflection in the mirror, as she dabbed on a little Yardley's Lavender perfume. "And my fingers are just itching to write!" She recalled Sachin telling her that *The Hunter Green* was procurable only at the Camlin outlet in the shopping complex at the Nehru stadium. She hired an auto-rickshaw to the place, and asking the driver to wait, quickly crossed the children's park, on the other side of which were the gaily painted shops. She paused for a moment by a breathtakingly grand red-rose bush in full bloom; and then she saw him.

A little distance away, Sachin was playing with a young child on a swing tied to the branches of a massive Banyan tree... The child was about four years old. And his features were unmistakable.

Naveena's hand trembled and the pen in her hand fell to the ground. She took a step away from the rose bush, and then swiftly walked out of the park. She climbed into the waiting vehicle, and said in a drawn voice, "Please drive me back."

Part Three

> *Nothing could have my love o'erthrown*
> *if thou hadst still continued mine;*
> *Yea, if thou hadst remain'd thy own,*
> *I might perchance have yet been thine...*

To an Inconstant One,

Sulekha Select

Sir Robert Ayton, 1570–1638

It was the child who later discovered the pen while frolicking around; Sachin recognised it at once.

The noises of the world abruptly ceased, and there was utter silence. The sunlight blazed violently, having unravelled the palimpsest of life.

He came home that evening at his usual hour. The house was empty, the air tangibly aghast. The manuscript of her play lay on the table in the parlour. Gently he picked it up. On the front page was scrawled lightly, in pencil, "I leave this play unfinished. You see, this morning I ran out of *The Hunter Green*."

Women in India want to be Men

Sailendra Singh

Women in India want to be men!

I axed my wife if this was true... (no this isn't the result of an oppressive strain deeply ingrained...it's just an enunciation-pronunciation folly. Once in an Indian restaurant in New York, my friend and I asked the heart-breakingly cute waitress if she could get us some Coke. Let me axe the cook, she said. We sat speechless as she withdrew into the kitchen. There was a sound and a yell and she emerged carrying a long face. Sorry, she said, I *Yeah, she said, of course of course you watch TV, what crap. You watch only Internet. You don't watch TV-sheevee. Don't teach me.* have axed the cook but he has no cock. We were relieved to hear this. We settled for some Pepsi. But, for a second, we did get a fleeting hint of what oppression can do to some women or how gory revenge can get.)

So I axed my wife today if in fact she wishes to be a man. She did not answer. I axed her again. She walked over my to my computer purposefully and yanked the main cable out of it's socket and looked at me with menacing eyes. I have work to do, she shouted, don't you? Where do you get the time to surf the net? Are you a bored American housewife? It seems *you* want to be a woman? I looked at her sheepishly. No no, my life, I said lying, I didn't pick up this thread on the Internet,

---

Sailendra Singh lives in Calcutta as a self-employed married man with two sons. He will turn thirty-four shortly. His sun sign is Scorpio. His favourite journey is travelling home from office. His favourite dish is Chello Kabab. Peter Cat, a nice restaurant in Park Street serves the best Chello Kabab in Calcutta. He spent four years in the Big Apple completing his graduation; the rest of the time he has more or less lived in Calcutta.

why are you berating the Net unnecessarily? It's from a documentary I saw on *Discovery Channel* today – a documentary on female infanticide in Tamil Nadu by Martin Frank, a famous activist. Yeah, she said, of course of course you watch TV, what crap. You watch only Internet. You don't watch TV-sheevee. Don't teach me.

I immediately stopped teaching her. I went and lay on my sofa instead. My thoughts wandered back to a time twelve years ago when I was a student in college. During the summers, back then, I used to return home to vegetate. The woman in my house, then, was my mother. (Men in India are dominated by women. Still they want to be men.) You are an artist, I had told my mother then, smacking my lips and licking my fingers clean of the buttery *dosa* she had prepared. You could have been a writer or a painter Mummy. My mom smiled, looked wistfully into the horizon and went back to flipping *dosas*. But this male-dominated society has oppressed you Mom, it has stifled your creative urges, shackled you, made you a lowly housewife, like a buffalo chained to a Persian wheel. At this my mom started. While I wondered if it was valid to use a buffalo in place of a bull in a Persian-wheel metaphor, I knew from her expression that it had struck home. She looked at me with pain in her eyes and said, it's burning. Of course, I said, of course, thumping the table, of course it is burning. The years and eons of slavery and gender biases seeped in your blood are burning, turning, churning and now they will rage, like fire. This repression is an incendiary bomb, Mom!

The motor of the *dosa* grinder, she said, pointing towards it – it's burning. And right she was. The *dosa* machine was emitting a sickly whine by now. Probably the motor had gone bust. You want another *dosa*? she quizzed from the kitchen. I was angry by this time – angry with her, angry with the society that had made her inured, uncaring of her rights and liberties. Yes, I said, another one and another and another. I wasn't hungry, yet I wished to punish her for being so insensitive to herself, so ignorant about her exploited position vis-à-vis the

Indian male and so blasé about her latent artistic talents. So I made her slog over *dosas*. Little did I know that I was punishing only myself. The *dosas* came marching one by one and I kept eating them.

When she finally emerged from the kitchen, wiping her hands on her vinyl apron, I told her that the exploitation of women in our society was complete, and that it was all a gender power play now, orchestrated by the hegemonic powers of the world, those savage capitalistic nations. The Marxists acknowledged sub-jugation of woman as a necessary condition for any theory of capitalism, thus it was not surprising, I said, *...thus it was not surprising, I said, wagging a finger at her, that you should find yourself at the fringes of this society's grinding wheel.* wagging a finger at her, that you should find yourself at the fringes of this society's grinding wheel. You can still rise Mummy, I said, all emotional and choked by this time, tears in my eyes (actually instigated by the *dosa* chilli-powder smeared on my hands with which I had accidentally wiped my brow), you can still revolt, rebel. Why do you have to sit at home wasting your life like this, changing nappies (Good heavens! I had never seen her change nappies, not mine in any case, and I don't know where these sentiments came from, probably from the pits of my soul for I was fervent and emotional by this time), watching TV, chatting with other exploited women, doing our Hindi homework, washing our clothes and those of the great exploiter, your husband! Why do you have to lead such a life? (I was careful not to mention anything about flipping *dosas*. It might have backfired.) Why don't you too attend office! You can start your own enterprise, you can be like a man, you don't have to cow down to oppressors, you don't have to swelter behind the *purdah*. You can drive a car (though I knew not what purpose that would have served; driving a bus or taxi would have been more meaningful). You don't know Mom, this whole society has brainwashed women, it has brainwashed you. I was getting a little exasperated with the zero rate of success I had achieved so far. My father does not even love you, I shouted at her, you are just his property! He exploits you! All men are like that in your society! She laughed at me. Will *you* teach me love, *dosa* boy? she said. You? You will tell me what's love or who loves me or what's good for me?

I went and lay on the sofa after this. It was useless, I concluded. These women have just been brainwashed beyond belief. This capitalistic, male-dominated society was just too much, too powerful, too hypnotic for them. These women could never be taught what was good for them. And I belched the acid remains of the spicy *dosa* as I drifted to sleep.

> Will you *teach me love,*
> dosa *boy? she said. You?*
> *You will tell me what's*
> *love or who loves me or*
> *what's good for me?*

As I slept, I dreamt. In the dream a woman who called herself Devi appeared with Kali's deadly scimitar in one hand and Hanuman's mace in another. She was singing a song in a plaintive drawl, stamping one foot on the ground after each verse and turning around 360 degrees every time:

> *Who is gonna cook dosas for you*
> *One plus one is equal to two.*
> *You are dominated by women? Don't lie.*
> *Women are dominated by men, apple pie.*
> *Women want to be men that ain't the truth.*
> *Women want to be rich, do u get it dude?*
> *If your dosa sticks, the pan is fake*
> *Get some mustard oil, would you like to eat cake?*

And after this the-woman-who-called-herself-Devi hit me gently me with the pointed end of her mace. I asked her why she hit me with the mace and not the scimitar? She said the scimitar was for *chokda* boys, Capitalist boys, women exploiters. Was I a capitalist? Did I exploit women? she asked, raising her scimitar and rolling her round eyes. No no, I said quickly, I don't exploit women, I only eat *dosas*. So she jabbed me playfully with her mace again. My bile churned. And she threw a riddle at me:

Do you sleep or do you wake?
Mummy's asleep or is she really awake?

And before I could think of an answer, I was drowned in tons and tons of Florida moss. Tons and tons of Florida moss. And then I stopped dreaming but carried on sleeping.

Sulekha Reader Comments

Chandra: Someone axed what the hell 'axe' means in the article. It is the American inner city pronunciation of 'ask'. :-))

Sailendra Singh: You are damn right Chandra. And what a coincindence too. I got this great joke in my mail today:

Bumper Stickers you don't see (but should):

1. Constipated people don't give a crap.
2. Practice safe sex, go screw yourself.
3. Please tell your pants it's not polite to point.
4. Ax me about Ebonics.

Thanks for the new twist to the 'ax' theory.

Damn

Tanushri Shukla

You don't have my sanction to make me a victim.

I couldn't get her voice out of my head.

She was a hard-ass bitch. So damn confident and totally in control. Always. I hated her for that smugness with which she lived life, as if she was privy to some huge cosmic secret and she kept me out of it. It made me feel like a child. But then I loved her for *her*. She was this amazingly strong, independent

> **She was a hard-ass bitch. So damn confident and totally in control. Always. Didn't she feel anything? Why didn't she ever cry?**

woman. The archetypal single, workingwoman. She wasn't unique for the city of Bombay which housed hundreds like her but in my mind, nobody could match up to Rita. Damn I hate her.

Why did she have to be so sure all the time? Why did she never stoop or hunch? Why was that back always ramrod-straight and that face set like stone? Didn't she feel anything? Was she frigid? Why was she so stony? So cruel? Like a marble statue? And a beautiful one at that. Why didn't she ever cry? Damn I hate her.

Tanushri Shukla, eighteen, is studying mass media in Bombay. She has attended eight schools in six Indian cities, detests vegetables with a vengeance and hopes to do great things in life with no real idea of what they will be. She is currently marking time as a freelance journalist and will probably make a career of it unless she takes up law, business administration or singing on street corners. Contrary to popular belief, she is basically introverted, loves dogs more than chocolate, wishes she could buy books for a living and isn't a writer, just an observer who sometimes needs glasses.

She doesn't give me the pleasure of wiping her tears and brushing her hair back and protecting her and soothing her. She never cries, never wears her hair loose, could protect the Prime Minister against a posse of terrorists single handedly and was always, always calm. Nothing frazzled her. Not pressure at work, not my screaming spells when I'd beg her to open up to me. She'd just calmly tell me to relax and not get carried away. *Damn I hate her.* Sitting there watching me with the impersonal air of a rock. She was a rock.

She had seen me cry hundreds of times. I'd rant and rave and demand that she open up to me. She'd tell me to ask her anything I wanted and that she'd answer. And I'd be at a loss for words. I knew what work she was doing, I knew about the fat woman in her office who always tried to steal her assignments, I even knew the date she started her period. And yet I didn't know her. Even after five years she was still a complete stranger to me.

Her parents had tried everything to get her to marry me. Coercion, force, pleas, emotional blackmail. Every motherly trick in the book from tears to orders. All of it had absolutely no effect on her. She was as stony as always, regarding me with unconcealed detachment. She didn't love me, I knew that. But why didn't she at least hate me? It would've been easier if she hated me, but she didn't feel a thing. To her I was as good as a stranger on the bus. To be looked at but not to be seen. To be aware of but not to be known. Damn I hate her.

She made me feel like a fool. A stupid, foolish child. Every time I asked her why she kept me at an arms length from her mind and heart, she'd give me a patient look making me feel like a child throwing a tantrum. She made me feel like a worthless, good-for-nothing moron who was at her beck and call. All she had to do was snap those slender fingers and I'd come chasing after her. She had no respect for me, no love, no anger, nothing. She was completely indifferent to me and the pains I took to make her happy; the lengths to which I would go to please her. To perhaps see her smile. At me.

I had known Rita for five years and I use the word 'known' very loosely here. Her family had shifted into the building opposite ours. Our flats were at the same level, such that we could look into each other's houses and watch TV. Her parents, ever the socialites, had met up with mine and they clicked instantly. Unfortunately the same couldn't be said for Rita and me. She was finishing up with her final year of graduation and I had already begun working by that time. Our families encouraged our friendship for the obvious reasons that an Indian family wants to keep its daughter locked up at home for the first 20 years of her life and thereafter expect her to walk out into the world of men and make a first-rate catch. I guess her parents didn't bargain for her temperament. They didn't really know her either. Did anyone? I don't think so. She was too independent, too shut off, too self-sufficient. She didn't need companionship. She had herself, her mind, her thoughts and that was enough. She didn't live life like most of us do – waiting for that *someone* and hoping for that *something* to happen. She lived reality. I

I knocked her onto the sofa and lashed out at her like a lunatic. She struggled to get up but I pinned her to the couch. Then I raped her.

was a dreamer, a romantic, an idealistic fool, as she'd probably put it. Ours was a match doomed from the start, but I refused to acknowledge that fact. I was madly in love with her way before her mother realized I was her Perfect Catch. I guess I didn't bargain for Rita's temperament either. I was no match for her.

We had just had another one of those screaming spells where I basically did the screaming and she did the listening and patient watching. I was shouting into her face, calling her filthy names, hoping for some sort of a reaction! I vented everything, all the anger and frustration at her total oblivion to my 'charms' and me during the years. I was called Casanova! And here was this woman who couldn't care less if I lived or died.

I hit her across her face and left a red mark on her. I had done it in a fit of passion and after that slap I got more furious.

It had opened the trapdoors to my rage. I didn't notice the change of expression in her eyes in the instant my hand struck her face. I screamed and raised my hand again but she stood up suddenly in an abrupt motion. She stood straight, staring directly into my face and her defiance and indignation made me angrier.

I moved my raised arm to strike her again when she caught hold of it and dug her nails into my skin, looking directly into my eyes with that insolence that made me scream like a caged animal. There was one area I beat her – physical strength. I shook off her slim arm and struck her on her face, harder than the first time. I knocked her onto the sofa and lashed out at her like a lunatic. She struggled to get up but I pinned her to the couch. Then I raped her.

I know I had taken her by surprise with that first slap. She had always thought of me as a harmless little plaything. A little kid who'd throw tantrums and threaten to hold his breath till he turned blue in the face but who never did carry it through. I decided to change all of that. It was time she realized that I meant business. She couldn't keep me away from her any longer. I was going to be part of her whether she liked it or not.

When I was done I stood up and spat on her. The ball of spit landed on her right cheek – my mark.

"You're *mine* bitch. You thought you were better than me didn't you? You thought you were above me, too good for me. You thought you deserved better didn't you? Well that should teach you! You're mine! You hear me? Mine!"

I thought I had broken her as she lay on that couch at my feet staring up at me. I thought I had finally become a man. No more Mr. Nice Guy. No more being the invisible guy, always in the background, hoping for a glance. I thought she had lost the battle.

I thought wrong.

For a few minutes she just lay there, bleeding, watching me scream and rave and spit all over the place. Then the expression in her eyes changed again. She lifted her arm and wiped my saliva from her face. She gathered her ripped clothes and stood up on wobbly legs. She was bleeding and was a mess. She couldn't have had the strength to stand up. She had just been raped, *goddamit!* She was supposed to curl into a ball and cry and beg me to let her go and promise to never be cruel to me again. But she stood up.

There was not a tear in her eye as she walked toward me.

"Remember Rajiv, I don't give anyone the power to hurt me. You don't have my sanction to make me a victim."

And she walked out of the door leaving me to clean up after her like a servant.

I sat in the apartment, crying like I had never cried before. I had raped her. But she had won. Her mind was stronger than my body.

She didn't let me go. The cops came in less than an hour.

Damn.

Author's Note: The inspiration for this piece came from Atlas Shrugged *by Ayn Rand. The phrase, "sanction of the victim" comes directly from the book. It was a concept that hit me in a big way. The idea that absolutely nobody can victimize you unless you allow them to and that so many of us give all and sundry this allowance every single day and then blame them for our misery, is so simple yet amazing. On the other hand, rape is one thing most women are downright terrified of. I wanted to bring out an attitude that probably doesn't, but could exist. The human mind can handle just about anything with the right attitude. Here was a woman who wouldn't let the most dire circumstances and a huge threat to her physical self, make her a victim. That, to me, is amazing and in a way, reassuring, that perhaps someone out there is as strong as this. I know I'm trying to be.*

Sulekha Reader Comments

Amita: I found that story rather problematic in the same way that I find Rand's argument of 'sanction of the victim' incredibly problematic: once again it places the responsibility on the shoulders of the target of violence to not feel the pain, to not be affected, to be in a sense, rational, unfeeling and superhuman. That is the foundation of the traditional argument of supporters of rapists and other offenders: that if a recipient of violence shows emotion or other effects of trauma, somehow it decreases her credibility and shows she is irrational, while the offender is often smug and intelligent in a twisted sort of way, in that he can rationalize away all responsibility or blame.

Supporting Rand's theory encourages women to keep it all inside, never making a public outcry, never 'playing the victim' and thus never making the offender own up to the outrageous crime and violation he has committed and should be punished for. Instead, we as members of society have a responsibility to create an environment where women who have been raped feel safe enough to step forward and speak out about it. We must acknowledge that speaking out about the trauma of being raped is a sign of strength and courage; indeed, it is taking steps to move from 'victim' to 'survivor'.

e-illusions

Jeeva

The alarm rings near my ear, jolting me awake. I shut it off before anyone else awakens. Groggily I sit up, half tempted to fall back into the comfort of the bed.

Then I remember; a letter – his letter – would have arrived. All grogginess disappears. Before even brushing my teeth, I switch on the computer. While the computer awakens, I finish washing and brushing my teeth. I sit in front of the computer exactly when *Windows* begins its welcoming music. I double-click the dial-up connection and within a few minutes I get connected to the Net. Its only 4.30 in the morning and the lines aren't busy as yet. I impatiently type my *Hotmail* address before the VSNL site gets loaded fully. This is a special address, but then it gets special mail...I tap my fingers nervously, waiting for the inbox to appear. The suspense is unbearable. Would he have written? Or would it be an empty Inbox with the message '0 new mail' that would stare at my face. I cross my fingers and hope and wait. 5K read, 7K read, 18K read, and so it continues K by K. The 'hot tip' appears, this time warning me to keep logging in regularly to keep my account active. I smile thinking how unnecessary the tip is, because I log in at least once everyday, if not more often. The *Inbox* appears at long last with the

---

Jeeva is an architect from Madurai and has spent most of her life there. She did her college education in Chennai and is now in Upstate New York trying to figure out how to light up buildings if not lives...Her writing doesn't cover any particular category, but is more of a need to express emotions and define things clearly at least for herself, if not for anyone else.

welcoming words '1 new message'. I scroll down to the end of the page, and my fingers tremble as they click on the message.

The message goes on, rambling in its content, and the writer touches upon so many topics, ranging from philosophy to movies, to books, to politics... 'Oh I love him so!' I think before reading further. At first I give the letter a general glance, and the details don't register. Nothing registers except his name 'Raghu' at the end. I feel a brief surge of agony and pleasure combined, as I look at the name, so beloved to me now! To think that a year back I didn't even know of his existence! He, living somewhere in England, and I, in far-away India, that too in Coimbatore, tucked away somewhere, and unlikely to ever meet, becoming close only through electronic mail! And yet he was the only person whom I'd ever completely confided in. I'd told him my beliefs, my prejudices and my darkest secrets, things I had never thought I'd tell anyone! How can two people who have never met, tell each other so much, I wonder? And it's not just a confessional. The issues we discuss range from Kosovo to Capitalism-versus-Socialism, to The Economy, to homosexuality, to religion – so many thoughts! I read the mail once more, this time more slowly, letting the words sink in. I have to reply sensibly if I want to sustain the e-friendship. That is part of the delight of course – writing to a mind that understands whatever you want to say. My heart skips a beat as I come to the final line: 'Oh, I forgot to tell you, I won't be writing for the next five days. I am going on a vacation with a few friends of mine. Take care till then.'

"Five days!" I exclaim dismayed. It seems like five years to me. Five more days of logging in and finding no new messages! It seems like torture. 'Why log in and be disappointed when you know he wouldn't be writing anyway?' argues one part of me rationally. But it has become a habit, a ritual, to wake up, to read his mail, to reply and maybe get an answer immediately and then write again. A day without a mail from him is terrible, but five whole days...I shudder! The day drags on with its innumerable details and at last it's time to sleep. This time I don't set the alarm, intending to drown my sorrow in sleep. I wake up the next morning, however, at 6 a.m., and though I try to sleep a little more, I fail miserably. As I toss and turn, my thoughts are focused on Raghu. 'Would he have reached his vacationing spot? What might he be doing? Would he even remember me at all?' I desperately want to check my mail but I don't want the heartache that I know will follow it. So I resist the impulse. The day passes away relatively quickly, because of a friend's wedding that I attend. I meet some old friends and we have a good time. Raghu doesn't enter my thoughts again till it's time to sleep once more, and then he doesn't leave my thoughts till the crack of dawn, when exhausted and confused, I finally fall asleep. I understand how drug addicts feel, for what do I feel, but an exalted addiction? The withdrawal symptoms are pretty painful though.

'I'd like to resume our discussion on love. Remember I told you once that it was possible and attainable?'

The remaining four days pass by, dragging on slowly as if they'd never end, till at last it's time for him to return. I go to sleep with a lighter heart and rise early as usual, with the alarm! I log in to find no mail, and I am devastated. How can this be? My thoughts race, searching for all possible alternatives. Could he have extended his vacation, did he fall sick, did his computer conk out? Everything except the possibility that he might have chosen not to write to me! I send an email asking him if he has returned and if he is well. It's torture again, waiting through the day, wishing the night would disappear and morning would come again. The reply arrives. Nothing dramatic: he writes that he had a good trip, and a whole lot of other trivia, which in no way relate to the relief in my heart. Yet the moment is something of an anticlimax.

I read on 'I'd like to resume our discussion on love. Remember I told you once that it was possible and attainable? You were the cynic then! Now I'd tend to agree with you. You know it's really funny, the way we think that it's the end of the world when we are in the midst of a crush. We think we cannot live without the other person and yet, most of the time, the situation demands that we must! And we do survive, and what seemed to be love becomes yet another illusion of love. And so on till we accumulate enough illusions to realize that that there is no place for the real thing. There is even no real thing!' I pause, unable to continue. Ringing in my mind are the words *yet another illusion.*

A Sigh to Remember

O. Jaantrik

A sigh of relief is not exactly a sigh *in* relief, but the difference is more than grammatical. One has to travel all the way to Otaru to appreciate the point.

Otaru is a smallish port located somewhere near the foot of Mount Tengu in the western coast of Hokkaido, óne of the coldest regions of the Japanese archipelago. The enchanting little town creeps steadily upwards from the harbour to the top of a mountain, where the Otaru University of Commerce perches, overlooking the magnificent Sea of Japan. During summer,

The resulting sleet then conspires with the incline of the city to transform a casual walk along the road into a gymnastic feat.

the weather in this part of the country is the closest thing to an earthly paradise. The winters, however, are long and cruel. Snowfall is a daily ritual and it falls not in flakes, but in heaps, often accompanied by rain. The resulting sleet then conspires with the incline of the city to transform a casual walk along the road into a gymnastic feat. Paradoxically therefore, the picturesquely serene township of Otaru has been nicknamed *jigoku-saka* or 'The Slide to Hell'!

I arrived there one lonely autumn with a visiting appointment in the University. Already the 'air' bit 'shrewdly', though I hardly noticed this, being more concerned about my ignorance of the Japanese language. Except for a handful of

O. Jaantrik was born and raised in Calcutta, India, and has been teaching economics in various corners of the world, but mostly India, since 1972. He received his Bachelor's and Master's degrees in India and Ph.D. in the US. He enjoys writing. He lives with his adorable wife wherever he happens to be and away from a charming US based son.

colleagues, few persons I came across spoke any English. Nevertheless, I had no choice other than English as a medium of instruction for my classes, which the students in their turn accepted with stoic indifference. The telltale lack of enthusiasm on their faces left little doubt about the futility of my teaching efforts. Each morning therefore, I plodded wearily up the road leading to the University, wondering if my situation was any different from that of a prisoner in solitary confinement.

This at least was the way I lived in Otaru till the arrival of the snow. One day though in early winter, a knock on the office door woke me up from morbid preoccupations with myself. I walked over and peeped out apprehensively. A smiling Japanese lad with a vaguely familiar face greeted me at the door and my surprise knew no bounds as he introduced himself to me in perfect English as a student in one of my classes! He wished to invite me he said, to a music performance by an amateur group. I accepted the invitation gratefully and counted on an evening of interaction with students.

I struggled down a slippery street on the appointed day and arrived at the theatre. My expectations were belied, however, for the young Japanese students who filled up the auditorium maintained a cautious distance from me. I resigned therefore to being the odd man out till the orchestra struck up the first few notes of the *Four Seasons* and all discomfort soon dissolved in the elixir of Vivaldi's creation.

Unfortunately, my involvement with the music grew feebler as we moved into the second of the four seasons. I had earlier treated myself to a few delicious cans of Sapporo beer, and these now made claims on my attention. Soon it was evident that I had no choice left but to take care of the problem. I sneaked out of the auditorium therefore and prowled along the empty corridors in search of the facilities. It was easy enough to locate them, but I found myself on the horns of a dilemma. The familiar pictographic aids of faceless entities, one sporting a Yul Bryner head and the other an over-starched skirt, were nowhere to be seen. In their place, two obscure inscriptions frowned menacingly down at me from adjacent doors. As I learnt to recognise much later, they were the Chinese characters for man and woman!

The emergency of the circumstance dictated a random selection. Without further ado therefore, I swiftly walked in through one of the doors, only to discover that I had committed a blunder. But the coast being clear and further delays being unbearable, there was no point fleeing. I rushed into the nearest enclosure I found and locked myself in. And then set out to heave a luxurious sigh of relief.

The sigh alas (though fortunately not the relief) was cut mercilessly short by the sound of approaching footsteps, followed by the incomprehensible chatter of a million feminine voices. My entry into the prohibited zone had obviously coincided with the Intermission. Leaving out the dubious case of Mrs. Doubt-fire, there are perhaps two classes of middle-aged males who are likely to show up in the Ladies' Room of a public building: the pervert and the unwitting. But a man in the Ladies' Room being a *man* in the Ladies' Room, members of the fair sex are not expected to verify his motives before calling in the police. And the Japanese police being *Japanese*, I would in turn be forced to present my case in pantomime! A Herculean absurdity, to say the least.

The only solution seemed to lie in a *deus ex machina*, for which I prayed fervently. When suddenly, a bell rang out. My heart jumped twice, first in alarm, apprehending the arrival of the Law, but the second time in pleasure, recognising the bell to be an answer to my prayer. The scuffle of feet, attended by a tone of urgency in the voices, signalled unmistakably that Recess was over. I heard the ladies leave in crowded confusion, their animated conversation gradually fading into the distance, till total silence reigned once again. I opened the door a chink and peered as well as I could to check if there were human traces in the vicinity. Once assured, I strode into the corridor and slipped quietly out of the fateful building. Thereafter, throwing all caution to the winds, I walked, trotted, cantered and finally galloped along the dreaded *jigoku-saka*, defying the icy surface of the steeply rising street. And I stopped only when I had put in several hundred metres between the theatre and me.

Then, leaning heavily against a roadside tree, I let out the sigh of a lifetime, *in* utter relief.

Neruda's Head

Desiensus Mobilus

This afternoon, here in this desert heat,
at this languid moment
when punctuation dies on my paper,
half-awake from a siesta
(*this heat, glasses of lemonade*),
I see Neruda's head looking at me in askance from
across the room with his flint-sheer eyes.
Resting uneasily on the window sill,
now breaking into a smile,
wobbling about on an imaginary axis,
showing off the blood-red hollow circle of
human flesh where the torso was once joined
(in motions, reactions and endless ailments).
"I have been lucky," he growls,
not paying any attention to my discomfort.
"At least I kept my head," he chuckles.
As a cemetery smell fills the room, I choke.
"Think of the heads that died screaming;
who were tortured or blinded, or
ended on a saber's edge for speaking their mind."
My ears reverberate in an uneasy echo.

Desiensus Mobilus grew up in the clamorous and noisome environs of Bombay where he learned to survive the big city by walking around aimlessly and by giving himself up completely to passionate and impulsive reading. After a perilous and stressful attempt to endure formal education at various places, he drifts around the US, working and living. When he gets time, he dabbles in various trivial pursuits, such as travelling and reading:

Pushing away childhood nightmares,
I check my Agnostic's clock.
The satin pillowcase tickled,
the sleep's season lost
I stretched myself to the oblivion of reality.
The window stayed opened to the empty world,
still bearing the moist marks of human flesh.

Train Window Bars

Apurva Mishra

On hot summer days, when you grip them tight, your hands come away with that peculiar smell – a mixture of rusted metal, diesel fumes, and human sweat – which is the smell of the Railways itself.

At night, you lie down and rest your feet on them, to be kissed by the cool moist night air. After it rains, each drop of water clinging to their undersides reveals a tiny, perfectly inverted picture of the landscape.

> *At night, you lie down and rest your feet on them, to be kissed by the cool moist night air.*

They are wide enough apart to permit the passage of a cup of tea, cone of peanuts, or the thickest tome of best-selling pulp fiction you can buy on the platform, but too close together to allow your gray Milton water-bottle with the broken strap.

Beggars standing outside (blind, deformed, young, old) hang on to them, as if that will make your shifting eyes meet their steady gaze.

You stick your arms out through them when your parents aren't looking. You press your forehead hard against them to better see people working, relaxing, bathing, defecating, or whatever else takes your voyeuristic fancy.

And you, you urban middle-class, convent-school kid, finally realize that this fragmented view, looking through these

Apurva Mishra was born in Pune and grew up in Ranchi, India.. He received a bachelors degree in electrical engineering from IIT Bombay and a masters in computer systems engineering from Boston University. He now lives in Portland, USA, and helps design computer processor chips for a living. His writing interests include poetry and short stories.

bars, is the only way you have ever really seen your country.

Taxi Wallah

Numair A. Choudhury

I am in the front now, pressing against the metal fence that separates us from the arriving passengers. Damp chests shove me from behind as arms snake their way around somehow. Loud and desperate voices grate my ears as I press back, sidling my way to the glass doors. Six passengers remain, guarded by disinterested *ansars*. Stickers on their tightly clutched suitcases tell me that they are from the six o'clock

"Sir, shaheeeb, whatever you wish. Up to you, I ask for nothing, no shaheb, nothing. Please sir, come, come."

Singapore Airlines' flight. From America, via London and Abu Dhabi. They stare at us, shocked, tired, and frustrated. I gesture and yell for several minutes before attracting any attention. "You," his voice cricks, "How much to Purbani?"

I leap forward. "Purbani Hotel? No proble*m, shaheb*," I nod, smiling, assuring, hands reaching for his luggage. "My taxi nice, air conditioned," I lie. Others step between us: scooter-*wallahs*, beggars, porters, and pickpockets.

He pulls his cases back a little "How much? *Koto, koto,* tell me first!"

"Sir, *shaheb*, whatever you wish. Up to you, I ask for nothing, no *shaheb*, nothing. Please sir, come, come." I manage to curl fingers around a plastic *Samsonite* handle and pull gently. He lets go.

Numair A. Choudhury was born in Bangladesh in 1975. He has studied and loved creative writing in Oberlin, Ohio and then at the University of East Anglia in Norwich, UK. He is currently in Bangladesh working in rural development and finishing his first novel. Numair is soon to enroll for a Ph.D. in literature, most probably in Upstate New York.

In the car he talks a little. "Where does the city hide its secrets?" he smiles. He has been to Dhaka before, but purely for business. This time he will have a week to spare. I look him over, trying to guess what he likes, what he can afford. Mid-thirties, quite carefree. Obviously not too wealthy or important: he was not met at the airport, but he possessed a certain breadth of vision; a length of stride that is not characteristic of the poor. Dhaka Museum? Snake charmers? Dance parties? Maybe handicraft stores, the Lal Bagh Fort? Angel dust? It is always hard to tell.

"I want to watch a Bengali movie. In one of those big cinemas where everybody goes."

"What kind of movie sir? Action movie? Good dancing, lots of fighting. Bruce Lee. We have James Bond also if you want English. *Goldeneye?*"

"No, no. A Bengali one; action sounds fine."

"I will show you where to go sir, no problem. Close to hotel."

I am glad I can help him with what he wants. We have all kinds of movies showing. Even if he wants the latest pirated copies, I can find him those that come in from Malaysia; filmed at theaters, they are full of another audience's shadows and sounds. If he wants adult films, we can go to Old Dhaka, where young, nervous boys fill dark rooms. I would do all this for him, but I have my limits. There are things I refuse. My friends cannot understand this. "If not you, Mintu, then it will be the next guy. They will get what they want, so make your share! If they want English Road, take them. So what if they want body parts? It is for medicine. Or stolen Durgas? Why does it matter to you, you are not Hindu? It is good money."

When I was young, I too thought like that. I was hard and angry. I could walk away from any face, no matter how full of pain, sadness or pleading. I could close my eyes to children who were being sold by the night. Or to those whose limbs were trimmed so they could beg – those who soon lost their trueborn smiles. I could stare unblinkingly at the starving who sat outside the *mosjid*; those who were not with us any more, not men or women now, but expressionless skin and bone. I could push torn women, who were crawling from their husbands' blows, out of my path when necessary, or step around heroin addicts who were bleeding to death. I was angry then, I did not see the people under all the filth. Nothing mattered because there was so much that did.

I made money though. Hard cash, every bit of it a reward for my indifference. But, soon I found that I became indifferent to *myself*, that I would not accept my own need to laugh, to cry, to release my breath and take in everything outside that was already a part of me. I became a shell, like the starving ones. But, things are different now. I am not sure what changed me. I know it happened when I went to visit my mother in the village before she died. Maybe it was what she said about my eyes.

> *I made money though. Hard cash, every bit of it a reward for my indifference.*

She said that they reflected like dirty water, hiding the insides, not letting light through. Or, maybe it was the quiet peace of the country that made my frustrations spill out; the limp coolness of the mango grove, the warm softness of the ground. Maybe it was meeting Sokina. But I began to feel sick. When I tried to sleep, all the faces I had ignored came back to me. I thought my mind would heal itself if I stayed away. But they kept reappearing, night after night. So, I knew I would have to return to Dhaka.

And I did, with Sokina as my wife. And I still drive my taxi. But I am so much softer. The faces do not come in dreams any more, they speak to me everyday. I am no longer distant from the streets. I listen. I blink. Because I have my own children now and like anyone who has held a newborn and let its weight sink into their arms, I know there must be a way out of what we are doing. At times I am still hard. With passengers who try to take me back to where I was, with my friends who still go there. Even so I am one of the in-between people, neither here nor there. Because I do not know any other way, I have found nowhere else to place myself. And as I am softer, I get pressed against the glass. I am still learning how to push back.

People like me make the foreigners comfortable. We are in the crowd at the airport, in the groups of men that stand outside hotels, restaurants, talking to the guards. We are at all tourist spots. We work in the embassies; we sit at cigarette stalls outside expatriate clubs. We are the ricksha*wallahs* idling near the bazaar, the *darwans* who always seem to sleep. We are everywhere, night and day, the painted eyes that everyone else closes.

Even the children feel it. I remember only a few days ago, when I was speeding a customer somewhere, I took a short cut through a side street in Dhanmondi. There was a field here, full of mischief in blue and white uniforms from the school nearby. They were playing football, *kabadi*, hopscotch and marbles. They were laughing, singing, running in pointless directions. Many were on the road, jostling each other about while they delayed going home. I kept my horn pressed down and they jumped aside, chuckling with the excitement of imagined danger. But then, there was this boy, of ten years or so, who was walking quietly with his friends. And as I rushed by with my horn, he spun about to face me. While he turned in one liquid motion, his right arm flung a *rajani-gondha* at my windshield. It flew at me,

Often, when I pass the kajol-eyed with untied hair, bargaining with their men, I am certain one of them is her.

landing on the glass, dead in front of my face. For an instant, for the slightest fraction of time that it takes a thought to form, I did not see it as a flower, and a shudder passed through me. I had been scared. This was the gentlest of reproaches, one from the children. But how many years would it take to turn them to rock?

As we speed away from the airport, the green and gold of grass and paddy gives way to the deep red of brick rubble on which shopping centers stand. They proudly display anything from imported lingerie to Sony stereos. All contraband though, as if impatient smugglers could not wait long after exiting *Arrivals* to peddle their wares. These shops are rarely raided – they are owned by politicians or bureaucrats. There are also restaurants in the complexes, catering to those too hungry to wait for the city. The majority of them make their money by selling black-market liquor. They pay the police dearly for this illegitimate right.

Behind the shopping centers, a little into the developing residential areas, there are slums – the *bosthis*. This is where the frustration and corruption from the commercial complexes hides its face. In the shanties that will be torn apart by the monsoons and overzealous *sepoys* (only to be rebuilt days later); in the naked infants with distended bellies, playing, screaming and in their mothers, the third or fourth wives of drunken laborers who will flee in times of particular hardship. But, none of this will interest my passenger, all this is a part of our world, one he will never have to touch.

The traffic thickens as we approach Gulshan. The air inside the car is very heavy now, its humidity weighed down by the black clouds of smoke that pour from buses and trucks.

"Where's your air-conditioning?"

I fidget with the controls, pretending exasperation at a sudden betrayal, "Sorry sir, it is strangely not working."

He sighs and moves closer to the tiny fan that rattles above the window. "What kind of a hotel is Purbani? Four star, right?"

"Oh yes sir, Purbani is super nice. Swimming pool, health club, big bar and restaurant. But, Sonargaon better *shaheb*, Sheraton also. But high price. Four thousand *taka* a night for single."

"Whoa," he laughs. "That's more than I'm willing to pay."

But there are many who pay easily. They are the businessmen with their briefcases full of projects and plans, full of tricks. They bring money with them, set up more factories and buy things needed in other countries. My daughter Alia works in a sewing house. I have a cousin there who can keep an eye on her and make sure the *dalals* stay away. She is lucky to find such good work. It is much better than other factories I have been to, with hundreds of women hidden in layers like rotten vegetables. The pay is little, but it helps. She comes home right after the evening *Azan*, like all good daughters should. Sometimes I think goodness is not a thing we can control. Alia will eventually be the person she was born. Now, she is at a dangerous age. But then all ages are dangerous for women in the city. Often, when I pass the *kajol-*eyed with untied hair, bargaining with their men, I am certain one of them is her.

Gulshan is a pretty place. It is where the diplomats and the new rich of the country live. *Gulshan* means flower garden and the name is appropriate for most of it, that is, the parts that you can see from the main road. Deep breaths and movements in the back seat tell me that the cement houses have not failed to impress. Most of them are painted white; they have tall pillars and decorated entrances with guardhouses.

Villagers who make it here find it difficult to believe they are in the same country. I once drove three men from Ramna station to a house on Road 50. It belongs to a man who owns tea gardens. Two of the men were his workers; the third had just arrived from Pabna with something. It was his first time in Dhaka. Whatever he carried must have been important for them to use me, instead of taking a bus or scooter. The villager was nervous from the start, but once we left the ugliness of center city behind and entered Banani, he became terrified, clutching onto the car seat, finally refusing to leave the taxi once we reached the house. He kept repeating, "What will happen here? What will happen here?" as if all his expectations had changed.

"Is this where the American Club is? Nearby?"

"Yes sir, we are close. Nice club sir, you have been to it?" I respond.

"Yes, for dinner on my last trip. I remember this area though, beautifully laid out."

But I wonder how much he has seen. There is a quiet world that passes him by.

There are also *bosthis* here in beautiful Gulshan. High walls, barbed and guarded, separate their urine reek from the sweeter scent of opulence. On one side there are flimsy bamboo huts, covered with sheets of plastic and on the other, there are brick mansions crested with hand made shingles. Even those from the city know only a little of what lies within the rich walls. My passenger will find his way into one of these houses soon – his week will take him many places.

I can tell that my **Shaheb** *has lost interest in the drive as he sinks into the seat. He cannot smell the aroma from the fryers at the* **misti** *stalls.*

We leave Gulshan to enter Moakhali. I live here. There are many more factories and *bosthis* in Moakhali. To the visitor's eye, it may be all stench and ugliness, but there is a lot that speaks to us. I can tell that my *Shaheb* has lost interest in the drive as he sinks into the seat. He cannot smell the aroma from the fryers at the *misti* stalls or hear the music shops playing their newest cassettes. Nor can he see the balloon*wallah* sitting in the shade, knotting his wares into the ludicrous shapes that will delight his young customers. The bright green and red of the *amra* sellers fails to affect him, just as the juicy attraction of the *paan* stands.

We pass the restaurant where I will have my dinner. There will be friends to sit and talk with, to exchange the day's stories with. Sokina leaves messages with them sometimes. Usually a thing I should buy, or a problem with the children I need to know about. My sons Kamal and Tupu need a lot of watching. They are eight and twelve, but have learned the cunning of men already. Both go to school – it does not seem to have taught them much. Yes, they have memorized their *suras*, but what they need to know for their day-to-day living, they have picked up off the streets. Along with a handful of dirt. I wish they were not growing up here, already they are small *mastans*, controlling the local cricket patch; planning fights against boys in the neighborhood buildings. I can see them when they are older, running with the hoodlums, trying to find a quick way to make money, but only making trouble. Sometimes I feel that my mind will only rest when I leave Dhaka. But that failed.

Soon, we are near Purbani. I point him to the nearest theater. Stopping at the hotel I ask him, "Why was nobody at the airport for you?" It was not wise, him being white and alone in the city. Or, anywhere in our country for that matter. But, in the city he will be cheated and pestered. Disturbed a lot.

"I know," he says. "Won't be doing that again. Some of you guys really know how to harass us."

I smile. And bargain a little.

Subbian Govindaraj, Where Are You?

Satya Prabhakar

Prologue: *The year was 1985. It was the best of times; it was the fairly OK of times. It was the age of the communist collapse; it was the age of Sridevi at the top. It was the age of Vespa scooters arriving in India; it was the age of Priya pickles going global. It was the age of NTR taking up* sanyas *(and then changing his mind to marry a young woman); it was the age of Ambanis and their love for Tina Munim. It was, as always, the age of fiery summers and fond, freaky monsoons in India. It was the age of the beloved (few) and that of the reviled (many). It was, as it always seems to be in India, the age of blinking hope mingled with remarkable resilience. It was the age of 'just the same.' Yet, change was around the corner.*

In that age of the momentous and the trivial, I found my way to America, armed with an ugly moustache, two pairs of Bata shoes, my mom's pickles and papads, a suit, and an offer of an assistantship. My seniors helped me settle down comfortably, hitching me up with an interesting roommate: let's call him Dhurandhar Bhattodia. When it came to understanding the American

> **The year was 1985. It was the best of times; it was the fairly OK of times. It was the age of the communist collapse; it was the age of Sridevi at the top.**

Satya Prabhakar is from Machilipatnam, Andhra Pradesh, where men are given to life, liberty and the happiness of pursuit. He got his BE from REC Trichy; MS and MBA from Univ. of Florida. He now leads Smart Information Worldwide, Inc. (Chennai, India and Austin, US) of which Sulekha.com is a part. He is married to Sangeeta Kshettry; they have two daughters Divya and Priya. His interests include writing, investing, eastern philosophy, tennis, chess and Kamal Haasan movies.

System, Dhurandhar was the most evolved. He knew that a 2-liter Coke bottle cost less in K-Mart than in Food-4-Less; that it's cheaper to get a roll of film processed by mail order; that it's better to order two 2-large pizza combos than one favorite-four special. Dhurandhar was the *desi* clearinghouse of all information pertaining to low-rent commerce in the hamlet of Gainesville. And he was a terrific buddy. He was kind, gentle and helpful when you dealt with him one-on-one. It's when he found himself in a group that a miraculous and somewhat scary transformation occurred: he insisted on being funny and he insisted everybody liked him. Further, he reveled in reciting Ajit *phattas* and singing Hemant Kumar songs. But, don't you agree, there's only so much of Ajit and Hemant a person can consume before the tummy starts to hurt? But this much I can say: Dhurandhar, for all his quirks, was a good man and we shall not look upon his like again. He introduced me to football by taking me to my first Gator football game.

Football is like religion in Gainesville, the home of the Fightin' Gators. Of course, it's lot more fun than religion. The whisper went that there was an Alachua county ordinance that made the absence of a Gator bumper sticker on any vehicle a misdemeanor, punishable by a fine of up to $250. So, I paid $2.50 to get a sticker that said 'Human by birth and a Gator by the grace of God!' for my $28 used bicycle. It didn't fit properly, but, I reasoned, why mess with the law? None of us Indians really understood football. All we knew was: 1. A team has four chances to cover 10 yards to get another four chances, 2. A team should move in the general direction of the opponent's end zone, 3. A touchdown is worth 7 points, most of the time. 4. The cheerleader girls, God bless their micro-skirts, are often more exciting than a successful 80-yard *Hail Mary!* pass.

Even though one didn't have to know a lot about football to enjoy it, we Indians suffered from this deep, gnawing fear that a sultry gal – say, Heather – sitting next to us in the stadium bleachers might turn to us, flip her lustrous auburn hair back, flash a stunning smile and ask innocently, "3rd and 5 on the 30.

What do you think is the best play now?" Indian men in America are, in general, pretty cool chaps; what they cannot suffer gracefully, however, is their knowledge being questioned and their ignorance exposed. We *desi* men of Gainesville wore the right orange-and-blue T-shirts, did the wave when it was time, chanted the slogans with ferocity and read the sports section religiously without even knowing what a Shotgun formation was. When it came to football, an external exuberance masked an internal, debilitating intellectual vacuum. And Heather's imagined query continued to haunt us and chip away at our fragile macho self-esteem.

Enter Subbian Govindaraj. A 6-year Gator veteran, Govindaraj exuded an inspiring, knowing, confident charisma and an unimpeachable belief in, and love for, the Gators. We felt so happy imagining gutsy Govindaraj's reaction to hot Heather: without even looking at her, he would reply calmly after a few moments of deep reflection, "Given that it's the fourth quarter and the defense is a bit tired, I think a play-action handoff to the tailback for a run around the right defensive end should get us the yards for a first down. When you are ahead in a game that is drawing to a close, you should always run the ball." With Heather looking dreamily at him, marveling at this rare combination of Machiavellian cunning, Socratic wisdom and Sampratic (after Pete Sampras) poise. Yessir, he sure knew what a *Shotgun* was!

When it came to football, an external exuberance masked an internal, debilitating intellectual vacuum. And Heather's imagined query continued to haunt us and chip away at our fragile macho self-esteem.

We junior *desis* swarmed around him as he held forth on 'why our beloved Gators shall win the next ball game'. He never ever betrayed even the tiniest doubt when it came to our Gators. "Our defensive depth is far superior." "Gators are coming off an easy weekend with few injuries." "Their coach is a new fellow with no experience." "Our offensive coordinator does well on road games in November." He knew everything and everything he knew foretold a Gator victory. Even if the Gators had lost the last three games in a row. "They learned valuable lessons in their last game against Ole Miss and will cut down on the penalties." No matter what, the Gators will win the next game. The rest of us unschooled minions sat transfixed by this transcendent wisdom and concealed moxie, and our hearts believed the resident *Desi Sage of Sport*, even as our minds were strongly advising us against it.

But the reason I am writing this article is not to talk about football or cheerleader cuties. It is to take care of some unfinished personal business. You see, when Govindaraj left Gainesville, he bequeathed unto me an automobile – a sprawling, lumbering 1969 Chevrolet *Caprice* – for a ridiculously small sum of $200, battery included. Don Govindaraj topped even that kindness by saying that I could pay him later when I get a job. An offer I couldn't refuse! So, I took possession of the vehicle and it was one of the happiest days of my life: I got a car and I cruised the mean streets of Gainesville even as my fellow *desis* in full-sleeved dress shirts struggled uphill on their skimpy bikes.

The rest of us unschooled minions sat transfixed by this transcendent wisdom and concealed moxie.

And that car helped me get my girl! One night I offered to drop off this girl at her apartment in the dead vast and middle of the night, because I was the only fellow in that small society with a car. Unbeknownst to this alluring beauty, I was madly in love with her but could not, until then, get myself to prosecute the romance in any meaningful manner other than to eye her covertly and covetously. But, you see, a big car breathes confidence into a timid fellow and inspires him to a greater glory. As we sat in this 85 square-foot Caprice interior, I summoned my courage and delivered the finest oration I was capable of. I don't want to bore you with a full transcript of my speech here, but it ended with this ardent plea: "Give me a chance, one chance. That's all I ask of you. What do you have to lose?" I thought I nailed it good, but my impassioned speech that night got some noncommittal gibberish in response. The prosecution persevered, and we got married some 18 months later. Who says women don't fall for men with big, sexy cars, ha?

But misfortune was just turning the corner with me in its crosshairs. I ain't one to look a gift horse in the mouth, but Subbian Govindaraj – *may God's mercy drizzle kindly upon him* – did me a grievous wrong. When he handed me the car keys, he failed to mention that the car needed to have its oil reserves replenished on occasion. All I thought a car needed was gasoline and a 'new car' fragrance stick hanging from the rearview mirror. So, I drove and drove and drove for close to eight months without even knowing that the giant under my command was thirsting for lubrication. Until one day, the brown *1969 Chevrolet Caprice SE* came to a resolute halt and refused to move an inch further. I was the Shakespearean beggar who, when mounted, runs his horse to death. A friend of mine, Jack Stranton, examined it and concluded that it was beyond repair and ought to be put to sleep. A towing company unceremoniously hauled away my Romantic Roadster. I still have the registration form of my first car.

Even more unfortunate was that I lost contact with Subbian Govindaraj after he left Gainesville. I owe him US $200 and there's a check waiting in my home with his name on it. And I want to hear him discourse on Gators' prospects this coming year.

Subbian Govindaraj, where are you?

Epilogue: Subbian Govindaraj is the real name of this person I am looking for. If you know of a Subbian Govindaraj who graduated from Florida in 1987, please let him know there's a fella known as 'Becker' looking for him and he's got two honeybees coming his way.

Listen to the Background Music

Venkatesh G. Rao

Listen.

Sa ri – ni Sa ga ma Pa dha Pa – dha ni Så
Så ni Dha ni dha Pa dha Ma ma ga Ri ga Sa ri Sa

Sindhu Bhairavi. Often I wake up to it. I wish I could sing it. Mornings are difficult times. Another day, you think, will things be different today? *Sindhu Bhairavi* helps. It tells you what you need to hear. Nothing really matters.
Cereal, shower, bus.

Summer is breaking out in a riot of cool pastel tank tops and deliciously short skirts.

Yeh haseen wadiyan, yeh khula aasman,
aa gaye hum kahan, yeh mere saajana

I wonder what I would do without Hindi film songs. Seriously.
I started out to write about being adrift with nowhere in particular to go. About missing, not home, people, but purpose. About where I am supposed to be going. I think I'll write, instead, about why it doesn't matter.

Venkatesh G. Rao works for Sulekha in Austin, TX, having found his way there from squealing babyhood in Jamshedpur and through angsty years of engineering at IIT Bombay and the University of Michigan. He has an incomplete Ph.D. waiting in Michigan and hopes to actually complete it someday.

Musafir hoon yaaron, na ghar hai, na thikana,
mujhe chalte jaana hai,
bas, chalte jaana...

America, land of sophisticated shades of emotion that evolved human beings live through. I cut a slightly comical figure here. I was listening to an old Lata Mangeshkar tape and stirring the *sambar* last night. My American housemate sauntered in,
   "That stuff sounds incredibly cheesy, not like the classical stuff you usually listen to."

Kahin deep jale, kahin dil,
teri kaun si hai manzil?

You know what? It's true. You can't be an urbane sophisticate and love Hindi film music at the same time. Oddly enough, the lyrics, which sound incredibly inane, mushy and artificial when translated into English, sound perfectly natural in Hindi and Urdu. Clear-cut, stylized fragments of emotion that appeal to the simplicity in you.

Sa Re Ga Ma; Ma Sa Re Ga; Ga Sa Re Ma; Ma Ga Re Sa
Geet pehle bana tha...ya bani thi yeh sargam?

Clip-clop clip-clop. The sensation of light sneakers on my feet, after a Michigan winter of heavy leather boots, is exhilarating. All girls are beautiful today. Really. Here comes one now, soft cotton, purposeful walk, coffee mug, backpack, earnest look. I fall in love fourteen times on my way to work. I arrive at the department still single. I am not heartbroken though.

Maana ho tum, behad haseen
waise bure, hum bhi nahin.
Dekho kabhi to, pya-aar se...

They keep me going, these songs. A reassuring, familiar soundscape in my head. You can't really take loneliness seriously if you have the right music in your head.

Wahan kaun hai tera, musafir, jayega kahan....

Up with Prozac, asleep with Valium. In some ways we are less complicated than we like to admit. Artificial, mushy, clichéd, yes. But these simple songs can control my moods.

Ruk jaana nahin, tu kahin haar ke
kaanto pe chalke milenge saaye bahaar ke.
O raahi, O raahi; O raahi O raahi

Or rather, I use them to control my moods.

I lean back in my nice American swivel chair, four lab reports graded in one hour. Need coffee. At the coffee machine I bump into one of the many girls I am secretly in love with,
"Hi, how's it going?"
"Just great, how about you?"
"Great!"
"See ya."
Sigh!

Bekaraar kar ke humme yoon na jaiye,
aap ko, hamari kasam, laut aaiye.

I live in strange times. My world is an odd world, a toy world. A world born of memories of a time when I did not make the distinction, *This is me, that is the world.* A time when I plugged neatly into the landscape.

Koyal kooke, koo-hoo gaaye,
yaadon ki bandook chalaye.
Baagon mein phoolon ka mausam wapas aaya re,
ghar aa ja pardesi tera des bulaye re.

I can never go back, not really. Once you break loose from a context, you can never define yourself relative to the outside world again. The Existentialists knew what they were talking about. Win some, lose some. I can still recapture snatches of unconsciousness though.

Ha...ay, neele gagan ke tale,
dharti ka pyar pale.
Aise hi jag mein, aate hain subahen,
aise hi shaam dhale

Spring sunset. I walk more slowly now. Another day, nothing much happened. Direction, purpose – they don't really matter at times like this when I am at peace with the world and myself. All around me, on State Street, there are relaxed faces. Some laughing gangs of high school kids, couples sauntering slowly up the sidewalk, absorbed in each other. Some oncoming pretty faces glance curiously at me. Pretty girls are surprised when men are occasionally too absorbed to steal a quick glance.

Kahin door jab din dhal jaye,
saanjh ki dulhan, badan churaye,
chupke se aaye,

Songs of contentment. Perfect company for the alone and idle.

I plop down in front of the TV with a slice of potpie. Hot and delicious. A housemate is watching *The Brady Bunch.*

"What's this show about?"

A shocked American face.

"You haven't seen *The Brady bunch*? Oh DUDE! It's like, this CLASSIC show..."

I like Americans. They are so happy and contented with their world, you can't help feeling more lighthearted when they are around. It must be good to grow up in a place where misery comes to you through CNN, where flipping the channel is all you need to do to make the world completely beautiful. Do you remember, the time when you used to get off your 6:05 local in Bombay, and hurry through crowds, efficiently avoiding outstretched brown arms and pleading eyes? How you used to retreat gratefully into your home, where drawn curtains and beautiful people on Californian beaches streaming in through the TV could make the world beautiful for a while?

The windows are open here, and I can watch pretty girls jog by, on their eternal quest for the ultimate body. We watch TV for a while. It is dull, but not annoying enough to make either of us reach for the remote. She tells me about her day and the little intrigues of her workplace. I tell her that a friend of mine just got back from a vacation in India with a wife in tow. She is amazed, confounded and very American.

"You mean, guys, like, just go back....pick up a bride and...?"

"Yup."

"So, like, all you guys come over here to study and work, and like, the women stay back, and then you go back and get married?"

"Yup."

"Man, that must suck..."

She is very polite, very American and careful not to offend. She doesn't add the obvious comment, "Man, you guys need to get a LIFE!"

Maybe lady, maybe. But don't blame me if I don't know how to live. I didn't ask to be born.

Kurt Vonnegut thought up that protest. An uncharacteristically fatalistic thought for an American. You know what he needed? Simple really, he needed my music, my soundscapes.

Hum na samjhhe the,
baat itni si-
khwab sheeshe ke,
duniya pathar ki,

Can you be really unhappy when you can sing that in the shower?

So, shower and sleep.

Sulekha Reader Comments

Krishnan: A very nice attitude to life.

I occasionally relapse into this kind of a state ...when deadlines are catching up faster than I hate to admit, and things are way over my head and a 101 impending tasks are begging my attention...a good dose of Kishore and Asha lends a totally different perspective.

"C- A- T cat , cat maane billi..." – such a silly, insanely stupid song, but it makes me feel so lightheaded!

"pilaoon murgi ke murgi ke ande hi ande, aana meri jaan meri jaan Sunday ke Sunday!" - nothing beats this old-time senseless classic.

Hindi songs are hypercool!

Nice job, Venkatesh.

Unwanted

Esther Lyons

Unwanted is my autobiography. I was born in Calcutta in 1940. I have memories of living in Saharanpore when I must have been just three and half. My sister was born there. I remember my father, a tall, handsome man with blue eyes, dark hair, and very white-skinned. I remember sitting in his lap and eating my breakfast of toast and fried egg. I loved him very much. He was seldom at home. My mother said he was a very busy man and that his work kept him out of the house most of the time. I especially remember one day, when he was leaving, I don't know why I clung to him. I had a terrible feeling that he would never return.

> **I specially remember one day when he (my papa) was leaving, I don't know why I clung to him. I had a terrible feeling that he would never return again.**

I do remember his voice calling out to my mother and saying in perfect Hindi, "Agnes, *isko ley jao* (take her away)." My mother, a beautiful lady in a *sari*, forcibly took me off his lap even though I was crying and clinging to my dear Papa. I could not stop him in spite of the strong intuition I had. My Papa never came home again. I waited for his return everyday. Then one day, I must have been about five or six then, a man in a dark suit came with my mother and my Uncle to see me, while I was busy playing out in the front yard. I was sure he was my father and I called out to him with joy, "Papa!"

"He is a *dost,* not your father. He is a very special *dost.*" Uncle said.

Esther Lyons was born in Calcutta and now lives in Australia. Unwanted is her autobiography.

I looked at my mother, questioning, and she said nothing. My petite and beautiful mother stood aside in silence. She looked very calm and yet sad. That man visited our house a few times before he disappeared forever. I was sure he was my father but they all refused to accept it.

In 1947, just before the partition and the Hindu-Muslim riots, we moved to Kalimpong in West Bengal. I remember I was very upset because I was worried about my father. I wondered how he would find us when he returned, but no one seemed to care. No one wanted to speak about him any more.

I remember being put into a boarding school at a very expensive convent run by the Loretto foreign nuns in Kalimpong, during the school holidays. I was only eight years old then. I hated it. No one came to visit me from home for a long time. I worried about my mother and my little sister, Violet. She was born in 1944 in Saharanpore. One day, after a fortnight's stay at the school, during which I spent most of my time crying, I managed to run out of the convent gates, all the way through narrow, hilly pathways to the house where we lived. I found my aunt sitting near the window, having breakfast. She too wore a *sari* like my mother. She had her own two children. Her husband, Uncle Eddy, was fair but not as white as my Papa.

Aunty was happy to see me. She informed me that my mother and sister had left for Muzaffarpore, where Father O'Brien, a Jesuit American priest, was going to send my sister, Violet, for adoption to his sister in America. I was heartbroken. Aunty was also going to leave Kalimpong for her relatives home in Bettiah, Bihar, in a week's time. "Please take me with you Aunty," I cried, "Don't leave me over here; please."

"Your mother has put you into this expensive convent, so you can be sent to America for adoption. The Jesuit Bishop of Patna wants her to do so," Aunt said with tears in her eyes. "I don't know how she can part with her children."

Somehow I managed to stay with Aunty and her daughter. We traveled to Bettiah together. A week later my mother came to collect me, and we went to live in Mirzapur for a few months. My sister, Violet, was with her. She could not manage to part with her and was happy to have me back. I watched her cry one day, saying to the parish priest of the Catholic church there, "Father, I cannot part with my children. I love them very much. Please employ me as a teacher in your Catholic school over here. I will bring them up myself. I don't care if Mino has forgotten them and his responsibilities."

"Sorry Agnes, I cannot employ you in my school even though I know that you are a good, trained teacher. The Bishop of Patna wants you to send your children away, and for you to start a new life without the children. That boarding school was good for Minnie, she would have had a good future in America as an adopted child. But now the only thing he wants me to offer you is a place for both of your daughters at St. Philomena's Orphanage at

To me piya meant my father who had forgotten to return...

Jhansi. Take them there and start your own life Agnes. The children will survive, you have to take care of yourself," Father O'Brien advised my mother, while she sobbed and I stood in the corner, listening.

A week later we were on the train bound for Jhansi. I was very upset and kept singing songs which made me cry – *humme chodh piya kis des gaye...piya laut ke aana bhool gaye.* (Where did my beloved go, leaving us behind? He has forgotten to return to us.) To me *piya* meant my father who had forgotten to return, and this my favourite song whenever I thought of my father.

We had a very hard time in the orphanage, where the two of us had to sleep on the floor, wear no shoes and eat *chappati* cooked once a week and kept in the wooden box, with spinach *saag*. I begged my mother to take us back. "Jesus will take care of us Mum, please trust him and keep us with you please, don't leave us here. I cannot stay without you." I cried, and so my mother again took us out of the orphanage and we traveled towards Allahabad. Aunt and Uncle Eddy were to meet us there. They had received my mother's letter and were going to keep us while Mum was to train and become a nurse to support us.

Unfortunately when we reached Allahabad they had not arrived and again we were without a home. Mum took us to the Catholic Church on Thornhill Road, Allahabad, and asked the parish Priest, Father De'Mello, for help. "Sorry I have no place for a stranger with two fair children," he said, handing Mum ten rupees, "Take this and find yourself some place. I cannot trust any strangers."

I remember walking the hot streets in Allahabad in the month of June. Anyway we did manage to grow up in Allahabad and attended the English convent school, St Mary's. My mother could only become the midwife nurse at Kamala Nehru Memorial Hospital.

In 1956 when I was sixteen years of age I came across some papers in Uncle Eddy's box which disclosed to me the fact that my father was a Jesuit American priest who was not given dispensation to marry and live with my mother, even after she had borne two of his children. He was given dispensation to work for the US Government though, and also had a role in the Central Intelligence Agency, while he remained a priest. He was to find radioactive ore, Beryllium, from Bihar and the sands of Travancore in the south, and collect it to be shipped to the US. Just before India got independence in 1947, he returned to the US. The Jesuits and the Bishop of Patna, knew it all and were the ones to accept his dispensation for the government work, but did not want to know about his children. Like many Anglo-Indians, we were to be adopted out or put into an orphanage.

In 1965 I managed to visit the US with the 'Experiment in International Living' scheme from Lucknow, and was able to find my father after 22 years. His voice, which I had last heard in 1944, helped me find him. He lived in Denver, a fat, bald man with the same blue eyes. He had a mine in his backyard where he mined Beryllium, which he supplied to the Atomic Power Station nearby. He had the dispensation to live with an American woman as his wife. He was still working for the government and had an FBI file as well as a role in the Central Intelligence Agency. I came to know later, through the Freedom of Information Act, that two years before he died, he went back to being an active Jesuit Priest, while his mistress, since there is no record of their marriage, lived with him as his housekeeper. He was buried as a great missionary of his time amongst the Jesuits, while he willed over a million dollars cash and two properties of 40 acres and more to his 'wife'. We were never considered. She in turn, willed it all to the Catholic churches in Lucknow and Allahabad, Mother Teresa, and many others in the US. My poor mother died in poverty after many years of struggling to support her children. She never went back to Latonah, her village in Bihar, out of shame. We knew no relatives in India while we were growing up, nor any in the US. Today I have contacts with them all. But the Church never wanted to accept us as the children of a Catholic priest, nor my Indian mother, as they accepted the American lady.

On Turning 40

Kris Chandrasekar

I turned forty on December 23rd last year, two days before Christmas. As in everything, there is a downside and an upside to being a Christmas baby. The downside is that you are more often than not, a victim of the 'one gift' curse. The upside, on the other hand, is that your age is identified with the previous calendar year. You are almost proud to point out 'but I was born in December', when asked the year of your birth, as though this were a deserved honor.

There was the idyllic childhood in India replete with street cricket and long summer holidays, followed by the entirely different tempo of student life in Southern California.

All this became moot this last birthday as I was relegated to that phase known as early middle age; I turned forty. It is a mid point, the great divide, this onset of early middle age. Truth be told, I have not changed all that much in the past decade. The body is no more out of shape, nor significantly less vigorous. Yet, there are those telltale signs, the slight graying at the temples, the regrets about some of the roads not taken, that gnawing worry that one may have caused pain to others. Above all, there is a need to put things in perspective.

From the vantage point of relative professional success and a tranquil family life, I surveyed the past. There was the idyllic

Kris Chandrasekar, a native of Madras, lives in the Bay Area with his wife, a Tech. Support Professional, and their two children. He has been a commercial banker for the past 15 years. His travels have taken him to various parts of Europe, Asia and North America. An avid student of history and politics, he has also dabbled in creative writing and literature. His other passions include football and India.

childhood in India replete with street cricket and long summer holidays, followed by the entirely different tempo of student life in Southern California in the late teens and early twenties. This period of life, which culminated in the obtaining of the much-ballyhooed MBA, can only be characterized as a curious mix of fun and misery. Then on to the emotional upheavals of the mid-twenties, a period of some turmoil, both on personal and professional fronts; this prompted both intense soul searching and long, hard work to ensure professional success. The soul searching revealed me to myself, warts and all, and helped me become more focused and less negative. In retrospect, this self-knowledge has helped me tremendously in my marital life.

Yes folks! I took that bold step one beautiful spring morning, at the age of thirty, with the lovely Jaishree, at the Malibu Hindu temple in Southern California. The parental units had flown out from India to grace the occasion. Over the next few years, we traveled relentlessly and managed to produce our first joint venture; we named him Arjun. We have since settled into a less hectic pace. After nearly a decade of married life, I must say I quite like it. So, here I am, living through the most tranquil phase of my life and trying to make sense of it all.

Yes folks! I took that bold step one beautiful spring morning, at the age of thirty, with the lovely Jaishree, at the Malibu Hindu temple in Southern California.

In looking for some common threads in the past, one thing that stands out over the past two decades is travel, a personal passion. Aside from helping me keep my sanity through the ebbs and flows of life, it certainly has provided great memories. I am able to recall with fondness the time I got lost in Italy on the way to Pompeii, during a leisurely footloose-and-fancy-free trip through Europe; the reckless (and foolish) drive through Arizona one snowy Thanksgiving weekend to get to the Grand Canyon. Or the night in a Bombay hotel trying to sleep off the jet lag only to be disrupted by noises emanating from the next suite, thanks to a particularly amorous couple. I remember lying awake that night not quite able to, in my dazed state, figure out whether to kick the fellow in the shins the next morning, or congratulate him on his remarkable prowess.

Another personal favorite was a trip to the Guruvayur temple during a hasty trip to India in the early eighties. It was an especially low point in life and I had wanted to make an offering at the temple in the manner of a local tradition known as *Thulabaram* wherein a food item (plantains, coconuts, etc.) is given to the temple equaling one's weight. The weight is measured on an old fashioned two-sided scale with the devotee sitting on one side. As I sat on one side, the other side, despite being piled on with plantains, wouldn't budge, much to the amusement of several children in the proximity. I didn't know whether to laugh or be embarrassed when the cashier behind the counter yelled out in English, "You pay maximum!"

In writing this piece, I've tried to gain an understanding as to why travel has played such an important part in my life. Travel has been my vehicle to look outward. It has kept me going. There is always one more place to see, one more country to visit. Thus there is always a built-in goal. Aside from all the solace it has provided, it has helped me continually redefine myself. I can only guess at the transformative powers of grander passions.

So what words of wisdom do I have to offer? What wisdom have I gleaned from all these experiences? Prosaic as this may sound, avoid negative people; they drain your energy. Take chances; to not do so kills the spirit. Live on the edge a bit, peer over the proverbial cliff's edge and feel the adrenalin pumping every so often. Ask for that promotion. Propose to that girl you've always had a soft corner for (this particular pearl of wisdom doesn't apply to you married guys! That's living too much on the edge). Don't let go of your passions even at your low points; these are what sustain you. And for your own sake, put your past mistakes behind you. You win some. You lose some. That's just how it works out. Concentrate on the here-and-now.

The *Epic of Gilgamesh* speaks to us across the centuries on the meaning of it all. When Gilgamesh goes in search of eternal life, he is advised by Siduri, the wine maker, to accept mortality and live in the here-and-now: to dance and be merry, to rejoice and make his wife happy in his embrace, and take delight in a child holding his hand as all life is transitory. Wise words to live by indeed, and I intend to do just that.

Real Words from Unreal People

Priya Sundaravalli Sudarsan

Here is a collection of statements from personal experience, confessions from close friends, or from inadvertent eavesdropping...

"It is our past life's sin that we are born women."

"Why do you want her to go to college?" "If she can cook and take care of the house, that's enough." "I hope you are not going to allow her to stay in a hostel." "You are giving her too much freedom." "A B.A. degree is enough; teach her home science, that will be very useful." "Teach her computer science, she will land a good husband." "She should not accept the scholarship and go abroad." "I don't know how you can send an unmarried girl abroad." "What all jewel sets have you made for her wedding." "You know, it's never too early to start buying jewelry for your daughter." "Don't waste money on her; invest it on your son; he'll take care of you when you are old." "It is

"Don't waste money on her; invest it on your son; he'll take care of you when you are old."

Priya Sundaravalli was born in the coastal town of Pondicherry and grew up in Madurai, the city of magical temples. She is currently working on a Ph.D. in industrial engineering at the University of Michigan, Ann Arbor. She recieved the M.B.B.S. medical degree in 1992 from PSGIMS, Coimbatore, and a master's degree in biomedical engineering from Drexel University, Philadelphia. She enjoys journalling, writing free verse, and writing and illustrating stories for children. She works at walking gently on this planet with her partner Nasy, and eagerly awaits their return to Auroville near Pondicherry by December 2001.

our shame to be living with our daughter in our old age; what will people say." "My sons' children come first before you all."

"You go inside; and don't come out till he is gone." "And don't show your teeth all the time; don't you have any shame." "He is a boy; he can do what he wants." "You don't have an opinion." "Be quiet and keep your mouth shut!" "What do you know?"

"No shame at all; she talks to men." "He is a decent man; he would never have done that to you!" "You must have started it all." "You're lying; I don't believe you." "Now don't make up stories." "You must have asked for it." "She made me do it." "She was always a flirt." "She deserves that."

"Always serve the men first; we can eat later." "You go play or study; your sister and I will do this." "Push you shoulders down and slouch; don't bring attention to your breasts." "Learn to walk like a woman."

"Our daughter has been raised with good Indian values." "Our daughter is fair-skinned." "Our daughter is an innocent divorcee." "Our daughter is very traditional." "Our daughter has never dated."

"I will marry a girl who has only studied up to 10th class; anything more than that, she'll be unmanageable." "We are looking for a girl from India for our boy." "Those American girls have no culture or morals; but boy! They must be fun to date." "The brainy types are usually very ugly!" "Cover the face and fire the base!"

"It must be her past life's sins; that's why she is still unmarried." "A woman is like a creeping vine; she needs a strong man to support her." "We don't like the girl; she is too dark." "We don't like the girl; she wears glasses." "Your parents did not conduct the marriage well." "Was that all your parents could do?" "No, this is not enough; where is the two-wheeler and fridge." "We want to see all the jewels you are giving your daughter." "Yes, we like to check if you have brought what you promised." "We just want one lakh rupees in dowry; there are many others who are waiting to pay us more, you know. Since our boy seems to like your daughter, we are willing to compromise." "Oh, we take no dowry; but if you want to give money to your daughter, we won't stop you!" "We don't take dowry; but just make sure that the marriage is celebrated in a grand way." "Once you are married, you belong to your husband's family." "The three knots of the *thali* are so symbolic; two knots are tied by your husband and the third by your sister-in-law." "Now don't be silly! A man cannot wear a *thali*." "Sit properly like a woman; you are the bride." "Fall at your husband's feet and get his blessing." "If you marry your uncle, all my gold bangles will be yours." "What audacity! She doesn't want to celebrate her first night here in our house." "What! You do not wear your *thali*?" "The bride's family always bears the cost of the wedding."

"Why are you trying to do everything, juggling both job and a home with kids?" "When your husband is making enough money, why don't you stay at home and live like a queen." "What's the use of all her degrees; she can't make decent coffee." "What!! Your husband wakes up before you and makes coffee?" "Who cooks in your home? Do you let your husband do it?" "She makes her husband cook and wash dishes." "Her house is a mess." "She went back to work two months after delivery." "Her poor husband, so hen-pecked; only listens to her." "Our daughter-in-law has brainwashed our son." "Hope you are feeding my son well? Only you seem to be gaining weight and our poor son is so thin." "What does your husband feel about all your activism/shactivism?" "Her husband has a raw deal; poor man." "I don't know how her husband puts up with her, poor man."

"You are unclean for the next three days; stay out and don't touch anyone or anything in the house; I'll do the cooking."

"No! No temples, no festivals, no school; yes, forget attendance, your teacher will understand; just stay in this room." "You are unclean for the next three days; stay out and don't touch anyone or anything in the house; I'll do the cooking." "You're still unclean; let 45 days pass and then we can name the child." "Just because we are in America doesn't mean we should forget out culture. So keep away from the kitchen and *pooja* room for the next 3 days. I will do all the cooking."

"What are you still studying for? Have a child and then study." "What, still no child? Did you have a checkup?" "She must be barren you know..." "A woman's life is complete only when she becomes a mother." "What is the use? In her stomach, even a worm will not grow." "What, another girl again?" "He is really unlucky to have married her." "Our ancestors will never attain peace."

"She is a widow only in namesake; she is still attached to her silks and *pottu*." "Oh! The poor man, he should remarry; he has a child to take care of, you know." "Her husband died and now she's planning to marry again; and that too after having a child! What is this world coming to?"

"Can't you take care of the child? See! She's disturbing me." "What's for dinner? What!! The same thing again!" "I am bringing four friends with me this evening, have dinner ready." "Don't complain to me about my parents; they come first before you. Don't you ever forget that!"

"Your grandfather says he will not talk to you till you grow your hair back." "How did your husband ever give you permission to do that?" "You should grow your hair back and put on some more weight, you look like a monkey now." "What! You shaved your head now! How did your husband ever let you do that?" "Your husband gives you too much freedom."

"You women have it so easy." "You just have to smile, and you'll get things done." "She probably slept her way to the top." "Oh! Your advisor is a woman?" "Oh! The professor is a woman?!" "Oh! You are doing a PhD?" "Engineering is for men." "What, you haven't changed your last name?" "She still keeps her last name." "I know India will always have such men, who know what is available in India, and women who support their men in good causes." "A woman's place is always behind her husband."

"Learn your place." "Why can't you be like her?" "Act like a woman." "She is after all a girl." "You are after all a girl." "She is just a girl."

"She is the social worker type." "I hate these feminist types." "She is a feminist."

Sulekha Reader Comments

Neela Gollapudi: Your article is thought-provoking, but the position of women in India is more complex than you let on. Indians would take your article in the right spirit - i.e., as being a kick in the backside to get people thinking. An outsider will get an entirely one-sided picture. My gut feel tells me that the situation you described relates primarily to middle class women, and not as much to the lower and upper classes. Being squarely from the middle class, can't say for sure though. There is more equity between the sexes in the upper and lower classes I would think; the upper classes probably because the woman comes into the marriage with an independent financial situation and the lower classes because the men and women work and the women are again independent. Also, I noticed that said inequity reduces with age. By the time the man and woman 'do' 10-15 years in their marriage, the woman's position in the household changes. In the 40-60 age group, in a reasonable proportion of the marriages that I have seen, the women are dominant, whatever image they may project outside.

Amitabha Bagchi: Gender inequities are just symptomatic of the disease; the real issue lies in the concept of gender itself. It is not men who oppress women; it is the concepts of *masculine* and *feminine* which oppress both. Within the framework of this system the oppression and mistreatment of women is the highly objectionable process that brings to light the problems implicit in accepting it. Your article disturbed me more than a little. Your methodology of placing pronouncements end to end, forcing the reader to build a context around each, is compelling but misleading. Early feminist filmmaking used the documentary as a political tool. The close up image of a woman telling her story was presented as the 'truth', inviolable, uncontestable.

How do you Say it in 'Indian'?

Ramesh N. Rao

A colleague of mine, a North Indian, has this habit of addressing me in Hindi, or mixing Hindi with English (Hinglish). "*Arre* Ramesh, how are you doing? Did you write the *chitthi* to Mark that you said you would? I don't want to hear any more *bakwas* from him about it, you know." It is jarring on my ears, and I very much dislike her for taking it for granted that I like her speaking to me in Hinglish. Then there is the graduate student from India in my school who likes to pepper her newly-acquired sorority-style American English with Hindi:

I would like to tell my colleague that her jarring mix of Hindi and English grates on my ears, and I am tempted to tell the graduate student that she sounds both hilarious and rather dumb.

"You know, I am like, give me a break. It is all *faltoo*. I am like, you are kidding me. I just spoke to my *bhaiyya* yesterday, and he..." Or some of my new acquaintances, who, having heard about some of my papers or publications, and calling from Boston or New York, immediately launching into a conversation in Hindi. I respond in English, and sometimes, I wish I could simply begin speaking in Kannada to them. I would like to tell my colleague that her jarring mix of Hindi and English grates on my ears, and I am tempted to tell the graduate student that she sounds both hilarious and rather

---

Ramesh N. Rao is an associate professor of communication at Truman State University. He was born in Ramanagara near Bangalore, India and spent the first 28 years of his life in India. He prefers to read rather than to write but realizes that once on the writing treadmill you can't get off it. At present he is working on the second draft of a book on the BJP and RSS. His wife Sujaya and he have two cats, Subba and Thimma, and live in the small town of Kirksville, Missouri

dumb. And those new acquaintances, I want to tell them not to take me for granted. But I hold my tongue. I don't want to be perceived as more of a curmudgeon than I really am.

What has this got to do with anything? Language. And the problem of language in India. It is said that the glue that binds a people into a nation could be geography, ethnicity, culture, or language. With Indians speaking more than 16 languages, 200 major dialects, and anywhere from 500 to 700 minor dialects, we are really a polyglot nation. A friend of mine, who wishes to remain anonymous, sent me a rather long note on the problem of language in India. Let me paraphrase him:

> *"Why does language, which eloquently reflects the culture of a people become the root cause of hatred? Because boundaries are sought to be drawn based on it. Seeds of Balkanization were sown in India when the Nehru government decided to form linguistic states. This was the second biggest blunder in the history of independent India, the first being the kind of Fabian socialism that Nehru subscribed to and foisted upon the people. The effects of socialism such as poverty, joblessness and corruption are apparent enough. The effects of linguistic states are far subtler, and more difficult to undo in the long run. Small side-effects are seen in the country already: the friction along state borders, river water sharing disputes between states, allegations of neglect of one's language on national television, states forcing linguistic minorities to study the local language, projectionist legislation for the arts to deter 'outside' influences and languages...and so on. There is talk of 'superiority' of one language over the other, and hence the superiority of a linguistic group over the other. Superiority of one group leads to an inferiority complex in other groups. Sometimes, we have people who hate all other languages except their own, and in a strange reverse, we have people who hate their own language, despise*

movies, dramas, literature, art based on their
language, and embrace the art, culture and language
of another group (the example of the influence of
English in India should prove this last point)."

This very articulate friend goes on to argue that Indian
culture was never language-centric. Throughout history not one
war was waged over language in India, he points out. When
kings waged war it was to enlarge their kingdom, not to impose
their language or religious
beliefs. When the Maratha **When the Maratha kings**
kings invaded the south, they **invaded the south, they**
did not impose Marathi on the **did not impose Marathi on**
southerners, though there is a **the southerners.**
small group of Marathi speaking people in Tanjore district
even now. All courts were conducted in the local language, and
for example, when the Kannada Sena kings invaded the north
all the way up to Bengal, they never imposed Kannada on the
Bengalis. In fact, they adopted the local languages and
customs. Sanskrit and Tamil co-existed for millennia, but after
the division of India into linguistic states look what has
happened.

Let me quote more from my friend:

> *"The first instances of linguistic imposition*
> *began in the sub-continent with the Mughal*
> *invasions. Persian, and later Urdu, was made the*
> *language of the royal courts. The Mughals never*
> *adopted Sanskrit or any of the local languages*
> *for communication. It was the Hindus and Sikhs*
> *who learnt, and later excelled in, Persian and*
> *Urdu. The Portuguese too, imposed their*
> *language in the areas they colonized. For a long*
> *time, Portuguese was the official language in*
> *Goa. Only in the last century did Konkani make*
> *its way back to the region, and is now*
> *flourishing.*

The primary reason for linguistic tolerance in the sub-continent was the varna system. Nowhere in our literature, be it in the Vedas, Puranas, Upanishads, Mahabharata, or Ramayana does it say that a person has to use language as an identity. People sought identity through their profession and their philosophy of life. A Vaishya from the Chola kingdom who spoke Tamil and worshiped Muruga felt closer to a vaishya from Sindh who neither spoke his language nor worship as he did. A Brahmin from Kerala was closer to a Brahmin from Bengal than to a Kshatriya living next door. An Advaitin from Kashmir felt closer to another Advaitin from Gujarat. A Dwaita from Karnataka bonded better with a Dwaita from Maharashtra. Alliances for marriage never had linguistic conditions set. Badami kings sought alliances from Rajasthan. Telugu kings sought alliances from Orissa. Kannada and Marathi Brahmins inter-married all the time."

If India is to survive as a country and Indians to be united, my friend says, then language as an identity has to be given up. His strategy for accomplishing this is rather drastic: "This can happen only if the existing linguistic state structure is dismantled and a new state structure is formed which takes into account the geography, topography and the terrain of the region. For example, if the whole of the Krishna river delta from the state of Maharashtra, Karnataka, and Andhra is formed into one state, it would suit the needs of the people better," he asserts. He comes up with a 'game plan' that would make sure that "linguistic states will be a distant memory in 50-60 years". Unfortunately, for my friend, I don't believe that such a plan is viable, given the present state of the nation. Also, the *varna* system, which then gave rise to caste divisions, got calcified over centuries, leading to the hierarchical and oppressive system that has now taken on a dynamic all its own. I do not know how that is going to be resolved. This article is not going to touch that bugaboo...

National language, linguistic states, and the history of language conflict: The Tamil problem, as it has been characterized by some, is related to the demands of regionalism and language. Nehru and Patel were against the idea of linguistic states, but there was popular demand for them after independence. Afraid of secession – till 1963 there was no constitutional ban on political parties' right to preach separation – and more riots following the holocaust of partition, they gave in. Hindi, being the tongue of a large segment of the population in the north, was made the national language, and linguistic states were okayed. The Tamils did not like the idea of Hindi as a national language. EVR or

They thought, and many still fervently believe, that Hindi is just the latest instrument of the imperialist north to subjugate the south.

Periyar (E.V. Ramaswamy Naicker), the man who started the Vaikom agitation in the 1920s for the uplift of untouchables in the then kingdom of Travancore, believed that 'Aryans' came to India from elsewhere and "concocted absurd stories in keeping with their barbarian status. The blabberings of the intoxicated Brahmins in those old days are still faithfully observed in this modern world as the religious rituals, morals, stories, festivals, fasts, vows and beliefs."

EVR believed that the Aryans had driven the Dravida communities away from the Gangetic plains by conquest and subjugation; so, he believed in, and wanted, a separation of the Aryan North from the Dravidian South. He also believed the Brahmins were the agents of the Aryan North and sought to 'destroy' them. Following this line of 'logic', EVR's and the Tamil people's sentiment against Hindi can be understood. They thought, and many still fervently believe, that Hindi is just the latest instrument of the imperialist north to subjugate the south. C. Rajagopalachari (Rajaji) played into the hands of EVR when he (Rajaji) became the Prime Minister (yes, this is not a typo) of Madras Province in 1937 and implemented the Congress policy of making Hindi compulsory in schools. EVR believed the imposition of Hindi would destroy Tamil language and culture. This was when he launched the anti-Hindi agitation. EVR also began his campaign for 'Dravida Nadu', which then got transformed into a campaign for Tamil Nadu, separate and independent from the rest of India. We have a Tamil Nadu now, but as part of the Indian union, and EVR's political descendants, the DMK and AIADMK, cannot issue any further calls for separation because of the 1963 Constitutional amendment. As late as April 1962, when C.N. Annadurai made an emotional appeal in the Rajya Sabha for the separation of Dravida Nadu from the rest of India, the idea of independence from the 'imperialistic north' was burning bright in Tamil hearts. But then came the war with China and the DMK suspended their call for separation in that hour of crisis. This was followed by the 16th Amendment which changed Article 19 to make any secessionist party ineligible to contest elections. However, the 'ogre' of Hindi still looms large in the South, especially in Tamil Nadu.

Language Formula: When the Constituent Assembly gathered in September 1949 to debate the resolution on the national language of India there was a lot of concern. The Hindi-as-national-language proponents claimed that Hindi was understood by 140 million people out of the 330 million people in India at that time and so should be made the official working language of the country. The moderates felt that if Hindi became the official language it could lead to the break-up of the nation. They wanted English to be continued as the official language till an acceptable version of Hindi could be evolved. The Congress Party had committed to the idea of Hindi as the national language at its 1924 CWC meeting. Incidentally, the CWC had approved two scripts for Hindi – Devanagari and Urdu. Gandhi plonked for a via media, Hindustani, the combination of Hindi and Urdu, as the national language. But since Urdu had become the national language of Pakistan by 1949, the rather Sanskritized Hindi became India's national language. There were the usual 'cautions' by the 'framers' of the Constitution, with Rajendra Prasad saying, "The question of language is to be carried out by the country as a whole. Let us not forget...there is no other item in the whole Constitution of the country which may be required to be implemented from day to day, from hour to hour, almost from minute to minute in actual practice."

Since the idea of Hindi as national language terrified many in the South, especially in Tamil Nadu, the crafty men in the government roped in N. Gopalaswami Ayyangar, a Tamil Brahmin, to draft the resolution making Hindi the national language! English was to stay as the official language for 15 years and then Hindi would take over. So, when in 1963 the Official Languages Bill was introduced in Parliament, Annadurai pointed out that though the proponents of Hindi claimed that 42 percent of the country could understand Hindi, this 42 percent of the people basically comprised residents of one area of the country: the North. Since the Constitution of India was enacted on 26th January, 1950, the grace period for the use of English was over on 26th January 1965. The DMK decided to observe the day as a 'day of mourning'. While the Hindi speaking people were elated, many felt that Hindi would be imposed, and they feared a new kind of *More people immolated themselves and drank bug poison in Tamil Nadu, and students in West Bengal took out processions* hegemony. Just before 26th January 1965, the Congress Chief Minister of then Madras state had arrested Annadurai and the top leadership of the DMK to prevent trouble. But more than 20,000 students took out a procession with the 'Hindi demon' garlanded with *chappals*. Congress flags were pulled down, and the national flag was burnt and desecrated in some places.

Two people immolated themselves in the cause of Tamil. Demonstrations turned violent, and when the police opened fire to quell them, people died. Home Minister Gulzari Lal Nanda said Hindi would not be imposed, and Prime Minister Lal Bahadur Shastri assuaged that "we can always sit together and iron out differences." More people immolated themselves and drank bug poison in Tamil Nadu, and students in West Bengal took out processions carrying banners that read, "We will speak no Hindi, read no Hindi, and hear no Hindi music." When the violence escalated in Tamil Nadu, where on one day 24 people were killed in police firings, two Union Ministers from Tamil Nadu, C. Subramaniam and O.V. Alagesan, resigned from the Central Cabinet, as they could not persuade Shastri to settle with the Tamil demand. The demand was that Hindi not be imposed on those who did not want to speak it or use it. There was no use seeking to abolish Hindi as the national language, but the DMK people wanted Nehru's assurance (of no imposition) to be implemented. In February 1965 the CWC asked the government to bring an amendment to the Official Languages Act which would give legal shape to Nehru's assurance. The government was thus able to diffuse the tension. And the DMK rode to power in 1967 in Tamil Nadu, and continues to be in power after 22 years (though in various forms).

What now? The uneasy 'acceptance' of Hindi as the national language by many, especially in the South, and to some extent in West Bengal, hasn't removed this 'thorn' of language from our sides. In Tamil Nadu, Hindi is still anathema. Many of its people lost their lives fighting for Tamil, and Tamil memory is long and strong. There is an interesting book by Sumathi Ramaswamy titled *Passions of the Tongue: Language devotion in Tamil India, 1891-1970* in which she says: "This incorporation of the language into the very being of the *Tamilian* carries tremendous consequences, for in its most passionate moments, *tamilpparru* (Tamil devotion) certainly instructs Tamil speakers that devotion to their language should supersede devotion to their parents, their spouses, and children;

but it also tells them that devotion to their language should transcend attachment to their own bodies and to their own lives."

With such devotion to language, and language embodying a culture and a civilization, there is little hope that Hindi will ever be *the* national language. I did not like to study Hindi in school. I still have nightmares in which I am taking a Hindi exam and I haven't prepared at all. I wake up and feel so good that the actual nightmare of Hindi language study will no longer bother me. Hindi is the language of the North, and it carries all the baggage of a northern hegemony.

My proposal is this: the next government to come to power, whether it is BJP-led or Congress-led, could bring about a transformation by tackling this language issue with a little bit of creativity. Make Tamil and Hindi the national languages, or Tamil and Sanskrit the national languages. Tamil is one of the oldest languages of the world, and of India, and its literature is vast, rich, and its heritage ancient and complex. The case for Hindi has already been made, though I myself believe it is not a language with any great tradition or literature compared to most other Indian languages: for example, Kannada, Telugu, Marathi, Bengali and Malayalam all have richer

My proposal is this: Make Tamil and Hindi the national languages, or Tamil and Sanskrit the national languages.

histories and literatures than Hindi. But Hindi, compared to Sanskrit, is a 'living' language, and a language spoken by the ordinary peoples. But Sanskrit has other emotional appeals, and of course has its great history, literature, and antiquity. Either way, Sanskrit/Tamil or Hindi/Tamil as national languages could mitigate, if not remove, the perception of regional rivalry and ethnic/cultural divides.

How would this dual national language policy be implemented? Would we then be burdened with a four-language formula, with us and our children having to learn Hindi/Tamil, local language, and English, or Sanskrit/Tamil, local language, and English? In what language/s would the affairs of the government be conducted? You may be even thinking as you read this, "God, what a waste of paper!" The solution I propose is simple. People can learn the local language and whatever else they wish to. There won't be any compulsion beyond learning the local language. The government's work will be conducted in whatever language the representatives are fluent in. After all, even now, the DMK/AIADMK members speak in Tamil in parliament. "Ramesh, you are promoting chaos and advocating babel", you may say. But wait. This is the age of computers. We already have software for simultaneous translations of languages. There is therefore no need for all of us to be burdened with the task of learning three or four languages. The 'national languages' will thus be just a symbol of the nation, and pose very little difficulty in conducting the nation's business.

So, now, what do you think of the Tamil/Hindi or Tamil/Sanskrit as national languages idea? As to my friend's idea of doing away with linguistic states, I believe the time is not yet ripe. It could happen one day, and I hope it will happen. But right now, people have invested too much in the idea and the formation of administrative entities based on language, and disentangling it at the moment is a task that the wiliest of politicians would be loath to take up.

The idea of two national languages is easier to implement, and should have a powerful effect on the nation. Those northerners whose idea of India ends at the Vindhya ranges will be forced to acknowledge that the country extends beyond it, and that those areas have much to offer. It has galled me for a long time that the north ignores the south. How many northerners learn any South-Indian language when they move and settle down in Bangalore or Hyderabad or Madras? They may speak some pidgin variety of the local language, but in the most demeaning way. How many northerners can pronounce a South Indian name correctly? The newsreaders on AIR or Doordarshan from Delhi have always garbled and messed up the names of southern politicians like Deve Gowda, Karunanidhi, Nijalingappa, Ramakrishna Pillai and

Chandrababu Naidu. It is time to put the south on the Indian map and into the Indian consciousness again.

When I mentioned my 'idea' to a friend from Madras she said that making Tamil a national language would play into the hands of the DMK types – those who hate the north, those who hate Brahmins, those who are inimical to Hinduism. I said that was okay. How else can we change the dynamics in India, if not through creative means, and by ignoring predictable scenarios? So, *vanakkam* and *shukriya.* May India prosper.

Sulekha Reader Comments

Arvind Kumar: Perhaps the solution is to do away with the concept of National Language and change the mindset of people to see a language as an utility than a symbol of 'pride'. Printing official documents in all 19 languages is not difficult at all. Of course, there will be calls for more languages to be included. Why not? Maybe the interest groups should pay some amount of money every year for their language to be supported by the government! I know it is a far-fetched idea but why not?

Saurabh Jang: When you start of with the wrong facts, you reach the wrong conclusions. In computer circles this is known as GIGO. I consider the construction of linguistic states to be the most pragmatic and sane decision possible in Indian democracy. As to conjectures about the lack of linguistic affinities in ancient India, this seems to be a case of intentionally striving for a conception of the past that fits one's current theories. No one cares about the real language tragedy: a college graduate from a rural or poor urban background who cannot speak English fluently might as well as be an illiterate for all the job opportunities his college degree is going to bring him. In our mutual language jealousies we did not stop to see the ogre that was eating at the very possessions we were fighting about: English.

Of One Night and its Day

Rakhee

the cheeks are wet,
yet parched, she remains.

the clutched pillow understands,
so lets her curl and sink in.
engulfing her like a favorite aunt,
the night gently rocks her to sleep.
the crickets sound the same
at home and in here...

day rushes in,
scooping her out of slumber.
she gives in to the charm,
that early morning weaves.
her favorite Gods are smiling...
reassured, she breathes again.

Rakhee was born in Bombay and brought up in Cochin. She received her Bachelor's degree in computer engineering and has been working as a software engineer since 1995. She lives in Boston with her husband.

Agnus Dei

Suraiya Ishaque

There was a naked man that stared down at her and seemed to occupy the central space in the garden. She would stare at him everyday during the twenty minutes that she had as a break from her classes. When the bell rang at 11 a.m. and all the children squeezed their way out of class, she would pick up her lunch bottle and go and sit in the garden. The plastic bottle was white and red and was filled with water; she had strict instructions not to drink the germ-filled version that flowed out of the water-coolers of the school. The bottom of the bottle had a large cup that could be unscrewed and this contained her lunch. As a result her sandwiches always tasted and smelt of plastic. Today she took her lunch and sat directly facing the naked man. She was determined that she would keep staring at him until she came to some sort of a conclusion of why he was there.

What she couldn't understand was why none of the other girls seemed interested in him. Everyone ran past him as if he had a right to be there, like Fernandez the school gateman. He was there, he had always been there, so why stop and stare at him and ask him why he was there and what he

She recognized that expression because she had seen it before; she had seen this man's face in the goat that had been slaughtered outside her house on **Eid.**

Suraiya Ishaque grew up in Karachi and received her high school education there. She attended Oberlin College in Ohio where she received her B.A. in english and third world studies. After college she spent time in New York, D.C. and Houston and has now moved back to Pakistan, where she intends to teach English and finish writing her collection of short stories.

wanted? She was different somehow because she wanted to know why everyone else seemed happy to ignore his existence. So she sat and stared at him and slowly took little bites of her cheese sandwich.

She had to strain her neck to look up at him. His face seemed to be hanging down and his eyes were lowered. She recognized that expression because she had seen it before; she had seen this man's face in the goat that had been slaughtered outside her house on *Eid*. It was the expression in the eyes of the goat when all it could do was bleed and keep its eyes open. She remembered that she had picked out the goat at a very dirty goat market called *Sohrab Ghot*. She had asked her father if Sohrab was the owner of the market and if all the goats belonged to him. Her father had laughed and explained to her that *Ghot* meant village in Sindhi and not the English 'goat'. She had not thought that her question was that funny, after all so many things were spelt incorrectly in Karachi. She had failed her previous spelling test by one point because she had always thought that 'dangerous' was spelt 'dangeroos' as that is what she had always seen behind all the oil and water tankers on the road. Following that logic, in her next spelling test, she had spelt 'kangaroos' as 'kangerous', only to discover that spellings had no logic. So if she had thought that *Sohrab* owned all the *Ghots* in the market, why did her father find it so funny? After he had finished laughing, her father remembered a joke about a man who went to England for the first time and this made him laugh again:

"*Kyun na tariqi ho? Bacha bacha angrezi bolta hai,*" (Why wouldn't there be progress when every single child speaks English?) he had told her and then laughed while she just stared at the camels and wondered why anyone would want to buy such a smelly creature.

She had never picked out a goat before and wondered how her father was going to make that decision. Soon she learnt how to do it and followed her father's example that showed her how to hold the goat's lips so that you could count its teeth. The more teeth, the older the goat. She asked her father why the age of the goat made such a difference but he only muttered something about some meat being tender and refused to elaborate. She decided that as long as she was going to look after the goat, she should pick the fluffiest and cutest one, regardless of its number of teeth.

When they came home with the goat and her father tied it to the gate at the back of the garden, she decided that the goat would be called "Billy" after the goat in her illustrated book *Billy Goat Gruff.* Her choice of name was not met well by her older sister who remarked:

"How can you call a goat a cat?"

She ignored her and accepted the fact that her sister was the queen of riddles that she could never answer. It was only later, while she was looking for her biscuit that had sunk to the bottom of her teacup as she dipped it in the tea, that she finally understood what her sister meant:

"Oh cat as in *billi*," she yelled nearly spilling her tea all over the sofa.

Billy soon became an integral part of her life. She would feed him various weeds that grew in her garden and she would count his teeth again and again to see if he was growing any older. Then one day she woke up and it was *Eid* and she was so excited as she leapt out of bed, determined to be the first child in the house to be bathed and *Now as she stared at the naked man's face and saw the blood trickling down his face, however, all she could think of was Billy.*

dressed in her new clothes. She headed towards the bathroom and her bare feet skipped over the cold green tiles in the hallway. Just before she opened the bathroom door she thought that she heard Billy bleating and decided to peep out of the window and see if she could see him. What she saw through the floral design of the metal grill made her feet even colder than before. She screamed and ran outside, barefoot and in her nightie. She ran up to her father and started screaming and was harshly told to get back inside the house and to put some slippers on.

Later when she realized that Billy was going to suffer a terrible end, she made up her mind never to look at a goat again. She could still picture his expression as his neck was severed and the blood started gushing like a volcano spitting out its lava. Even worse was the monotonous bleating that Billy undertook from the moment the butcher tried to make the goat lie down on the ground. For the next few days, she tried not to vomit every time a neighbor sent a tray filled with quivering red meat, and no matter how hard her mother tried to convince her that she had cooked chicken, she could not eat any form of meat. The worst was that there were animal guts at road corners and on rubbish heaps and the entire neighborhood seemed to be invaded by intestines, hides and swarms of flies.

When she met her friend at school after the *Eid* holidays were over, she told her all about how she had chosen Billy as a new pet and how she had been betrayed by her own family. Her friend unsympathetically informed her of her neighbor's cow who ran without its head till the end of the street and then collapsed in a heap. After hearing that, all she could think about were the camels at *Sohrab Goth* as she tried to imagine what a headless camel would look like. She came to the conclusion that she should just never think about Billy, cows or camels ever again. Now, however, as she ate her plastic-smelling sandwich and stared at the naked man's face, all she *could* think of was Billy.

The cheese suddenly got stuck in her throat, as the tears started to trickle down her face just like the blood trickling down the face of the naked man. She suddenly heard a voice and through her blurry eyes she saw the white figure of a nun.

"What's the matter my child?" the nun asked.

"It's Billy, he was just like this naked man." She managed to sob out.

"My child, this is our savior who suffered for our sins. Did Billy suffer on the cross as well?" she asked.

"Billy was my pet goat; he was killed at *Eid* and distributed to all our neighbors. Why sister, why was Billy killed?" she asked.

Sulekha Select

"Oh my child, Billy was not killed, he was sacrificed to God in memory of Abraham who was going to sacrifice his son to God. This man is like Billy but he is called *Agnus Dei* or the Lamb of God. His name is Jesus and he is the man you Muslims call *Isa*." the nun explained.

"But there were lambs too, and cows and bulls and even some camels. Did all of them have to be killed?" she asked.

"God created them and he took them away because they loved him so much. Jesus took the sins of this world and sacrificed himself like a lamb. These animals, like the Lamb of God, help to wash away your sins." the nun replied.

She stared at the naked man and she thought that he didn't look like a lamb at all. Why would God want any creature to get that expression in its eyes? How could slaughtering Billy or this man help other people? She wanted to ask the nun all these questions but she noticed that the nun had already started walking towards the gate of the garden. She heard the bell ringing and knew that she had to get back to her classroom for *Islamiyat*. She wanted to ask her teacher who this 'Agnes Dee' was and if Billy had gone to heaven. Five minutes later, she decided not to ask all her ebullient questions. The girl next to her had forgotten her *dupatta* and the *Islamiyat* teacher had thrown the chalk-duster in her direction. The girl got up slowly after the duster had smacked her on her arm, and caused a white layer of chalk dust to fall all over the desk. She quietly, and with her head down, went towards the corner of the classroom and climbed into the dustbin.

Suddenly she understood why Billy had been killed. Just like the girl who forgot her *dupatta* and was punished by the teacher, Billy was also being punished for forgetting to do something. She wanted to run out of the class and find the nun and ask her what the naked man had forgotten to do. He must have made a very big mistake to be called a lamb and slaughtered.

Desi Bonsai

Krishnan Sundararaman

And the remnant who have
escaped of the house of Judah
Shall again take root downward,
And bear fruit upward.

Isaiah 37:31-32

7:30 pm, Weekend, Aug. 1999, New York

I emerge from the shower to get ready for yet another *desi* party. My good friends Mohan and Savitha, who have incidentally been united in marital bliss for a couple of years now, occasionally condescend to invite bachelors to their strictly of-the-wedded, by-the-wedded, for-the-wedded gatherings. I was the chosen one this time. Unfortunately, Savitha's limited supply of spicy *samosas* and delightful *gulab jamuns* would also be partaken of by the 'legal' guests at this occasion – Mr.

Why invite a Japanese, unappreciative of sophisticated dishes and the finer palate, to a decidedly heavenly Indian meal?

Krishnan Sundararaman a.k.a ag was born in Pune, raised in Bangalore, fell into West Virginia, rose again in Michigan, fell into Rochester, rose yet again in LA, and has finally fallen into New York City, where he slogs away for an investment bank. Along the way, ag accumulated a masters in computer science, a few friends, a tidy collection of stories on Sulekha and a horde of brickbats on its revered Coffeehouse forum. Despite the absence of a matrimonial forum on Sulekha, ag managed to seduce a Sulekhite and conned her into tying the knot, an act that conferred upon them the official status of First Sulekha Couple. He continues to lurk on Sulekha off and on, and controversy dogs him wherever he goes.

and Mrs. Mathur, and their sole teenaged production, Ajay. Mohan made the introductions. I shook their hands while suspiciously eyeing the *samosas* piling up on the plate in front of them. Regular *desi* couple. Ajay reminded me of my frisky youth – he had the same demeanor, silent yet spirited, relaxed yet alert, seeming rather interested in the routine conversation, when in fact he couldn't care less. There was a knock, and I, seated closest to the door, attended to it. A funny-looking Japanese person bearing a bunch of potted plants identified himself as Mr. Nagachi, and Mohan, pausing in mid-conversation, waved him in.

As I made yet another pilgrimage to the *rasoi* and helped myself to an exquisitely-shaped *samosa* right off the hotplate, Mr. Nagachi set down his pots and sniffed the air gingerly. Why invite a Japanese, unappreciative of sophisticated dishes and the finer palate, to a decidedly heavenly Indian meal? "*Mankege hoomalay kot hagay*" (Like giving a garland to a monkey), I remarked to Savitha, who shushed me instantly. Turned out Nagachi had a greater purpose in mind – he was on a mission to bring forth wisdom to the gardenless denizens of the Manhattan concrete jungle.

Savitha had been pestering Mohan for some semblance of greenery, and Mohan, the methodical, analytical, left-brain Wall Street stockbroker, declined to impulsively shell out a few hundred bucks for a bunch of potted plants without first subjecting himself and his guests to some informative and erudite lecturing from a specialist Bonsai dealer in the area. Enter Mr. Nagachi.

Bonsai literally translates to 'tree in a pot'. It is both the plant and the pot together. Short trees planted in the ground don't qualify – they're topiary, not bonsai.

Any plant can be reared as bonsai, though obviously some plants are more receptive to the process than others. You should buy good seeds (at this point, Mr. Nagachi extracted a bunch of the seed packets he sold at his dealership, and passed them around), wash them with fungicide and provide ample nutrition and lighting in their formative years.

Ajay appeared restless. Ask a 13-year-old to sit through *Vedanta* and this is what'll happen, I thought. But compared to his buddies in India, this kid was positively lucky. I remembered how miserable my own childhood was. Our family back then was cramped in a single room. We lived in an unhygienic neighborhood, where dirty, unkempt vagabonds roamed the streets. The gutters, the mosquitoes and the filth – the images are so vividly etched in my mind. It was the same food every single day: rice and *sambar*, rice and yogurt. Third-class 'ration' rice which tasted absolutely yucky. The rich kids at school had apples and juice for breakfast. The only time I ever got an apple was when I fractured my ankle and some kind relative dropped by at the hospital. Even that one apple had to be split between me and my non-fractured brother. Yep, Ajay was very lucky. Brought up in the U, S of A. Clean surroundings. Plenty of apples. Lucky kid.

Once the seeds germinate into tiny plants, you cut off the main root – the taproot. The main roots are chopped to promote development of a more pleasing radial structure.

We were simultaneously watching TV during Nagachi's discourse. Muted, of course. The married women gossiped, the married men paid serious attention to the Japanese gentleman, and I, the sole bachelor, flitted intermittently back and forth, from the tube to the Bonsaiman.

"Ajay was 5 years old when we got our GC," Mrs. Mathur explained to Kavitha. They had had the kid back home in Vijaywada, where the Mathurs were part of a large joint family. Traditional, orthodox, rooted in values and culture. The US was nowhere on their horizon. The arrival of Ajay galvanized the balding dad into action. A low-profile instructor at a no-name computer-course outfit, he upgraded his skills and netted the coveted post of a SAP architect via a *desi* bodyshop. The fall of '94 saw Ajay's pram getting off a Boeing 737 at JFK, his *desi* mom and dad huddling in the unfamiliarly chill weather, and covering the little boy with shawls and sweaters. Sure he may be an Indian by birth, but to them, Ajay's roots lay out here.

Sulekha Select

Layering techniques are then employed to transform the plant prematurely into a tree. Ground layering is accomplished by anchoring the tiny branches to the ground with a stake to prevent the tree from moving. Air layering involves enclosing the leaves of the plant in moss-filled plastic bags.

Ajay's serendipitous channel surfing bore fruit as soon as he stumbled upon Channel 59. *The Cartoon Network. Loony Tunes*, Bugs Bunny. "Wow!" he exclaimed. "Bugs Bunny, my favorite!" he told me.

Hmmm, OK, whatever, but shouldn't a seventh-grader be watching something slightly more attuned to his age? Like say, Ricky Martin or the Back Street Boys? Something didn't feel quite right here. On the other hand, Ajay was positively beaming! Boys at his age reserved that expression for those of the fairer sex, and this kid was wasting it on a stupid cartoon character? I was baffled.

"We don't have full service at home," Mrs. Mathur clarified. "All those *nanga* ladies on *Showtime* and *HBO*," she whispered. "It is so vulgar. No censorship in this country. We have only CNN, Cartoon Channel, and the International Network. You know, for Indian movies."

Poor kid, I reflected. A 13-year-old has to subsist on a diet of cartoons. In his shoes, I'd have openly rebelled. Why were they stifling his freedom, I wondered. What did they gain by pinning him down when his buddies floated free?

The ringing method is a very effective technique to promote the growth of bonsai. Wrap a piece of strong wire around the trunk and twist it until it bites into the bark. Cut a number of nicks in the bark and then apply a soothing hormone compound to those cuts.

"How many *samosas* have you gobbled?" Savita demanded of me. "I've driven 500 miles just to eat *samosas*, OK?" I mock-protested. "Aaahh!" I exclaimed, as I bit into a chilli. "I need some water," I said, only, I pronounced it *wadder*, the proper American pronunciation I'd practiced meticulously after my arrival in this great country.

Ajay instantly looked at me. He was impressed, I could tell. I was almost as good as him!

Savitha didn't quite catch it, however. She asked, "What?"

"Wadder," I repeated. Then, 'wa-turr', I translated. She understandingly walked up to the refrigerator. She tossed me a bottle of the cold liquid, and passed me some "sweet ketchup," as she called it. It was tomato sauce. "This is so haaat!" I exclaimed, still reeling under the chilli-effect.

"Yeah," Ajay chimed in. "Mom, this is so haaat. I want tomato sauce too! I've driven 500 miles just to eat tomato sauce, OK?"

Wow! My eyes almost fell out of their sockets. I was definitely rooting for this kid! He had some spirit, I could tell. He packed a mean punch. This kid was definitely like me! He'd go a long way!

The mom, however, was less than impressed. "Ajay!" she yelled. The shocked kid turned towards her, and the bonsai man pressed the pause button on his erudition. "That is so rude. Tell sorry. Tell sorry!" she chattered like an Indian parrot.

The poor kid apologized to me. I was thoroughly embarrassed.

I dealt with the parental figure first. It took a while before I could subdue the dominant bastard.

Mr. Mathur wanted to know what was going on. The lady gave him a quick recap in her native Gujrati. She sounded like an express train in frenzy. The enlightened Mr. Mathur threw fiery glances at the kid. I could feel the wire biting into the bark.

Ajay was now truly scared. I could see the fear in his eyes. I was convinced this wasn't the first time this had happened to him. I rushed to his defense. "It's, OK, uncle," I dealt with the parental figure first. It was a while before I could subdue the dominant bastard. When he finally realized I wasn't offended, Mr. Mathur walked to Ajay's side and made an effort to appear the ever-friendly, jovial dad. I spied a single tear tricking down the kid's cheek, but then, he caught his dad's harmonious expression and smiled. The soothing lotion was working its magic.

You can prevent the strengthening of the base by digging under the tree and severing off its major roots. You should also remove branches going off in the wrong directions. The tree will resist – have patience while the tree recovers, and continue with the pruning. Once you get a triangular shape, maintain that shape consistently, at all costs.

"We have given him plenty of freedom," Mr. Mathur explained to me, lest I get the wrong impression. "It is freedom within parameters," he said. "Freedom," he paused and repeated, "Within *parameters*," stressing the last syllable.

By now, I was sort of convinced this guy was a classic psycho. He had no clue how to bring up a kid, and his psychological BS probably originated in some dime-a-dozen self-help book he had picked up at the Manhattan news store across from his office.

"Freedom within parameters is how you raise sensible, obedient kids, in this country," Mohan supported his friend. I was getting sick of that clichéd expression by now. Moreover, Mohan's opinion in this matter scarcely amounted to much – he didn't have a kid in the first place.

Carefully plan how the tree will look now, and how it should look in the future. You must have a very clear vision of the tree's progress. As the tree grows, mark those branches that don't appeal to your sense of aesthetics. You can then chop them off using specialist bonsai tools such as a *wen*, which is an intricate parrot-beak cutting device.

"Ajay will definitely go to MIT," Mr. Mathur wanted me to know. "Or Haaarwaaard," Mrs. Mathur offered an alternative. "We are planning very carefully for his future. After his vacation next month, his high school will begin in full swing. We have a full schedule for the next semester," elaborated Mr. Mathur, and Ajay nodded obediently.

I was like, "Gosh, guys, gimme a break! What schedule? The kid's in high school, for crying out loud!" Of course, I didn't breathe a word.

Savitha was all praise. "Ajay is such a nice kid!" she explained to her husband. They were planning for a daughter in the next couple of years. They had already come up with a name – Anu. "You know, when Anu grows up, I want her to be just like Ajay. Polite. Well-mannered," she continued. Then, turning towards Mrs. Mathur, "We will enroll Anu in *Bharatnatyam* school," she said triumphantly. I detected a note of 'There! Can you do that with your kid?' in Savitha's overflowing enthusiasm. "Yes, definitely," Mohan was already figuring out the costs in his head. "America is such an unsafe country. Unless we teach our kids the appreciation of fine arts and our Indian culture, they will become wayward souls like these American teenagers you see smoking and doing drugs and everything," he explained to the sole bachelor.

Maybe Anu would like to learn Disco, not *Bharatanatyam*. Yet, I patiently heard him out.

Nagachi was nearing the end of his speech. In the later stages, factors like poor soil, extreme climate and bad lighting will promote the classic stunted root that severely constrains the vertical development of the tree. Systematic pruning will limit the number of branches. Gradually, you can get a masterpiece of a miniature tree, he summarized. Mohan paid him handsomely for his lecture. Mr. Mathur bought a budding bonsai and gifted it to Ajay. A gesture of truce, I guess. It was kind of ironic, a bonsai for a bonsai. Nagachi having departed, we grabbed our bowls, filled them with tasty *gulab jamuns* and walked out into the open moonlight.

"We will enroll Anu in Bharatnatyam school," she said triumphantly. I detected a note of 'There! Can you do that with your kid?'...

The moon cast its warm glow all around, and Ajay caught his breath. "Wow! A convertible!!" he said, espying my pretty Miata.

Here was my chance!

"Hey, we can go for a ride," I teased him invitingly. "Wow! Really?" his beseeching eyes begged him father. Mr.

Mathur cast a discreet look in Mohan's direction, as though seeking his approval of my character. Mohan said, "Yeah sure, why not?" The kid joyfully hopped in. I revved up the engine and we were off like a bullet.

Being a bachelor and all has its privileges. You learn to microscopically examine freedom for what it is, without prejudice or bias. In my book, curtailed freedom is the same as no freedom. Sure, there's a line, but it is nowhere close to where the Mathurs have drawn it. Mathur must have flunked his geometry, for his lines are way off base.

Spirited kids make for good citizens. The sole suspension from school, getting caught in the locker room with a *Playboy*, losing one's virginity in the back seat of a Corvette on prom night, catching an occasional X rated flick on *Showtime* – these aren't crimes you protect a kid from. Forbidden fruit is doubly luscious. By curtailing freedom, you make every forbidden pleasure that much more desirable.

Instead, you let the kids develop a sense of ethics over time. Their sense of values is shaped by life-changing experiences they go through, and by blocking these out, you can actively promote a classic stunted personality. The obedient child is an anomaly – he's consciously bottling up his desires. Once he reaches 18 and legally gets out of your clutches, nothing is beyond him. He's definitely going to run amuck with his newfound freedom, and find delight in every con game with no moral sense or fear of repercussions or reprimands. Never having been given a chance to err before, his errors at this later stage are going to be ten times as expensive.

"Can we go to McDonalds?" Ajay interrupted my profound stream of thought. "Sure Ajay," I said, slowing down and pulling in at the drive-in. "What'll you have, crispy chicken?" I asked.

"Dad only buys me fries," the poor kid bleated. My outrage had crossed its limits by now. These orthodox veggie lunatics! Where exactly do they get off! "Two Big Macs, large fries, and two cokes," I barked into the speaker. Ajay grinned from ear to ear. I had planted the bonsai on open soil.

> *For there is hope for a tree,*
> *If it is cut down, that it will sprout again,*
> *And that its tender shoots will not cease.*

Job 14:7-9

Sulekha Reader Comments

Lalita Pandit: I think the bonsai analogy works very well in this story. It is a universal truth that in raising their children, it can be said, quite a few parents, consciously or unconsciously, do some harm. I will admit that I have my own theories about where my parents failed me, what they did wrong. Yet, I don't know to what extent these are not my justifications for my own failures. Also, I don't see American parents not curtailing their children's freedoms. Many of my American students complain about their parents. It may be that it is a different set of freedoms they curtail. Often, middle to lower-middle-class American parents are not very forthcoming, or generous, with helping out with college tuition. Students take loans, or work a lot while studying. Many American parents don't want their children to hang out with 'foreigners' or darker skin color people too much. Many insist that their children go to church with them on Sundays. Yes, dating is mandatory, and many American parents pester their son or daughter if he or she does not have a date! They think this makes their kid odd, eccentric, they worry, and their friends 'talk', etc. For small kids, there is a time to go to bed; it is strictly implemented in most homes. When a child does something wrong, he or she is grounded. Many consider that necessary. Children are expected to do chores that they hate doing, but developing in them the habit of doing unpleasurable things is also considered part of parenting. Even regarding food, there is that 'eat your Brussels sprouts, or else...' idea. Even in my family in India, I vividly remember when my brother wanted to become a vegetarian; my father forced him to eat fish. I remember the scene vividly, and thought my father was being cruel. I hated that scene. Yet, my brother grew up to love fish! And, my father attributed his life-long stomach problem to his having been a vegetarian, having been allowed by his parents to remain a vegetarian for 25 years. He believed his son would have the same stomach problem if his food did not contain enough protein! I liked the bonsai analogy very much and agree with the general point of the story."

Devayani Katripadi: I understand your problem with adults who you see as being too demanding and constraining. But if you think hard about it, every person draws a line somewhere. It is not a question of *if* we draw a line or not, but *where*. You seem to say that you are happy with your idea of where to draw the line but you don't much like where others draw the line.

Arun: Great analogy and very well written! Don't get perturbed with people disagreeing with your viewpoints. That happens all the time. Nobody and nothing can get universal approval. It's all the more so when you seek to traverse a divergent track than that of the majority. While I don't want to get into the "where to draw the line" business right now, it is nevertheless inevitable that we all have to do it somewhere at some point in time. That we don't agree with others' viewpoints and/or vice-versa, is reflective of the diverse mental orientations that we all have. Nobody is right or wrong but everybody just feels a certain way at a certain time. Also, we ourselves change our views all the time, many times without complete conscious understanding that such a thing is indeed happening. The same setting if it were to be in India, I am sure most of the people would have strongly reacted to your article saying that they don't find any curtailment of freedom going on there. They would judge it relative to the environment there and so is your post relative to the prevailing environment in the US. All said and done, it is a job well done and if it makes a few parents think, you have accomplished a worthwhile task

Pillow Talk

Bharadwaj

I

Super Rin! I washed my clothes with *Super Rin*. Four garments with an entire bar of detergent. Now the clothes will always froth when put in water. Then, I fed on guava leaves, which were plucked from my backyard tree, with a dash of salt and pepper. Some reclusive bloke had made a startling discovery, after years of chewing different kinds of leaves, that these were the best to get rid of bad breath. The research came to a halt one day when he chewed on hemlock and died.

"Heh, the only way she's ever going to know is if I tell her myself," I muttered, rather smugly I should say in retrospect, to myself.

Some background would probably wipe the puzzled expression off your face (if it isn't something permanent). I got married recently to a beautiful and religious lady who is devoted to God and the Good Ways. My wife, I call her Sri, okayed the wedding, because she believed that the only alcohol I ever imbibed was the self-generated kind. She didn't ask me whether I consumed meat or not, but had she known that I do, she'd be making cutlets for a potbellied bank clerk as I speak. (My wife has a habit about dwelling on the handsomeness of this man, whom she rejected for the virtues of yours truly, every time we argue.)

Well, of late, I've started to miss my bingeing in college days. Especially my favorites: chicken and hard liquor. When

Bharadwaj was born and raised in Vishakapatnam, India. He works as a computer engineer in the Bay Area. He received his Bachelor's from Andhra University, and Master's from Virginia Tech. The time he allots for writing is divided between humor and 'gentle' horror. His other hobbies are skiing and hiking.

the cock crows at dawn, I dream of chicken. When I take my cough syrup at night, I think of whiskey. To make matters worse, a hedonistic friend keeps popping in once in a while to remind me of the 'good old days'. Conversations with him usually leave me licking my lips. My heart aches and a thirsty numbness pains, to misquote Keats.

Now this friend, a guy nicknamed Pandu (from '*chintha-pandu*', Telugu for tamarind), is a talented bachelor but Sri developed an instantaneous aversion to him, not surprising, going by his track record with old-fashioned housewives.

Conversations with him usually leave me licking my lips. My heart aches and a thirsty numbness pains, to misquote Keats.

Things became worse for our camaraderie when one day she overheard him trying to persuade me to attend a booze party. A sermon and a decree followed, and I was convinced that this was the last I would see of the dude's behind, with the newly-formed *Bata* footprints on it.

A few days later, an opportunity to satisfy my inner cravings presented itself when, by a slice of luck, one of Sri's uncles was roasted by a lightning bolt when he was fixing his TV antenna. My wife set off the next evening to attend the funeral. She had only six words of advice for her husband, who was about to start his two-day parole:

"KEEP AWAY FROM PANDU, YOU HEAR!"

That same day Pandu shamelessly came knocking at the door, grinning in all his tamarind glory. He argued that the next time I would get a chance like this would only be when someone else died in her family.

A good point, because her family members have a tendency to live until their teeth fall off. Not considering the odds of getting zapped by Zeus Himself. I succumbed to his evil schemes without a second thought.

Two nights in a row, I feasted on chicken, vodka and whiskey at his place. I should admit that it didn't feel the same as before, maybe because a guilty conscience was the overpowering factor this time.

Anyway, I was sweating alcohol when I finally staggered home the morning of the day Sri was to return. I had just enough time to destroy all evidence...

With *Super Rin* and guava leaves.

II

If you had been at the station that day and had spotted a lady accompanied by an entourage of half a dozen old and scrawny porters, you would never have imagined that she was returning from a funeral. She stepped out of the train, dressed in a bright orange sari, shimmering like a light bulb. Her cargo was hauled in with forty different bags, balled-up saris, and all kinds of odds and ends.

They got their measly tips from my wife, mixed with a few curses in chaste Telugu to neutralize their gains.

The porters became shorter and wider after they unloaded the luggage their heads. They got their measly tips from my wife, mixed with a few curses in chaste Telugu to neutralize their gains.

"Did you inherit all this stuff from your dead uncle?" I asked, in wonder.

"Don't be silly. You forget that we're in June already. I brought two bags of cut mangoes from our farm to make your favorite pickle. The rest of the stuff is what I couldn't bring with me when we first set up *kapuram*."

So much for the dead uncle. Here was the typical housewife, whose life revolved around her immediate family: husband, kids (once manufactured and deployed) and to an extent, parents and siblings.

She started firing the standard questions every wife is bound to ask her husband after returning from any distance greater than a mile.

"Dear! Did you water the plants?" "How did you survive while I was away?" "Did you eat the curries I kept for you in the refrigerator?"

"You look like you lost weight." "Oh dear, if I'm not around, who'll take care of the plants and you?"

I yapped a few unintelligible answers, and quickly steered the subject to the latest death in the family.

She talked animatedly about the goings-on in her village. Seemed like her dead uncle, bless his soul, was not just a pious Vishnu devotee. He had more worldly talents. He distributed a fair amount of his wealth amongst the servant girls, for apparently no G-rated reason. The wife inherited his hearing aid, into which she had shouted obscenities till his body burned to ashes.

I interrupted her news report to offer my two cents. "Now, if the wife becomes a servant to the *nouveau riche*, she can give them a taste of their own medicine."

That started Sri bickering about my tasteless humor for the rest of the ride home. I was left wishing I had a hearing problem too, so that I could shut off my hearing aid when she goes off on one of her tirades.

We reached home and ate our dinner amidst her incessant chatter. Finally, it was time for bed, which was really the time I had missed her most during her absence. I turned off the lights and snaked my hand across her arm. "WHAT! Are you nuts? You can't touch me; I have just come from visiting the dead. I'm in *mylu*. You should take a shower for touching me."

If it were not *mylu*, it would be *madee*. These customs were driving me nuts. I thought this was the best way to pay obeisance to her dead uncle – by doing what he enjoyed doing a great deal in his life. I turned over to the other side, to resign myself to boring sleep, when suddenly I remembered something. Oops!

Something really, really important, which I should have never forgotten, in the first place. The hair on the nape of my neck curled upwards, as the full import of my sudden crisis dawned upon me. I had a problem. Oh yes, a dangerous problem, which stemmed from a seemingly innocuous habit.

The habit of talking in my sleep. The instrument with which my guilty conscience takes revenge on me. To put the extent of this problem in perspective, I should narrate a few incidents from earlier days, because in recent times, when sleeping with Sri, I've done nothing that I've had to conceal from her.

It was this habit that let a nervous suitor for my sister know that she thought he looked like a termite. I had accidentally dozed off during the 'bridal looks' ceremony.

It was also this same habit that revealed to my Pop that an excuse like 'group study' is only fifty per cent accurate. 'A big-time booze party' would be a more appropriate phrase.

And yes, this was the same habit that alerted our neighbors that it was not a monkey who had been pinching mangoes from their tree. Rather, it was my good old Pop doing a slick con job right at the crack of dawn.

Well, just my luck that I married a girl who can't sleep when the leaves rustle in the wind. There was only one solution that came to my mind. I had to stay awake until she fell asleep, and then, I could sneak into the hall. So I lay my head on the pillow and closed my eyes, concentrating on her breathing.

Sleep is a funny thing. You sometimes just don't know how you got into it or how you got out of it or what happened during it...just one of those black periods that break our active lives into discontinuous functions. The next thing I saw, after a blackout, was a beam of sunlight through the window capturing a trail of dust in Brownian motion.

It took me a second before I realized the Fatal Truth. I had slept. I might as well have been sentenced to death. Hanged from the gallows. But, hey, maybe I hadn't blurted out anything. Maybe for once I had been too tired to even talk in my sleep. Maybe I had talked about how much I missed her (too hopeful?). I turned around to the other side to check on the sleeping Sri.

Empty! Sri wasn't there. I didn't hear her in the kitchen. I yelled out for her.

No answer.

Something caught my eye, an audiocassette next to her pillow. It was titled, 'Songs from *Devadas*'. Yeah, right.

I knew what was really on there, as I put it in my cassette player. Sweat broke easily on my forehead.

Silence for first few seconds. Then, I could hear a faint whipping-kind of sound. That was our fan. Then I heard my voice. I turned the volume higher.

It was a chant...a strange kind of chant. I can only roughly reproduce it here:

"Chicken. Spicy chicken. Chicken, chicken." "Vodka, showers of vodka. Smirnoff vodka." "Whiskey, single malt whiskey. Whiskey, whiskey."

Then, my voice started fading away until it wasn't audible any more. Only the whipping sound of the fan accompanied my desperation. I felt a sudden, unbearable longing for her. I was sure she had stalked out of this place; how could a simple-hearted, pious, village girl continue to live with a sinner like me?

"Chicken. Spicy chicken. Chicken, chicken." "Vodka, showers of vodka. Smirnoff vodka." "Whiskey, single malt whiskey. Whiskey, whiskey."

"Oh, how can I do this to poor Sri," I cried to myself, feeling sorry for my poor wife.

"...CHELIME ledhu, CHELIYA ledhu, veluthure LEDHU..." Ghantasala's song in *Devadas* suddenly burst from the cassette player, continuing after the brief interruption.

I pressed the stop button.

The irony was sickening; Devadas singing this song, drunk, after breaking up with his girlfriend.

III

While I was lost in my thoughts, someone had opened the front door and wandered into my room. The kind of person who seems to have eked out a living doing just that, floating silently from one place to another like a hovercraft. He was a tall, bespectacled chap. A phlegmatic guy who could breathe confidence into a death row inmate.

"Ahem," he started slightly with a cough.

I jumped out of my skin. When I saw who it was, I tried to repeat the action, and landed on my butt on the floor.

"Tejas! Man, I can't tell you how glad I'm to see you. Gather your horses and listen to this: I think my wife just walked out on me!" I said, breathless from rushing through the earth-shattering news.

Tejas lived next door. His talents were occupied by pulling guys like me out of sticky situations. His clarity of thought and application of first principles to the solution of domestic problems never ceased to amaze me. He had sort of dedicated his life to the upliftment of downtrodden husbands. He was my guardian angel.

Tejas spoke in his usual calm and measured voice, sizing up the situation like a private eye.

"I gather that you talked in a your sleep last night about alcohol and chicken and your wife deduced, correctly if I may say so, that you had enjoyed these forbidden pleasures during her brief absence?"

"Now how the heck do you know that?" I asked, perplexed but marveling at his abilities to deduce the situation flawlessly.

"Elementary, I overheard Sri talking to Janaki in my kitchen a few minutes ago," Tejas explained.

His wife Janaki was the president of the Women's Club and a student of Law. The kind of woman who was always looking for a way to get the ladies' act together. She was probably rubbing her hands with glee at the news. This was, doubtless, fertile ground for a rally against the atrocities committed by husbands against their wives. The club hadn't been very active lately. I had even heard that the treasury was going empty.

"You mean she is in your house right now?" I asked, with a touch of relief showing up in my voice, for knowing she hadn't committed suicide. At least, not yet.

"Yes, she came in this morning and fell into Janaki's arms crying about how men prefer a few drinks over wives. They were still there when I left. They had switched their discussion to the similarities between men and roadside pigs," he said. "It's remarkable! I had never even realized that two different species can have so much in common," he added, deep in thought.

I groaned.

"Maybe I should go in there and try to explain my way out of this problem, but I can't think of anything reasonable to say to her."

"Perhaps I can help you on this matter. If I'm not mistaken, all you have to explain is why you blurted out three offending terms in your sleep. Which is a simple issue, if we can think of an article or a movie in which the frequency of usage of these three terms is noteworthy."

"Brilliant!" I slapped my forehead. "Why didn't I think of a stupid thing like that myself," I noticed that my last words seem to have offended the poor guy.

"Oh, I mean, it's a good idea! I can't believe I'm so stupid compared to you. Do you know of any movie or an article which yaps about these things?" I inquired eagerly.

He shook his head.

"As I said before, it's a simple matter if we can think of one. Nothing comes to my mind. However, I'd advocate you quote a movie with a fictitious title. This will also eliminate the risk of Sri grabbing hold of the movie herself. Obviously, an English movie and fortunately, all the terms you have used are English."

"Of course! How about a movie like, 'Chicken, Vodka and Whiskey'?"

He didn't stand there and start clapping at my imagination (or lack of), but he agreed since we were in a hurry, and he had nothing better to suggest himself. I was grateful to the guy for helping me out once again; here was a pure philanthropist, a guy who lives for the others. A guy who deserved a good turn himself this time.

"Tejas," I said, not without some effort for I loved my blasted tree, "you know the old lime tree whose branches are dropping leaves all over your garden?"

I paused for a gut-wrenching moment, "I'll cut them off today."

I could see the guy was genuinely touched. The ghost of a smile formed around the corners of his mouth.

"Thank you," he said with a far-away tone in his voice. "Shall we go now?"

IV

"Wifeeey...!" I came running into the kitchen, with my arms outstretched.

Tejas followed me in a more subdued manner.

Sri was sitting on a stool, deep in meditation. She didn't even bat an eyelid at my exuberant entry.

"Stop there! How dare you enter this place after your unpardonable sins?" That was Janaki, the Women's Club president, at her eloquent best. She peered over her spectacles when she said that. When a guy looks over his glasses and speaks, he appears benevolent, like Mahatma Gandhi. But when a woman with a thin and hard stature does the same thing, she reminds you of the third-grade school teacher who gave you the dreaded answer, "NO!" to the question prompted by your raised index finger (later in the class, when the urgency increases, it'd be accompanied by the middle finger, but then she would still say, 'NO!'; these teachers ought to be banned from schools for interfering with the calls of nature).

I sat down and explained to them with an amused look, the kind that dispels worry, that this whole thing was a misunderstanding. I told them that I had watched this movie called, 'Chicken, Whiskey and Vodka', and this movie, in all likelihood, influenced my dreams.

"Therefore, you see, I mentioned those things in my sleep," I finished with an emphatic thump on the table.

I searched their expressions hopefully for any signs of comprehension. I would have made more progress shouting at a deaf man vacuuming his floor.

My prize witness, Tejas, spoke up to help me out. His soothing voice could convince the most cynical of minds. "I remember watching it myself: 'Chicken, Vodka and Whiskey'. A most interesting movie, starring Kirk Douglas and Ingrid Bergman." His embellishments were nothing short of perfect. This guy was also cleverly suggesting that the movie was made long ago, in case the lawyer wife decided to ask us to bring home the videocassette.

"I thought he said the movie was, 'Chicken, Whiskey and Vodka'," the chief prosecutor observed astutely, her glasses dramatically dropping another centimetre down her nose. The wife was always one-up on the husband. I butted in with a quick explanation.

"Oh, I forgot! He's right, it's 'Chicken, Vodka and Whiskey'. In alphabetical order, you know. Not to forget the climactic effect. You start with chicken, wash it down with vodka and finish with the king of all spirits. Sort of like Caesar saying, *Veni, Vidi, Vici*."

"*Veni, Vidi, Vici* is not in alphabetical order," the prosecutor was pressing her case adamantly, trying to break me down with insignificant observations.

It was time to bring this matter to a logical end. I couldn't go on any more on this subject without the danger of blundering somewhere.

"This is ridiculous! I can't help it if I have a habit of talking in my sleep about arbitrary stuff. In fact, if I read a murder mystery, I'll probably say that I killed someone. Would you turn me in to the cops then? Ha! You tell me? Would you turn me in to the cops?"

I looked around hungrily for an answer. I drove home my point. I could see it was working. Janaki adjusted her glasses until she was looking *through* them. She appeared a trifle disappointed that the Women's Club could not, after all, convene on this issue. The treasury would remain empty.

The expression on Sri's face became softer. She broke out of her meditation, and dabbed her eyes with the end of her sari. She sniffed, and asked me where I had watched the movie.

I heard somewhere that Rahul Dravid on his day can play any kind of bowling. Yorkers, inswingers, outswingers, leg spin, googlies – dish him anything, he will put it away safely. But once he gets to the nineties, an experienced bowler would recommend a surprise element that puts him off guard completely: bowling the simple full toss. You can bet your life that this nervous chap will play all over it, and walk back to the pavilion crying like a cheated kid.

If I were Rahul Dravid, I'd be batting in the nineties now. And I just received a full toss.

"At Pandu's place," I said without thinking. And then, I bit my tongue.

A stunned silence followed.

"Boo-hoo-hoo, men are such pigs."

Long-Distance Romance

Vandana Jena

On the day of my engagement, when my fiancé and I exchanged rings, little did I know of my spouse-to-be's obsession with rings of a different kind. Pyromaniac I had heard of, but phonomaniac? A fortnight later when we got married, my father made the fatal mistake of sending a small cell phone as a parting gift, to keep in touch and to ensure that my Prince Charming had not turned into a toad overnight. Papa must have pursed his lips when the next morning instead of hearing his darling Vandana *beti's* dulcet tones he heard the bridegroom's nasal ones. But husband dear had begun his married life with the belief that I, and all my material possessions, belonged to him, for

If, in the film Deewar, *Shashi Kapoor had dismissed Amitabh Bachchan with the one-liner "*Mere paas Maa hai," *Sanjay in a minor variation to the theme, would have said, "*Mere pass cellphone hai.*"*

better or for worse. Within two days the cell phone became so much a part of him that I wondered if the vow of 'till death do us part' had been taken with me or with the cell phone.

After marriage I began to learn new things about him. Not only did he love himself, he was even more in love with his voice. He loved to hear it morning, noon and night. Having been a student of mass communications, he loved to communicate. That he did not always have a ready audience

Vandana Kumari Jena was born and raised in Delhi, India, and has been working as an officer of the Indian Administrative Service since 1979. She belongs to the Orissa cadre. She received her Bachelors and Masters in Political Science from Delhi University and Masters in Development Administration from the University of Birmingham (UK). She writes middles, short stories and poetry. Currently she lives in New Delhi with her husband and two sons.

before him did not deter him. If, in the film *Deewar*, Shashi Kapoor had dismissed Amitabh Bachchan with the one-liner "*Mere paas Maa hai*," Sanjay in a minor variation to the theme, would have said, "*Mere paas cell phone hai.*" Money of course was of no consequence, partly because communication, not calculation, has been his forte. Just four days after our marriage I got a call from him. "Vandy," he said, "I'm speaking from Nirula's pastry shop, what kind of pastry do you like?" While many a woman would have melted with love at their husband's voice laced with affection, I was busy calculating the cost of the call. At eight rupees per minute, the pastries would come in expensive if I didn't decide quickly. "Pineapple pastry please," I hissed.

"Speak loudly," he bellowed,

"I can't hear you."

"I said, pineapple pastry," I yelled.

"There aren't any," he replied.

"In that case doughnuts will do," I said.

"Plain ones or chocolate ones?" he countered.

"Either," I said, knowing that brevity, is indeed the soul of economy. A minute later I got another frantic call.

"Oh my God, I don't have my wallet on me, someone has pinched it, or maybe I have dropped it."

The possibilities were immense and my husband was about to describe each of them in detail. "I'll look for it," I yelled and put down the phone.

"I'll call you up later," he muttered.

I looked for the wallet everywhere and finally I spotted it, on the bedside, where he had obviously left it after replacing it on his person with the new love of his life, the cell phone. Five minutes later he rang up again and was pleased to know that he and his money had not parted, not just yet anyway.

That evening I told him that not buying pastries had cost us 80 rupees. He was hurt. "Here I am, yearning to hear my wife's voice and all you think of is money."

"Do you know," I began cuttingly, "at the rate at which you are going, we will get a bill of five thousand rupees at the end of the month?"

"Oh my God," he said, and then suddenly he cheered up, "since your father gave us the cell phone, won't he pay the bills as well?"

The next evening, while we were sitting on our lawn, nursing a *nimbu pani*, our neighbour dropped in, her huge Labrador, Tiger, in tow. "I'll get you a drink," my husband, the epitome of chivalry, said. For one dreadful moment I thought he would ring up on the cell and ask the servant for one. But better sense prevailed. Apparently even Sanju knew the cost of lemons. He left the cell phone on the table and went into the house. Mrs Bali suddenly twittered like a bird and asked me the way to the restroom. I led the way. A few minutes later we returned. Tiger was sitting placidly by the table.

"Where's my phone, Vandy?" asked Sanju on his return.

"It was here, on the table," I said.

"It isn't there any longer," he said.

"Well I knew it was a mobile but I didn't really expect it to run away," I said facetiously.

He almost broke into tears at my retort. "This is serious. How could you leave it alone and go? It's not even insured," he said.

"Well, neither am I," I said. This time he glared at me and I realized that any more of my humour and my marriage, and not just the *nimbu pani*, would be on the rocks.

"Somebody has pinched it," he said, "this is a matter for the police."

"This has happened because of you," he said darkly, while waiting for the police to appear, "you were jealous of the mobile."

"And what do you think I did, practice voodoo?" I hissed. Mrs. Bali was enjoying herself. After all she had the rare privilege of being the sole witness to our first matrimonial battle. Just then the police arrived. "Spoilsports," I heard her mutter under her breath as she bid us goodbye.

Sulekha Select

"I don't think the cell phone is stolen," said the inspector after hearing Sanju.

"The telephone couldn't have done a Houdini," said Sanju.

"But no one could have taken away the phone while the dog was here," countered the inspector. He pursed his lips in Sherlock-Holmes fashion and said, "Strange, but why did the dog not bark?"

"Because someone known to him had picked up the phone," both Sanju and I uttered in unison.

"Ring up the cell number," said the Inspector, "and let it ring." I went inside and dialed the number, while the Inspector and Sanju prowled around the lawns. They began to hear a faint sound nearby. It came from the adjoining garden. And then realization finally struck them. The cell phone, small enough to rest in my palm, now rested in the abdomen of that monster Tiger. A smile spread across the face of the inspector. "There, sir, your mystery is solved."

"But," wailed Sanju, "how do I retrieve the mobile?"
"Well, if it had been a thief," he grinned, *"Hum usse ugalva lete."* (We would have made him vomit it out.) On that humorous note, he left us. Only, like Queen Victoria, we were not amused.

> "Strange, but why did the dog not bark?"

We went to Mrs. Bali's house immediately and narrated our tale of woe." "Ah my poor Tiger," she said, her face going red, "I wonder what will happen to him now? She rang up the vet on her mobile while Sanju kept pacing up and down the drawing room, wearing down the carpet, much like an expectant father.

"Your dog will survive," said the vet.

"What about my cellular phone?" hollered Sanju into the receiver."

"It will probably come out the next morning," he prophesized. Now it was Sanju's turn to seethe. He could not imagine an overnight separation from the cellphone. He looked beseechingly at the neighbour,

"Can't you induce vomiting?" "Why don't *you* give it a try?" she countered.

"Vandy," said Sanju, "are you willing to give your right hand for a cell phone?" I gathered his meaning; he was asking me to put my hands into the jaws of death. "I really can't," I returned sweetly, "as I said before, I'm not insured."

"Well neither am I," he said, "and remember I am the main bread winner." I was stumped momentarily.

"All you have to do is tickle his throat, with a feather of course," he added hastily, seeing me glare. "And you do not have to worry about your being incapacitated," he continued in his wheedling tone, "you're already married."

"But will not remain so for long," I returned, "If this conversation continues. And it will be difficult," relishing the turn the conversation was taking, "to get married once again, minus a hand."

"That would be a problem," he muttered nastily, "even with both your hands intact." Just then Tiger, his stomach full, put his head down to sleep. Now we understood the wisdom of the old adage 'Let sleeping dogs lie'.

The next day at the crack of dawn Sanju was ready, "Come on," he said walking stealthily, "we are going for a walk." But it was certainly not romance which was in the morning air. We were to follow Tiger on his morning rounds. I am a dog lover of sorts. I have lived with a German Spitz. But a Labrador, I realized, is a class apart. Not for him a little jog around the park before his morning ablutions. He went for a five-kilometer run everyday. Tiger ran like an Olympic runner along with the servant, while we huffed and puffed behind. "Sanju," I said, sweat pouring down my face. "If anything happens to me I want you to know I have written my will in your favour."

"This," he said, quelling me with a glance, "is not the time for words but for action." I saw that his eyes were glued to a banyan tree. Beneath the tree a mini hurricane was in the offing. Tiger was letting off a big whoosh. Along with the sound and fury, out came the remnants of his Last Supper. Two pair of eyes stayed glued to the scene after Tiger had left. We heaved a sigh of relief when we saw the outline of the precious mobile.

"Vandy, pick it up" ordered Sanju.

"You forgot the magic word," I said.

"Oh," his brow cleared, "the word 'Please'?"

"No," I clarified, "the word 'I'll'."

Without another word he pulled out a pair of plastic gloves from his pocket, picked up the cell phone and dropped it in a polythene bag.

Once we came home he began Operation Cleanup. He cleaned it with a damp cloth, not once but twice. Then he smelt it and almost gagged.

"Nothing," he said, "will make me touch this again." An hour later he bleated, "Can we get another one?"

Then I had a brainwave. I liberally sprayed my husband's favourite perfume, Fahrenheit, on it. He froze in shock. "You've half emptied the bottle," he said.

"It's for a good cause," I retorted.

Later I went to the cell phone shop. "This cell phone works only in a limited range. Can't we get one with a longer range?"

"For that," the shopkeeper smirked, "you would need a more expensive model." I paid the extra amount and opted for a more expensive model. The shopkeeper took the phone smelled it suspiciously and said, "Why does it smell different?"

"Oh, does it?" I asked innocently, "I didn't know, this is our first cell phone, you see."

We brought a new model home a few days later. It is not only better. It is bigger. Hopefully Tiger would find it quite a mouthful, if he repeated his antics. Sanju was touched by my gesture. Papa was not. "You didn't find my gift good enough?" he mourned. The time had come to tell him the truth, the whole truth and nothing but the truth. So we did.

"What," he chuckled, after hearing our tale, "do you think happened to the old mobile?" "I'm sure it was sold," I said. We all laughed.

So if in recent times you have brought a cellular phone that reeks of Fahrenheit, it is time for you to freeze. And if after reading this you say, "Oh shit," I, for one, will not blame you.

The Zamindar's Wife

Mira Prabhu

The murder of her only son Vikram completed the destruction of Sundari's once blazing spirit. One dreary year later, sole inhabitant of the mansion built two dusty miles from the village of Hastinapura by her husband's great-grandfather Ram Thakurdas, Sundari sank into a torpor so deep, she felt like a fly struggling feebly within the viscous maw of a monstrous tropical flower.

As she rocked herself in the old swing chair on the veranda, sipping delicately spiced tea, she recalled her disturbing encounter with the young social worker who'd puttered up the drive on his scooter last month to visit her.

"I'm from the new *Sevak* office in Hastinapura. You've heard of us?" He'd perched anxiously on a worn maroon velvet couch in the

"Sevak *offers you a chance to redeem yourself,*" he cried, coming to his feet. "*You* zamindars *have bled India for centuries!*"

front hall lined with flamboyant portraits of her husband and his ancestors. Her simple black cotton sari thinly bordered with gold seemed to reassure him.

She nodded. *Sevak* was a grass-roots social service organization founded by Maharashtra's college-educated radicals.

Mira Prabhu was born in Bangalore, in the deep south of India, and lived there until 1986, when she moved to New York. Her creative career began twenty years ago in Bangalore, when she wrote copy for product ads as well as for audio-visuals in a well-known advertising agency. Her passions are yoga, meditation and eastern philosophy, in particular Tantra (both Hindu and Buddhist). Her first novel, Whip of the Wild God, *was inspired by her urge to express the passion she feels for yoga , meditation and the vast eastern philosophy from which they spring.*

"Hastinapura must rise from the dead," he'd announced dramatically, startling her. "It's a tragedy – generations of weavers with no money to operate. The government grant's not enough, we need private donations."

She gestured to the inquisitively hovering maidservant to bring tea. "For what precisely?"

"Small-scale handloom industries."

Sundari cringed – how to confess that despite the faded grandeur of her home, all her husband had bequeathed her was the humiliation of having died in the act of laboring over a prostitute? That she'd only survived by selling pieces of jewelry she'd managed to hide? "I have no money to spare. Perhaps when I die, I will leave *Sevak* my home," she said, avoiding his eyes.

Her response shocked him. "*Sevak* offers you a chance to redeem yourself," he cried, coming to his feet. "You *zamindars* have bled India for centuries!"

Dazed, she noticed his baggy khaki pants and the bright splashes of turmeric on his shirt. The boy was cooking for himself. "Won't you wait for tea?" she pleaded, but he was already gone.

As a radiant bride, she'd kept far from the low of spirit, afraid to catch their contagion. Now she was one of them. Hastinapura's heat must have put her to sleep for the distant cries of children on their way home from the village school jolted her out of the nightmare she'd been plagued with since Vikram's murder. Once again she heard the stranger's high voice, Vikram's frantic responses, that final gunshot. Then the police officer, informing her that Vikram belonged to a gang specializing in stealing gold biscuits. "The almost perfect crime, Mrs. Thakurdas," he'd mocked, showing his contempt for the highborn son who had sunk so low. "Hoarding gold's illegal to begin with, so their victims couldn't complain. But your son made off with all the loot. Cheats don't like being cheated."

"Aren't you going to catch his murderer?" she'd cried. "I can identify his voice!"

"Catch him?" The official had raised an eyebrow. "He's probably out of the country by now, with enough gold to fund a revolution. In any case, Mrs. Thakurdas," he'd said more gently, touched by her misery, "we need more than a voice to go by."

Sundari didn't tell him that the murderer had fled empty-handed, unnerved by her urgent hammering on Vikram's door. Let the gold lie where it was – perhaps the murderer would come back for it one day.

Now footsteps on the gravel drive startled her and she looked up to see her old gardener standing beneath the spreading tamarind tree.

"What brings you here, oh Shivan?" she asked.

Shivan spat a stream of betel juice into the dry earth. "A city fellow drove into the village today, madam," he lisped through half a mouthful of teeth. "Wanted to know if the *zamindar's* house was for sale."

"Really? What did he look like?"

Shivan puffed out his scrawny chest in imitation of the stranger. "Fat and rich, madam, driving a shiny car."

"A real-estate chap," Sundari surmised. "What did you say?"

"Me? Nothing. The hotelkeeper gave him directions here," Shivan's face took on a pleading expression. "I need money for the doctor," he confessed. "My grandson ran after his car because these city folk usually throw the children change. This bastard stopped, then, when the boy ran forward, reversed! My boy fell into the gully and cut his foot on some broken glass..."

"Give him a tetanus shot," Sundari ordered, opening the knot in her sari and extracting a ten-rupee note, which she placed in his gnarled hands.

In gratitude, Shivan touched his forehead and bowed, then motioned toward her once glorious gardens. "See?" he pointed his walking stick at a clump of ivory-hued flowers. "*Datura!*" He made to uproot it but Sundari stopped him. An English botanist, a guest of the late *zamindar*, had spotted the flower's long white flaring blossom. "Angel's Trumpet," he'd informed her crisply, nudging the shaft of the bloom with a muddy black boot. "Causes hallucination, sometimes death."

"Weed after the rains, when the earth's soft," Sundari dismissed Shivan with an imperious wave. "And take the mangoes in the backyard to cheer up the boy."

"Superb!" Dharilal announced. "Now the other wing!" She hesitated, so he added quickly, "I'd be willing to go high. Three lakhs...maybe more..."

She moved curiously to where Shivan had pointed. His eyesight was good – it was indeed the dreaded *datura*. She bent down to uproot them, then returned to the swing to dream away the hours till nightfall. The roar of a car shook her out of her reverie and she opened her eyes in twilight to see a silver Studebaker roll to a stop before the house. A corpulent man eased his body out of the car. Beyond, village lights winked faintly.

"*Namasthe*," he said, beaming at the gaunt old woman peering at him. "I am Dharilal – from Bombay."

This must be the fellow Shivan had told her about. "Come in," she invited, noting the sweat beading his forehead. He followed her into the cavernous sitting room.

"Permit me to come to the point, madam," he said, lowering his bulk into a *divan* as Sundari returned with the tea. He took a large gulp. "Your home impresses me."

"How much?" she asked peremptorily. Considering its remoteness and state of disrepair, she'd been advised it would fetch a meager lakh of rupees.

Dharilal chuckled patronizingly. "An astute businesswoman in Hastinapura!" The dying sunlight caught the gold fillings on his teeth, blinding her momentarily. "First I must see the interior."

"If you will explain why a businessman would move so far from the city."

"Heart condition," Dharilal confided mournfully, massaging his chest with bejeweled fingers. "City life is too strenuous. Already I've suffered two attacks."

The man wheezed as he spoke and with all that fat, his heart certainly labored. "You shouldn't be driving yourself about, Mr. Dharilal," Sundari chided. "The ride from the city is exhausting, is it not?"

"It is indeed," Dharilal agreed mournfully.

Sundari stood, beckoning him to follow. She led him through high-ceilinged rooms with ornate plaster carvings and long corridors, even letting him have a glimpse into her own bedroom with its four poster carved bed and bay windows with their sweeping views.

"Superb!" Dharilal announced. "Now the other wing!" She hesitated, so he added quickly – "I'd be willing to go high. Three lakhs...maybe more...."

Three lakhs? For a property worth less than a third of that? "Come then," she invited, leading him into the west wing. But he was overtaking her, trying the door to Vikram's old suite. He stood in the center of the room, eyes flicking over every part of it. "Mr. Dharilal," she called, but he didn't hear her. "Mr. Dharilal," she repeated sharply, "maintenance is prohibitive!"

"But worth it, Mrs. Thakurdas." His eyes were still darting around the room. "May I bring a construction fellow in to make an estimate?"

Sundari smiled. "You must be hungry and village fare's not good for a heart patient. Let's talk over dinner."

Dharilal demurred weakly, but Sundari insisted, leading him past the many side chambers and into the large kitchen. She set steel containers with *rotis*, lentils, rice, a dish of fried mutton, green beans and a bowl of yogurt on the table and watched as he ate, plying him with more and more until there was nothing left. Dharilal sank back, replete.

"Some *paan*, Mr. Dharilal?" Sundari inquired, bringing out her silver salver and cutting the water-softened arecanut with miniature shears.

"Only a fool would refuse," he replied ingratiatingly.

Sundari was skilled at creating the heart shaped, aromatic leaf-package used both as a breath freshener and digestive.

Deftly, she packed the leaf with arecanut, adding rose petal jam, tiny silver balls and a pinch of white lime. Pinning the aromatic package together with a clove, she offered it to Dharilal.

"Excellent!"

"Have another," Sundari invited, rolling a second. As he bit into it, she said abruptly. "Did you know my son was killed here?"

Dharilal hesitated, then nodded sympathetically. "People in the village spoke of it."

"So, Mr. Dharilal," Sundari leaned forward, riveting him with her eyes, "you're here to locate your misbegotten gold, are you not?"

"Do not joke with me, Madame!" Dharilal stuttered.

She laughed grimly. "Joke with a murderer? No, no, no, I prefer to talk about serious matters."

Dharilal gaped at the old woman in growing disbelief.

"How do I know you killed Vikram?" Sundari continued softly. "Your voice, the fact that no villager would discuss my son's death with a stranger, and most of all, your ridiculous offer. I was not a *zamindar*'s wife for nothing, you know." She laughed at his incredulous expression. "What were you trying to do, fool? Dazzle a woman who never cared for money with money?"

"You're mad!" Dharilal whispered hoarsely.

"Mad with grief, Mr. Dharilal, but not stupid."

Dharilal struggled to rise, but Sundari's glittering eyes pinned him to the chair. "And by the way," she added, "you've just consumed enough *datura* to drop an elephant."

"*Datura*?" Dharilal croaked. "You fed me poison?"

She rose slowly to her full height until she towered over him. "To hell with you, Dharilal," she ordered sternly, eyes blazing, raising her arms like the wings of a savage bird of prey. "It's your proper place."

Dharilal stared up at the woman he'd so terminally misjudged, his fleshy lips working in terror. Then his fingers clawed at his chest and his huge body simply collapsed, face forward, sending the empty vessels clattering on to the kitchen tiles.

Sundari's own heart had almost ceased as she watched his struggle with death. Hands trembling, she unhooked the gold-edged face mirror that hung over the sink and held it over his open mouth. It's surface remained dry. She stared down at the corpse, then decisively moved away to pick up the telephone. "A realtor from Bombay suffered a fatal coronary at the Hastinapura *zamindar's* house," she informed the desk sergeant with quiet authority. "Tell the Inspector to send a vehicle for the body at once."

She returned to the swing on the verandah, awaiting the police. Some would debate it, but on examining her conscience, she decided that her vow not to kill was intact – the *paan* had contained no *datura*. She'd gambled on Dharilal's own guilt and fear doing him in, and had won. *Karma*, the law of cause and effect, was unerring. Those who killed died horribly, in this lifetime or another.

In her mind's eye, she recalled Dharilal's hungry survey of her son's bedroom. The gold was hidden there, this she knew. Vikram's suitcase had been so heavy the maidservant had helped him with it; thanks to Dharilal, he'd never left home. Tomorrow she'd locate the gold, then inform the social worker that she would indeed finance the renascence of Hastinapura. A gust of wind pushed the swing gently forward and, as fireflies threaded luminous magic into rustling tamarind trees, Sundari visualized his troubled face explode into joy.

Winter Garden

Lalita Pandit

Looking at war photos of Drass and Kargil, what I see are the mountain peaks, rain-washed roads at high altitudes, a soldier rinsing dishes in a little stream. I know exactly what the air is like up there, how it feels on my skin, rushes through my hair. I remember a few words of an old song about the victors of Drass: "*...kaa hraas door kar/ Drass vijay karne valo.*" I do not see the roads paved with blood, or the stones catching shadows of those who do not know of the myths and legends about this majestic mountain. The trees are the same as they were in my father's village, in my grandfather's village. I remember those days now as if they have come to life again upon the screen of my mind.

It is November and we are watering turnip patches in the vegetable garden of our Kulgam house, in southwest Kashmir. This is the second turnip crop of the season, the one that will brave the winter. Unripe turnips will stay in the ground;

My grandfather calls his wife by sweet names, his pet names for her. He tells us stories about her youth, and she speaks of him as if he is someone she just fell in love with.

we will cut off the tender leaves, protect the plants before severe frost sets in. In early spring, new leaves will grow out. In the patches of winter kohlrabi too, baby greens (*kanul*) will grow out in spring.

Lalita Pandit grew up in Kashmir, lived in different parts of India and has lived in the US for the last nineteen years. She teaches at a University, and is interested in Indian culture, mythology, and poetry. Among her most favorite authors are Kalidasa, Abhinavagupta, Kalhana, Bilhana, Jaydeva, Tagore, Aeschylus, Sophocles, Euripides, Shakespeare, Swift, Henry James, Marquez, Neruda, V.S. Naipaul, Bessie Head, and many others.

The protective scaffolding of many patches and parcels of the garden will be done on some Sunday, latest by December 10th. We will bring in bundles of hay, wood dust, ashes, and sticks. My father will do what has to be done. We will assist him. I know I will do all this work reluctantly, grudgingly, wishing I was somewhere else where it is not just study and work all the time – some place where people do not try to stifle complaints by shouting: "Be grateful, you are allowed to go to college. In your mother's and grandmother's times, girls your age were married already and they lived under the strict governance of their mothers-in-law." I am seventeen and I have no fear of marriage. I have an idyllic view of it, based on the good marriage of my grandparents. My grandfather calls his wife by sweet names, his pet names for her. He tells us stories about her youth, and she talks of him as if he is not the man she has been married to for half a century. She speaks of him as if he is someone she just fell in love with.

In my room, at nights, I write poems but I have to hide them. My older brother searches for them when I am not home, reads them out loud to everyone in an affected manner. I think if I were married, my husband would not let this happen. He would know how to read my poems. He would respect my privacy. My mother says it is very foolish to think that a husband can be a friend, that one can trust him to this extent. When I confront her, in my adolescent arrogance, and say, "what need is there, then, to have a husband," she gives me a long, rather remorseful look, and changes the subject. If, at such times, she is engaged in sewing something, she will finish, say nothing, snap the thread violently, raise her face towards me and command me to do something, in a very matter-of-fact way.

Father is most satisfied with my work in the kitchen garden. It is big enough, but not too big to justify paying someone to do the work, and it provides us with vegetables all year round. Discontent makes me a good worker. My father thinks I am his only offspring who has so far evaded the label of a 'problem child.' Everyone else, in one way or another, is 'a problem child.' In the weekly postcards that are written to and received from my uncle in Delhi, only the initials of a child's name are used and the so-called 'problem' is discussed. If my mother wrote those postcards, she would express her secret worries.

When my brothers are scolded for staying out late, my grandmother says: "boys have to have their pleasures." Girls have to have their pleasures too, but it would be insane to say this out loud. For example, why is it so impossible for me to go for a long walk alone, all the way to the big river, Veshav. Why do these long walks happen only when a lot of our male cousins visit and we are allowed to go with them. There is so much chatter then, so much noise. One cannot truly enjoy the great beauty of the river, take in the entire view, the rounded stones, the rocks, the boulders, the trees, the shrubs, and the blue sky above. Sometimes these trips are permitted when there is a new bride in the house. She has to be taken out. There is a lot of fuss, the bridegroom pretends to ignore her, though he hears nothing that is said and is often eager to be left alone with her. The bride herself is not so interested in the river. One has to

My younger sister is thirteen. She is all fire and brimstone. If we ask her to do something, she stares at us with such hostility, it is quite intimidating..

hold her purse, her shawl, as she playfully dips her henna-dyed feet in that clean water, as she pretends to slip and fall over, so that the bridegroom can have an excuse to come and save her. It is only when the evening shadows grow around us, as silence falls, that they are left alone for a bit. It is then that I can stand apart from the rest, become one with the landscape.

My only constant pleasure is reading, I take a book in my lap and lose myself in it. I see what can be seen from the windows of the Kulgam house, sun setting over the Himalayan peaks, birds flitting over rice plants, roads in the distance, trucks carrying steel rods, or long thin pipes that hang out, strike against each other in rhythms that create a melancholy drone. A late moon rises on *Janmashtami* nights. In it the rice plants look silvery. As the night air rushes through them, they experience the first tremor of joy. These are my pleasures, but I have no one to share them with.

Our Sundays are not only for gardening and yard work, they are also washing days. Evenings are for ironing. Three sets of day clothes for each of us. Monday through Saturday, we'll be so tidy. All because we were willing to labor on Sundays. In truth, it is not as much work as it seems to me. Often, it is fun. Still, I like to grumble. In the evening I shall say, I could have read the last hundred pages of *War and Peace* and tomorrow I could start *The Brothers Karamazov*, or I could have re-read Tagore's *Choker Bali* to compare it with *The Wreck*, as I had wanted to. Only the other day, my English Professor said *The Wreck* is not as good a novel as *The Eyesore*, titled *Ankh Ki Kirkiri* in Hindi. I thought then that both are good in their own way. Now, again, I think both are good.

My father does not care for any kind of fiction. He thinks only philosophy and history are worth reading, but he will be happy if I can come up with arguments and evidence to defeat my professor's high-handed dismissal of Tagore. I will not speak to my professor directly about it; that would be improper. No talk outside of the classroom is permitted between a male teacher and a female student. I shall have to write up my comments and arguments. Father will take this essay to his 'brilliant' colleague, and the colleague will make written comments. Both men will have the satisfaction that they made a contribution towards 'honing my intellect' in this covert way.

I ponder over all this as I work in the garden. A thorn pricks my foot and I over-water the turnip patch. A few plants at the edge are drowning. I drain some of the water before father takes notice. A harsh-voiced crow swoops over an insect that has come up onto the surface, its skin glistening in the evening sun. Father announces that it is time to take a rest. We gather in a group, sit around a green mound up above where there is a plateau covered all over with strawberry beds. Above us are bare branches – with a few, lingering red and yellow leaves – of peach, almond, apricot, cherry trees. Behind us is a fence covered over by grape vines that climb all over the popular trees. The fence is adorned by honeysuckle, jasmine, and along the edges there are various kinds of flower trees, and one pomegranate tree.

Mother has brought out tea, snacks made of corn flour, and fruit – pears and fresh walnut kernels sent to us by our uncles, my mother's brothers who live in the nearby village, Devsar, right across the gurgling mountain river, Veshav. A November sun has set, it is getting cold. We put on our sweaters. Mother rushes in to cook the evening meal. Grandmother comes into the garden to have tea with us. She admires our handiwork. My older sister is twenty. She stands away from us with her friends. They giggle and laugh a lot. Whenever I come close to their thick circle, they fall silent. I have the reputation of being too studious, hence, not interested in gossip and light talk. They exclude me from fun talks and they make my sister swear she won't tell me a thing. They think I will disapprove. My younger brother enter- tains me with his constant chatter. My older brother confides in me. Only I know that he smokes, no one else does. I cover up for him

I have the reputation of being too studious, hence, not interested in gossip and light talk. They exclude me from fun talks and they make my sister swear she won't tell me a thing.

whenever it is necessary. My younger sister is thirteen. She is all fire and brimstone. If we ask her to do something, she stares at us with such hostility, it is quite intimidating. We try our best to keep her in a good humor. She is my grandmother's pet, though grandmother would never admit that. She thinks she loves us all equally.

Our father is a professor. His father owned some land in Kulgam, right behind our house. In addition, he had some sort of a business, a shop in the town. He micro-managed the household expenses with a tight fist, so that he ended up becoming reasonably prosperous. He would dole out spices, tealeaves, almonds, sugar, salt, ghee, oil, and other expensive items every morning for that day's cooking. He did it with good cheer, making fun of himself along the way. It was like a daily ritual. No one questioned his authority, or his interference. New clothes and shoes were also strictly rationed; he knew of each item's value and condition and decided which child's old shoes will fit whom, and so forth. He was generous with books, pens, paper and ink. He said these were good investments. With his own children he was not generous even with these 'investment' items. My father and his brothers had to return every sheet of paper to him (he counted them) at the end of a school year so that he could use these as paper bags to pack things in his shop, things like tobacco, sugar, cinnamon, cardamoms, sesame, yellow mustard seeds, and other things that he and his shop assistant sold. In my grandfather's regime, writer's blocks that make people tear up sheets of paper, when they have written only a few words on them, would have been forbidden. At the end of the year, when he collected the sheets of paper, he would have been shocked to see such waste.

My great grandfather, Prakash Ram, was a farmer. That is, he made a living that way. He was very well-educated in Sanskrit and Persian but it would have been impossible for him to get a job. There were not that many jobs in those days, fewer for Kashmiri Hindus in Kashmir. He had four sons. My grandfather was his eldest son. Prakash Ram was poor, so poor that the accumulated despair made him commit suicide when he was forty-eight years old. Though, that is not what they called it then. He ate nothing for 40 days, sat in his room with his prayer beads. My father was four. At the end of the 40 days of fasting, he asked my father to take a jug, clean it very well, fill it with cool water from a stream near the house. My father did what he was told. The woman of the house, Yenderamal, Prakash Ram's wife was working in the fields, as were my grandfather, my grandmother, Amravati, and others. Prakash Ram gulped down entire contents of the jug, as my father stood watching with fascination his "*Lalla*," (a common affectionate name for a grandfather) drink this water as if it was *amritam*. A child of four watched his grandfather die.

A year later, Yendermal, Prakash Ram's widow, got up on the morning of the first anniversary of his death. My father hung by the skirts of her long Kashmiri *bhatani pheran* (the long, somewhat ornate dress Kashmiri Hindu women used to wear in those days). It was the day when she was to remove the wooden bird-feeder type of thing set up on top of the outer door. It had been set up at the end of the initial mourning period, on the twelfth day. This was a mourning ritual widely practiced in those days. The bereaved family made food offerings to the dear-departed for one year of ritual mourning. Perhaps it was a Vedic ritual, a householder ritual associated with death. This offering was made early in the morning, before sunrise. The food was cooked freshly, in small toy-like pots and pans. With flowers and other oblations, the offering was made in the name of household gods, the sentries at the gates of Yama, appropriate *bhutas*, *bhairavas*, and so forth. Perhaps it was a way in which the world of the living and the world of the dead merged, and also a way in which boundaries between the two were defined. The dead person's soul was believed to be in limbo for one year, still attached to the family, still in need of being remembered daily.

Usually a daughter or a daughter-in-law would do this, but my grandmother was pregnant that year. A pregnant woman could not perform rituals of death; nor could she be asked to wake that early. The only other woman in the house, my great grandmother, had to do this. Every morning for the whole year, my father woke

When my father's youngest child, a girl of three, died, I wondered if in her short life she had been hugged enough, kissed enough.

with her, watched the food being prepared, the flowers, the fragrance being arranged in a little thali, *mantras* being read and the daily offering of food being made to the one who fasted himself to death. That morning, upon seeing this perch being destroyed, my father broke down. His child heart shed many bitter tears. He pulled at his grandmother's dress. He raged, and in anguish he cried: "How will my *Lalla* eat now?"

When my father's youngest child, a girl of three, died, I wondered if in her short life she had been hugged enough, kissed enough. I wondered if we had said enough endearments, if we had sung lullabies to her. She was surely a beautiful child. Since she was so little, there was a penance ceremony performed, a sort of *yagnya* that went on for three days. My father sat with the priest. At some important juncture my mother would join in, sit with my father to read the *mantras*, make oblations to the fire, then she would return to the kitchen, or attend to other affairs of the household. When I asked her what all this was, she said "because Priya died before all the sacraments were done, these have to be performed posthumously, as if she had passed through all the stages and had lived a full life with us." It was then that she broke down. I stood in front of her, stunned, imagining my sister grown into a beautiful young woman. I imagined the *devagon* ceremony, a fire ritual before the wedding day, when a girl prepares for marriage. I was eight years old at this time. The penance ceremony began on the day of the first anniversary of Priya's death. No other anniversary was observed afterwards; Priya was too young for that kind of remembrance.

Every spring, in those years, my father's winter garden burst into joy, sprouted, blossomed, matured. Ice melted slowly. Spring breezes made one's heart ache for an impossible, unattainable love. Rain washed the earth. Little greens of kohlrabi and/or kale, tender like broccoli rabe, would be brought home in baskets, cleaned up, washed, cooked alone, or with home made cheese, or fish, or mutton, potatoes, or lotus root. Turnip greens with little turnips attached to them, and spring flowers. Hope. The festivals of *Shivaratri* and *Navreh* within a month's distance from each other. The disciplined, restrained festive joy of our home, expressed not in words and gestures, only in colors and fragrances that must still linger over there, on top of that rubble covered in snow, cleansed by spring showers. I am sure wild flowers grow all around it, and grasses, too thick to clear them away.

Mist

Aruna Nair

Drab day, mist-ridden
I flop in the car
my eyes wandering over
those cloud-hung hills
merged, for this brief day,
with the softness of the sky.
Drab, drab, drab
this dullness
places its white, stretched hands around the bowl of
the world,
and presses thickly,
squeezing the sky and tired hills
dry.
Then a bend in the road
and
suddenly
a patch of tree and bush and shrub,
twined together in wet greenness
trembling ecstatically in the brushing caress of the
mist.
And suddenly the fog
stops being the white, cold-wet hands of
death-drabness,
and becomes a fantastic goblin of life
dancing through the hills and plants,
kissing them in little, tender droplets.

Aruna Nair was born in New Delhi, India, where she lived for 14 odd years. She then moved to Swansea, Wales where she is currently studying for her GCSES. She is 16 years old.

This cloud
has looked upon the world
and loved it so,
that it cannot bear to fling its rain down, as others do,
from its cold distance in the sky.
It has loved the world so
that it has dragged itself down,
down from the chill heights of sky,
and thrown its white, wet arms around the grass,
and kissed, with soft, liquid lips the hilltops
and flung itself, in abandon,
across the horizon-body of the world
fitting itself into each crevice,
and kissing each individual leaf
with its swollen, sea-burden.
Mist.

Once Upon a Flight

Rajesh K. Venkateswaran

I brooded darkly on life. I looked out my window at the bleak desolate airport, and tried not to sit on my seat belt. The editor had, a few hours ago, rejected my masterpiece. She sent me an e-mail saying it was not logical enough. Hell, it was *brilliant*. But she couldn't see that. And now she, a woman, was teaching *me* logic. The cheerful flight attendant upset my concentration with assorted cheerful juices, and I waved her away. I had no wish for the company of happy humans. I wanted all my energies to be focused on editors. Logical female editors called Meher. For that was her name. She was a dis-

Her face was hidden behind whatever she was trying to coax into the overhead compartment, but her red shirt was fooling around just above where her jeans ended.

grace to it, of course. What a waste of a name, I said to myself, as I brought my *Catch-22* out to add spice to my thoughts on editors. I wondered how people could trust women with editing. It's all very well if they want to fly aircraft and engage men in hand-to-hand combat. But editing is serious stuff. Men's lives depend on it. You don't give such things to women.

Rajesh Kumar Venkateswaran was born in Kerala, India, and grew up in Calcutta. He received his bachelor's degree in computer Science and engineering from the Indian Institute of Technology, Bombay. He is currently employed as a software engineer near Boston, in Massachusetts, USA. Rajesh likes to write about ordinary people, caught in extraordinary situations. He would like to make people laugh, yet some part of him tries to make them think. He had wanted to write novels, but the demands of his profession being what they are, he is having great fun writing short stories.

I was sympathizing with the dull grey wing of the aircraft, when there was a slight disturbance to my right, and I realized I had female company. Her face was hidden behind whatever she was trying to coax into the overhead compartment, but her red shirt was fooling around just above where her jeans ended. And if her waist were any indication, she would have a perfect face. But I turned back to my grey wing. I had had enough of women. They could all go edit.

The problem with women is that they cannot prevent themselves from harassing a good-looking man who wishes to be left alone. And the prettier the woman and the more aloof the good-looking man, the more is the danger of assault. There is, in fact, a strain of woman that gravitates towards the dangerously handsome man with glasses. Could this be one of those? The luggage having gone in, her face became visible. And I couldn't help noticing that she looked Indian, and was as beautiful as her waist had suggested. I gave her the most distant smile I could manage. She looked at me funnily, and I disengaged eyes immediately. When a female's first glance is at your nose and your ears, you know you're in big trouble. For she will try anything in her power to take off your glasses, and put them back on, and giggle at them from various angles. This is a common female genetic defect that this one had in chronic abundance. I could see it in her eyes.

I guess women are to be pitied really. Maybe I cannot understand the extent of my own charm. But surprisingly, things were not going according to the script. She soon opened up her little table and started writing something. Not a glimmer of being attracted to my dangerously handsome face. Just as well, I thought, for I didn't give a damn, really. Maybe she was a writer, too, and her editor had given her the boot. Or whatever it is that editors give aspiring female writers. But that got me thinking, if you get my drift. She might very well be making war on men, while I was making war on women. I could now understand her disinterest in me, beyond the automatic glance enforced by her genes. There was probably a fire burning within her at the moment. And in a professional way, she was committing her thoughts to paper. Unlike me, who was wasting my fire on mere fantasies? I was impressed, and I think I craned my neck just a little to see how she was going about it. You see, her hair was falling freely over her left shoulder, and some strands were even playing upon the open pages of my *Catch-22*, and I couldn't see through. Hence the craning of the neck.

She was writing poetry. I could fathom that from the trivial observation that the ends of most of her lines had commas, and some of them rhymed. But was she writing about editors? I couldn't say. However, I must have been perilously close to her head which was well-concealed in that mass of hair, for when she did the normal woman thing and shook her head to increase blood-flow to the brain, she gave my nose a nasty whack. She apologized before she emerged from her hair, but when she saw that it was my *nose* that was the victim, she wondered in a voice that sweetly dripped ice whether my book wasn't sufficiently interesting to keep my nose a little away from her head.

She soon heard about her extraordinary sense of rhythm and, I think, her alliteration and her rhyme scheme figured prominently in the critique.

I don't know if you have ever been thinking favourably about a beautiful woman whose hair has been doing things to your fingers, when she has suddenly elected to look into your glassy eyes and shoot barbs of fire at them. Let me caution you, if you haven't. It is highly disconcerting. I am not a weak person given to stepping on the panic button. But this combination of beauty, fire and ice was a little too much, and I think I stuttered. In fact, I stuttered and stammered. I stuttered and stammered and confessed. I told her I was curious to know what she was writing. I told her she wrote excellently. Her poetry was wonderful, her choice of words amazing. The fact that I hadn't seen her work well enough didn't seem to be important.

I think she was a little taken aback at this unexpected praise, but I was just warming up. She soon heard about her extraordinary sense of rhythm and, I think, her alliteration and her rhyme scheme figured prominently in the critique. I concluded with the clincher that her imagery was deeply poignant. Almost benign, I added and mercifully stopped, for I had run out of breath.

Her eyes must have been opening steadily wider as she listened to what she had sparked off. But it was only now that I noticed them. Blue they were; and very beautiful. There was no flame within for miles.

"Benign?" she asked in a voice that was warmly incredulous; it was accompanied by a gentle quivering smile on her lips. She couldn't control herself, it seemed, and she laughed. If I were a poet, I would probably say that rivulets of rippling laughter cascaded from her lovely lips and fell in joyous streams all around me. Or something to that effect. I think the world should be eternally grateful I decided, way back in my innocent youth, that poetry and I would go our separate ways. But her laughter did ripple. In waves. She laughed and she giggled and she wept. She rolled in the aisles. She stopped and grabbed as much of her breath as she could, and looked at my astonished face and whispered, *"Benign?"* And began all over again.

"Are you quite done?" I asked her after about half an hour, for she had already woken up a sleeping child and two more threatened to follow suit in the vicinity.

"I think so," she said. "Oh my God, but why *benign*?"

"I don't know," I said. "I don't even know what it means. Maybe I like words that have *gn* in them."

"He doesn't *know* what it means!" she informed her red nails, and arched her dark eyebrows. "Do you know what *poignant* means? What are you anyway?"

"Actually, I'm a writer. And yes, I do know what *poignant* means. I'm not all that ignorant, you know. In any case, I have given you enough entertainment for the day. If you don't mind, I'll get back to my book."

Saying which, I tried to concentrate on my *Catch-22*. Why the hell did I say all that, I asked myself. And what made me say *benign*? God, I must have sounded like an idiot. Though I don't believe any self-respecting idiot could have sounded quite like that. She was not *that* pretty, I mean, to make me lose my head so comprehensively. The worst thing was that my glasses didn't seem to have made any difference. I might have been wearing contacts for all the difference they had made. What had made this stupid airline plant such an item next to me on this flight, when I had wanted to be alone with my agony, I couldn't imagine. Some idiot sitting at his computer must have divined that it would be a good joke to play on unsuspecting men to have young women sit next to them and written the reservations software accordingly. Must have been the brainchild of some misguided software engineer from India. Very weird people, these Indian software engineers. In fact, the only thing they seem to think of is women. Did you know that software companies in India make women project leaders for a purely non-

I mean, everyone knows that women cannot write decent software. Women cannot edit, for heaven's sake. How can they write software?

technical reason? I mean, everyone knows that women cannot write decent software. Women cannot edit, for heaven's sake. How can they write software? No, the reason is, Indian men like to be governed, ruled, bossed over, by women. It's an inherent genetic trait. Take my word for it. Whenever women have been given the reins in India, manly things have happened. Take Razia Sultan. Take Lakshmibai. Take Indira Gandhi. Although none of them could write software. You see my point. What India needs is a strong-willed good-looking woman at the helm. Remember how Vajpayee sent Tendulkar an encouraging note during the World Cup? It didn't really have much effect, did it? Just imagine what might have happened if Prime Minister Manisha Koirala had sent that note. If I were Tendulkar, married or not, I would have scored a string of centuries, just to keep her happy and smiling. If you really want to know, this was the basic thrust of the piece over which the editor and I did not see eye to eye. Do you know that she suggested the article was more suited for the humour section? Do you know... Oh forget it!

I must have fallen asleep over my thoughts, for the plane shook a little and I woke up blinking, to find my head on her shoulder. Hell, I didn't know I had fallen asleep. I quickly removed head from shoulder. My glasses were not on their familiar perch. I was wondering where they were, when she said, "Oh, you've woken up? I feared your glasses would fall off, so I plucked them from your nose. Let me put them back on for you."

Time stood still, as she said this, and I was suddenly wide-awake. "Aha!" I said to myself. The satisfaction was quiet. It was sweet also. "Aha!"

She adjusted them on my nose. There was obviously something that disturbed her for she delicately tipped them a little to my right, and then a little to my left, and then she brought them forward a little, and then smiled prettily, "Hmmmm."

"Now, your glasses look perfectly *aligned*," she announced, with her gorgeous head tilted to one side and her slender fingers on my ears. "And *benign*, too," she added. And our noses twitched as one, in synchronous amusement. And my thoughts were back to their crisp clear selves; I was sure the clouds to my left were fleecy and white, and the sky golden. The brown coastline stood sharply against the deep blue sea. And I said I really wouldn't mind knowing her name.

She smiled, her blue eyes twinkling in harmony, "It's Meher. What's yours?"

On Your Wedding day, Sincerely

Neeta Patwardhan

The seven-page invitation should have served as a warning. Its front done in red, green and gold depicted a geometric Lord Ganesh the way Picasso would have drawn it. Each page invited you to a different ceremony of Radha's weeklong wedding. The *mehndi* party, an evening of songs, a post-wedding lunch, the before-you-catch-your-flight quick dinner on Sunday evening, and of course, the main garland exchange at 10 a.m. on Saturday. Hidden inside the invitation booklet and peeking coyly was a white business card with a toll free number for the bridal registry.

'We are registered at Nordstroms,' the card nudged gently, conveying its message in a sweet but business-like manner.

'We are registered at Nordstroms,' the card nudged gently, conveying its message in a sweet but business-like manner.

'Whatever happened to the good old days when people insisted on *no gifts or bouquets please!'* I wondered. It was hard to believe how much Radha had changed. Just three years ago she had told me about the Peace Corps and how she wanted to volunteer time in Africa. She was the last person I ever imagined would register at Nordstroms.

Neeta Patwardhan was raised in Zambia and later spent several years in Pune, India. She received her Ph.D. in computer science from the University of South Florida. Currently living in Houston, she divides her time between writing software for the oil industry by day and short stories by night. She enjoys writing humor and irony. Her personal essays and short fiction reflect observations about the immigrant experience.

I wasn't going to attend the wedding in California for various reasons, and therefore decided to make use of the registry, even though I detest the very idea. After all, the white card had generously given me a toll-free number so at least the phone call would be free. I called early so that a wider selection of items would still be available.

"How much would you like to spend?" the Nordstroms sales assistant inquired with an indifferent tone.

"Maybe $30," I replied. There was a long silence at the other end. The kind of suffocating silence that gets you worried because most assistants are always so perky and verbose.

"Let us see," he finally muttered. "There's really not much left, but wait, let me go down the whole list. There is a muffin pan, you can make twelve muffins in it," he sounded relieved that he had finally found something within my budget.

"Anything else?" I inquired, disappointed with his selection.

"In the cookware section, there is a slotted spoon for $25."

"Is it made of gold?" I asked. The person at the other end didn't appreciate the humor, so I refrained from further friendliness.

"Can you look a little harder?" I whispered into the phone, hoping my anxiety wouldn't show.

"Why don't you just go for the muffin pan, with shipping and handling it will come to about $30, right within your budget," he tried to persuade me.

I just could not digest the idea of a muffin pan as a wedding gift. I wasn't sure why. Radha had selected it after all, and I wouldn't have felt awkward about sending her a gift check for $30, so why did I feel awkward about this?

"Is there anything worthwhile for $40?" I asked, the calmness in my eager voice attempting to conceal my increasing frustration.

"There is something in barware, a set, it's $35.99," the voice at the other end muttered. I assumed it was a set of four glasses and a decanter. "The only other things left in that range are napkin rings for $35 each and the Ralph Lauren toilet paper holder for $39.99." I visualized the pizzazz with which the newly married couple would begin their life together, everything from input to output meticulously peppered with a dash of elegance.

"Are you sure? There's got to be something else!" I insisted. The lazy voice at the other end didn't respond.

"Ma'am, everything is $50 and above!" He was getting impatient. The realization dawned on me that any decent gift was going to cost that much, at the very least.

"Can you please tell me what is still available in that range then?" I was really curious now.

"There is a set of nine goblets and another set of nine champagne flutes." Finally I had a nice gift. I breathed a sigh of relief. I wouldn't look so cheap anymore with the muffin pan that baked twelve whole muffins.

"Each," the voice at the other end said suddenly.

"Each?" I asked, still reeling from the surprise, the full significance of the word not having sunk in.

"Yes, each. There is also a set of twelve soup bowls for $50 each!" I wondered what Radha would do with these. At her dinner parties, she usually opened Campbell's soup cans with effortless finesse. For a moment, I reflected on the unique notion of enjoying Campbell's soup from these expensive bowls. What did I, the country bumpkin, know anyway? The bowls might have been made from some rare, magical material that is found only in the Kalahari Desert and enhances the flavor of a soup, transforming it from the mundane into food fit for the gods. I imagined Radha and myself, at some point in the future, with Campbell's Tomato Bisque turned Ambrosia chatting away about the good old days when we didn't know any better.

"And looking down the list I see one place setting for $299 and I also see a Lennox Teapot for $79.99."

I thought I'd given the wrong name to the Nordstroms assistant. As far as I knew the bride's definition of cooking meant boiling your own pasta (from scratch of course) instead of using frozen entrees. Was this the same person who was planning to entertain with fifty-dollars-a-piece glasses? I asked the assistant to make sure this was Radha's registry he was referring to.

I have never understood why brides put these expensive items on their registry. If I ever owned glasses that expensive, I'd be too scared to touch them, let alone drink from them, and they would certainly be insured first! It always irks me when I see people succumb to the magical spell of the brand name. I tell myself not to be too harsh. It is everywhere around us: the glorification of materialistic wealth, to use a cliché. So many seem to live for that bigger home, the sailboat, the diamond necklace, the BMW and let us not forget for a moment please, that expensive soup bowl!

"Wait, you are lucky, there is more, we have two items left in the bath shop section. A Ralph Lauren lotion dispenser for $59.99 and Laura Ashley soap dish for..." he didn't tell me how much it was for.

"For?" I asked.

"Never mind. It's not within your budget Ma'am!"

Finally a gift was chosen. The barware set for

"And finally Ma'am, would you like it custom wrapped?" I was asked. A question like that generally implies there is a hidden cost involved so I politely declined.

$35.99. It was going to cost $40 with shipping and delivery. The price was certainly above my budget but under the circumstances, and not wanting to look cheap, I had no choice. At least the gift consisted of more than one glass. Glad the ordeal was over, I was about to end the call when it became apparent there were more surprises in stock.

"Which of the following greetings would you like on the card: *Best Wishes, Happiness Always* or *Congratulations*?" I chose '*Happiness Always*' because it seemed to convey the most important thing a marriage ought to bring into one's life. In the maddening mountain of fine brand name gifts the couple had asked for, I knew they would not find the secret that might lead them to it.

"And how would you like to address the couple?" the voice at the other end continued *"Dear, Just the Name,* or *On your wedding day?"* I chose the last one hoping it would be the end of automated choice making. But no!

"And how would you like to sign off? *Sincerely, Affectionately,* or *With Best Wishes?"* he rambled on. I asked if I could put a personalized message on the card instead.

"Ma'am, we do not allow personal greetings." I can't remember what I chose. It didn't really matter. I imagined some lifeless computer in a big Nordstroms warehouse, printing out this message on a white card. Then I visualized a robot searching for a brown box with a label "barware" in long aisle of similar brown boxes. The robot, having found the gift, then slaps the greeting printed earlier onto the box, and off the gift goes to the bride's address. Very personal indeed.

"And finally Ma'am, would you like it custom wrapped?" I was asked. A question like that generally implies there is a hidden cost involved so I politely declined.

"Of course I didn't ask what a barware set consists of! I assumed it would be four glasses and a decanter," I told Nandita on the phone later that day. She had also been graced with an invitation to the seven-day wedding. I told her to act soon, or else even the fifty dollars glasses would be sold.

"Are you sure?" she asked. I wasn't sure if she was just playing with my mind or was serious. "I mean if a flute is $50, how on earth do you expect to get four glasses and a decanter for $40?" she laughed.

That night her words kept haunting me like a bad dream. The thought nagged at me and wouldn't let go, like an insect enclosing its tentacles over helpless prey. The next morning, I decided to call Nordstroms again to clarify my doubts.

"No, no, not at all!" a voice bubbled with frothy laughter when I dialed the toll free number for the second time in two days and asked if the set had four glasses and a decanter.

"For $35.99? You've got to be joking, Ma'am. That set you picked has four stirrers made of glass."

Sulekha Reader Comments

Rita Ayyangar: Well said!! I do wish commercialism wouldn't take precedence over the simple joys and charm of a wedding! With all this emphasis on gifts, it can be stressful both for the couple planning a wedding who are pressured to register and for the friends wanting to get them a gift to commemorate the occasion. I thoroughly enjoyed the story and can relate to similar experiences, which left me standing gaping aghast at the saleswoman as I learned that not a single item in the registry was less than $30-40 and...in retrospect, in at least one case I am glad I did not contribute to the agony of dividing the half complete flatware set as the couple battled thro' a divorce about a year later!! Instead, at least one tiger or a swan or...I don't remember what...in the Cincinnati zoo enjoyed a month or maybe even a year of being fed, on behalf of the couple!!

Jeeva: This is a good article. The whole concept is very new to me, and I found it very amusing. At first I thought you were joking, but looking at the comments by other readers, I realized, this is in fact something that's actually happening...Just what the whole idea is, beats me...

Isn't a wedding supposed to be a celebration and you invite people to share your joy...and instead with all this, it's turning out to be something else...too crass to name.

Sonali Kolhatkar: Great reading. I had a tough time deciding whether or not to register before my wedding. My mother told me of the 13 milk cookers she and my dad got at their wedding (I guess those things were very trendy then). In general I think it is too practical an idea and really takes away from the whole idea of giving a gift to someone you care about. Plus, people tend to get really carried away and burden their guests with a wedding invitation. Right away that means a good enough outfit for the wedding, a wedding shower gift and a wedding gift. At least $100. Yeesh! (I ended up registering for my wedding at Pier 1 Imports and only telling those who asked and insisted. Mostly things under $30 anyway!). :-)

Glossary

Note: The language of origin of each term is noted in parentheses. Where a term originates in Sanskrit and exists in slightly different forms in various languages, we have noted the language of origin as 'Sanskrit'. Words that are in common use only in one language are attributed to that language, even if the root word is from Sanskrit. Where they appear, complete sentences or phrases in Indian languages are accompanied by translations within the body of the article. Quoted verses from songs and poetry have not been translated.

ABCD: 'American-born confused *desi'* (slang for second-generation Indian-Americans, used especially by native Indians).

Abhinaya: 'Expression' in an art form such as dance (Sanskrit).

Advaitin: Follower of the monist tradition of Hindu philosophy (Sanskrit).

Akshathai: Yellow rice, usually thrown as a blessing during various Hindu ceremonies such as marriage (Tamil).

Amra: A kind of fruit (Bengali).

Amritam: Ambrosia (Sanskrit).

Angavastram: Loose garment worn by South Indian men (Tamil).

Ansar: Literally 'helper' or 'friend' (Arabic).

Ayyaiyyo: A cry of lament, commonly used by South Indians (Tamil).

Bajrang Dal: A conservative politico-religious Indian organization. (Hindi).

Bakwas: Slang for 'loose talk' (Hindi).

Beti: Daughter (Hindi).

Bhairava: A malevolent being in Indian mythology (Sanskrit).

Bhaiyya: Brother (Hindi).

Bhakti: Devotion (Sanskrit).

Bharatnatyam: One of the classical dances of India, associated with the southern state of Tamil Nadu (Sanskrit).

Bhuta: Ghost (Sanskrit).

Billi: Cat (Hindi).

BJP: *Bharatiya Janata Party*, literally "Indian People's Party". A conservative, nationalist Indian political party that rose to prominence in the early nineties (Hindi).

Bollywood: Colloquial term for Bombay's Hindi film industry.

Bosthi: Shanty town (Bengali).

Brahmin: The priestly caste in Hinduism (Sanskrit).

Carnatic Music: The classical music tradition of South India.

Chappals: Slippers (Hindi used in an English plural form).

Chappati: Thin, unleavened Indian bread (Hindi).

Chintha-pandu: Tamarind (Telugu).

Chitthi: Letter (Hindi).

Dalal: Middleman, often with the connotation of 'pimp' (Hindi).

Darwan: Doorman (Hindi).

Desi: Literally, 'of the country,' a colloquial word for 'Indian', especially among members of the Indian diaspora (Hindi).

Devanagari: The script used for Hindi, Sanskrit and several North Indian languages.

Divan: Couch (Hindi).

Doordarshan: The State-owned television network in India, literally 'remote vision' (Sanskrit).

Dosa: a light rice-and-lentil crepe, a specialty of South India, but now popular all over India.

Dravida: Adjective referring to South India (Sanskrit).

Dupatta: A veil-like piece of cloth used as an accessory for the common North-Indian dress, the *salwar-kameez* (Hindi).

Durga: Hindu goddess who destroyed the buffalo-demon, *Mahisha.*

Dwaita: Dualist Hindu Philosophy (Sanskrit).

Eid: An Islamic festival (Arabic).

Faltoo: Slang term meaning 'useless' (Hindi).

Gaali: Term of abuse (Hindi).

Ganesha: The elephant-headed Hindu god of the arts, also associated with auspicious beginnings.

Gharaana: Literally 'house'. A generic term for the various schools of North Indian or 'Hindustani' classical music, particular instances usually being named after their places of origin (Urdu).

Ghot: Market (Urdu).

Gulab Jamun: A dark-brown Bengali sweet made with cottage cheese, soaked in sugar syrup (Hindi).

Grihapravesam: A ceremony performed at the time of first occupation of a newly-built or newly bought house (Sanskrit).

Harappa: An ancient city of the Indus Valley Civilization, excavated early in the 20th century. The Bronze Age culture that flourished then in the Indus Valley is often referred to as *Harappan* culture.

Hazaar: Literally 'thousand'. Often used as a slang adjective meaning 'a lot' (Urdu).

Hinglish: Colloquial term used to describe the simultaneous use of Hindi and English, especially among middle-class Indians.

Homam: A sacrificial ritual revolving around a small ritual bonfire (Sanskrit).

IIT: Indian Institute of Technology, any of the six prestigious public engineering universities in India (at Delhi, Bombay, Madras, Kanpur, Kharagpur and Guwahati).

Islamiyat: Religious instruction in Islam (Urdu).

Iyengar: A South-Indian Brahmin subsect, comprising devotees of Vishnu (Tamil).

Iyer: A South Indian Brahmin subsect, comprising devotees of Shiva (Tamil).

Jansmashtami: Festival commemorating the birth of the Hindu god Krishna (Sanskrit).

Jyotishi: Astrologer (Sanskrit).

Kabadi: An Indian team-game, involving alternate attack and defense of marked 'home' and 'alien' territorial zones (Hindi).

Kabuthar: Pigeon (Hindi).

Kajol: Black eyeliner (Hindi).

Kapuram: Family (Telugu).

Kathak: An Indian classical dance form, associated with North India.

Kathakali: An Indian classical dance form, associated with the southern state of Kerala, and characterized by the use of elaborate costumes and make-up.

Koto: "How much?" (Bengali)

Kshatriya: The warrior and imperial caste of classical Hinduism (Sansrkit).

Kumkum pottu: Red dot on the forehead, worn throughout India and known as *teeka* in the north (Tamil).

Kurta: A loose, long upper-body garment (Hindi).

Lakh: One hundred thousand (Hindi).

Lakshmi: The Hindu goddess of wealth, usually the object of prayer rituals during the dedication of new projects.

Leela: Play, sport usually used to describe the doings of divinities; mysterious happenings (Sanskrit).

Lungi: A loose lower-body garment worn by Indian men (Hindi).

Machi: Colloquial word for friend (Tamil)

Madee: A state of ritual cleanliness (Telugu).

Mandal: Association or organization (Sanskrit).

Mantra: Chant (Sanskrit).

Masjid: Mosque (Urdu).

Mastan: Don.

Mehndi: Decorative staining of the skin using the crushed leaves of the Henna plant (Hindi).

Misti: Sweets (Bengali).

Muhurtam: Auspicious hour, especially for starting new ventures (Tamil).

Mundaka Upanishad: The *Upanishads* are scriptural comm.-entaries associated with the dominant school of classical Hindu philosophy, *Vedanta.*

Muruga: Son of Shiva in Indian mythology, god of war, primarily worshipped in South India.

Mylu: A post-funeral period of ritual abstinence maintained by mourners (Telugu).

Naamam: An elongated mark worn on the forehead, especially in South India (Tamil).

Namaste: Common Indian greeting, usually accompanied by folded hands (Hindi).

Nanga: Naked (Hindi).

Nimbu-pani: Lemonade (Hindi).

Odissi: A classical Indian dance form, associated with the eastern state of Orissa.

Paan: An aromatic leaf-package chewed after meals (Hindi).

Pakoras: fried vegetable fritters, a common Indian snack (Hindi, used in an English plural form).

Papad: A thin, hard wafer-like snack (Hindi).

Parathas: Layered, unleavened Indian bread (Hindi).

Phattas: Slang for tall tales (Hindi).

248

Pheres: Literally 'circles'. The seven ritual circuits of the fire in a Hindu wedding (Hindi).

Pooja: A Hindu prayer ceremony (Hindi).

Poonal: Sacred thread worn by Brahmins (Tamil).

Puranas: Hindu quasi-historical scriptures containing a mix of genealogy and mythology.

Purdah: The practice of women covering their faces with veils (Urdu).

Raita: a cold salad with yogurt dressing

Rajani-gondha: A delicate, aromatic, white Indian flower

Rasoi: Kitchen (Hindi).

Roti: Thin, unleavened Indian bread, a synonym for *chappati* (Hindi).

Saag: A dish prepared with any of several leafy vegetables, such as spinach or fenugreek (Hindi).

Sabji: Vegetables (Hindi).

Samosa: A popular deep-fried Indian snack, comprising a crisp shell stuffed with vegetables, usually spicy potatoes and peas (Hindi).

Sandhyavandanam: Meditative ritual performed several times a day by Brahmins and involving the chanting of the best-known verse from the Vedas, the *Gayatri Mantra* (Sanskrit).

Sanyas: Renunciation of worldly life and material pleasures, the last of the four stages of worldly life according to Hinduism.

Saraswati Vandana: Prayer to Saraswati, Goddess of Learning (Sanskrit).

Sepoy: Anglicized spelling of *sipahi*, or soldier (Urdu).

Shaheb/Saheb: A term of respect, like the English 'Sir' (Hindi).

Shiv Sena: Literally, 'Shiva's Army'. A conservative, Hindu nationalist Indian political party, primarily active in the western state of Maharashtra (Hindi).

Shukriya: 'Thank You' (Urdu).

Siddhivinayaka: One of the names of Ganesha.

Sulekha: Literally, 'good writing' (Sanskrit).

Sura: Chapter (of the Quran) (Arabic).

Swaaha: An incantation that accompanies the pouring of sacrificial offerings (such as clarified butter or ghee) into the ritual fire used in Hindu ceremonies. In Hindu mythology, Swaha is the consort of Agni, the god of fire.

Taka: The currency of Bangladesh.

Tamil: The language of Tamil Nadu, a South Indian State.

Telugu: The language of Andhra Pradesh, a south Indian State.

Thali (Hindi): plate.

Thali (Tamil): A symbolic thread tied around the neck of a South-Indian bride.

Tollywood: Term for South India's film industry.

Urdu: Language spoken in much of North India and Pakistan, with a Hindi syntax and a vocabulary heavily borrowed from Persian.

Vaishya: The mercantile class in Hinduism (Sanskrit).

Vannakam: Tamil greeting, synonymous with the Hindi *Namaste.*

Varna: Literally, 'color'. The term for 'caste' in Hinduism (Sanskrit).

Veshti: A traditional lower-body garment worn by South-Indian men (Tamil).

Vibhooti: Sacred ash, often smeared on one's forehead (Tamil).

Vigneshwara: Literally 'remover of obstacles'. Another name for Ganesha (Sanskrit).

Wallah: Suffix meaning 'man', as in '*doodhwala*' (milkman).

Yagnya: A Hindu ritual involving a bonfire (Sanskrit).

Zamindar: A feudal landlord (Hindi).

Questions and Answers

Q: I love this stuff, where can I find more?

A: Fire up your browser on your computer and type in 'http://www.sulekha.com'. You can read nearly 1200 articles (and growing every day) by over 500 authors, including more by the ones in this book, by clicking on 'Contributors' on the Sulekha homepage. You can also view the art and photography of Sulekha contributors by clicking on 'Gallery' on the home page.

Q: I'd like to write for Sulekha, how do I do that?

A: Excellent! Type up your article in any text editor or in Microsoft Word and email it to us at editor@sulekha.com! If it meets the approval of our reviewers (who are volunteers from the Sulekha community), you will be published on the site, where you will be read by several hundred readers in the first few days, and if your article becomes popular, several thousands! You will also have the opportunity to hear exactly what readers think of your writing, and improve your skills with the benefit of feedback from a discerning audience!

Q: I'd like to share my thoughts with the writers in this book and other readers, what do I do?

A: Come to www.sulekha.com, click on the 'Contributors' link and find the author whose work you want to comment on in the list there. You can share your comments by clicking on the 'Post a Comment' link on each article page.

Q: What are the other things I can do on Sulekha?

A: Lots of stuff! You can share your photography and art as well as your writing. You can also contribute book, music and movie reviews, share and discuss news stories using our unique reader-contributed NewsHopper. You can also participate in the many active discussions in the forums on all kinds of topics and join in the many activities, contests, games and clubs on Sulekha.

Q: Can I read Sulekha articles via email?

A: If you do not have access to the web and would like to receive selected Sulekha articles via email, send us an email at editor@sulekha.com.

Q: I'd like to reprint Sulekha articles in my publication. How can I do that?

A: Send an email to editor@sulekha.com to enquire about syndication of Sulekha articles.

Q: This is not enough! I want to know more!

A: We'd love to tell you a lot more about Sulekha. Unfortunately though, Sulekha itself has over 250,000 pages of content, with several hundred pages of new material being added every day. If you'd like to find out more, fire up your browser and type in http://www.sulekha.com/tour.html where we've created a guided tour of Sulekha especially for you!